LETTERS

OF

GENERAL C. G. GORDON

TO HIS SISTER

M. A. GORDON

LETTERS

OF

GENERAL C. G. GORDO

TO HIS SISTER

M. A. GORDON

" Warrior of God, man's friend, not laid below,
But somewhere dead far in the waste Soudan,
Thou livest in all hearts, for all men know
This earth has borne no simpler, nobler man."

TENNYSON

London

MACMILLAN AND CO., LIMITED

NEW YORK: THE MACMILLAN COMPANY

1897

RICHARD CLAY AND SONS, LIMITED,
LONDON AND BUNGAY.

First Edition printed March 1888.
Reprinted March, April 1888; *July* 1888 ; 1889; 1890; 1897.

TO

HER MOST GRACIOUS MAJESTY

THE QUEEN

THESE LETTERS OF

CHARLES GEORGE GORDON

ARE BY SPECIAL PERMISSION

MOST HUMBLY DEDICATED,

"He being dead yet speaketh."—HEB. xi. 4.

"Now ye are the body of Christ, and members in particular."—
I COR. xii. 27.

"As we have borne the image of the earthy, we shall also bear the
image of the heavenly."—I COR. xv. 49.

PREFACE.

In placing this selection from my brother's letters before the public I have been moved by two reasons: one, the often-repeated request of many friends—both known and unknown—to have more "of his own words." For though many—perhaps too many—books have been written about him, little is really understood of his religious life. The fact of his faith and trust in God is indeed known, and many sects have claimed him as belonging to themselves; but he acknowledged none, looking beyond, to the foundation of all, Jesus Christ; and taking for his guide his Bible with the "traditions of man" stripped off. The other reason is the hope that many may derive from the perusal of these letters some of the comfort and help that I have gained from them; for it does not seem right that I should keep to myself what may cheer a fellow-pilgrim on his way. If any hearts are comforted, or if any readers are led to study the Bible from seeing what it was to General Gordon in his life of difficulties and of toil, I shall indeed be well repaid for having "unearthed my jewels"—and precious jewels have they been, and still are, to me.

The selection is made from a large number of letters in my possession. Some may think I have included too much, and there may be some things which it would have been better to have omitted; but it is difficult to weigh every word, or to select quite judiciously. No two persons think alike, and what suits one mind might not be acceptable to another. General Gordon himself says: "I am not wise

in my words or writing; I write from my heart . . . . which
is not good." "I do not claim that what I say is always
true, but to me it appears so. *I* see this or that, another
does not see it; I can say no more." He wrote just as he
felt, and according to the mood he was in at the moment—
sometimes in the flesh, sometimes in the spirit, often apparently contradicting himself. When this was brought to
his notice he, being fully aware of his own weakness,
would answer: "No man in the world is more changeable
than I am." He often remarked that if he went by his
first impressions all was right with him, but that if these
opinions were altered by the arguments of others he failed;
so it was far better for him to be left to himself. The key
to much—inconsistency, shall I call it?—is to be found in
the opposition of the two natures which exist in every man:
the one human, the other divine (see Romans vii.). He,
like all mankind, had to contend against the flesh, which
was wholly evil, whilst the indwelling of God enabled him
to sustain that conflict which ended only in the death of
that flesh. Now the real man is with his much-loved God.

Many have asked me about my brother's first religious
impressions, and I have therefore commenced the series
with portions of two letters written at Pembroke in 1854.
But, with this and a few other exceptions, I have for various
reasons excluded his earlier communications, and have
selected my material principally from letters dating from the
period when he began a regular correspondence with me, in
which he recorded the spiritual, as well as the material, life
he was leading. The series is printed in chronological
sequence, and, as far as possible, dates have been given;
but it sometimes happened that one subject was carried on
from letter to letter: in such cases the first date has been
deemed sufficient.

Many passages in these pages may seem disjointed: this
fault proceeds from General Gordon's habit of writing

whatever struck him at the moment. His religious thoughts were always with him—not as a separate thing, but his life. I know also that there are repetitions; but, when such occur, I think the reader will find that it is not repetition only, but that some fresh thought has been added. My aim and desire is to give my brother's own words and thoughts as he wrote them. Would that I could give his looks and the expression of his countenance when he spoke earnestly on those subjects nearest his heart! They had a great charm; and his eyes would sparkle with real delight, as, after speaking on some of God's great truths, he would exclaim, " Is it not lovely ! "

It was part of my original plan to omit 'all the letters written between 1874 and 1879, as so large a portion of his correspondence during that period has already appeared in *Colonel Gordon in Central Africa*, edited by Dr. G. Birk-beck Hill. But to have done this would have caused a blank; the steps and stages by which God taught him would, as it were, have been wanting. *Those* letters were published to show the *man's* work in the Soudan; *these*, to show the Spirit of God working *in* the man. For the same reason I may have repeated some parts of the letters written to me and published in *Reflections in Palestine*.

It is far from my intention to write anything like a memoir of General Gordon in these few introductory pages, but how kind and thoughtful a brother he was will be partly seen by his letters; and I think that some of his remarks will help to show him as he was, though, as a friend of his, Colonel ffolliott, writes: " To understand properly what has been written [of General Gordon], in fact what he has written himself, requires a personal acquaintance with him ; for your brother was so unique, so utterly unlike any one else, that a personal friendship was necessary, to understand fully the greatness and goodness of heart that moved all his actions, even the smallest."

He greatly loved his Bible, and made it his one great study, saying :

"The chief proof, after all, that the Bible is good food, is the eating of it; the healing efficacy of a medicine, when it is used, is a demonstration that it is good.   I believe the origin of evil is disclosed in the Bible, and I have notes on it, but it is not yet clear to me.   'He that is of God heareth God's words: ye therefore hear *them* not, because ye are *not* of God,' John viii. 47.   I like my religion, it is a great-coat to me."

Death had no terrors for him :

"I would that all could look on death as a cheerful friend, who takes us from a world of trial to our true home. All our sorrows come from a forgetfulness of this great truth.   I desire to look on the departure of my friends as a promotion to another and a higher sphere, as I do believe that to be the case with *all.*"

There are many gaps in the correspondence.   These are due partly to the cessation of letter-writing when General Gordon was at home, and partly to my determination to avoid, as far as possible, all reference to party politics or public affairs.   For the same reason, I make no allusion to his employment by the Cape Government or to the much-discussed subject of his acceptance of the post of private secretary to Lord Ripon, and of the resignation which so quickly followed.   The time has not yet come when such matters can be treated fully; names cannot be mentioned without opening the door to discussion and criticism, which I would avoid; and, as a "half-told tale" can never be a true one, I prefer passing over all such matters in silence.   I merely give the following extract, to show the view my brother took of all earthly governments, without regard to time or place:

"I feel sure that you, like me, want comfort with respect to political affairs, so I will tell you how I try and comfort myself. First, I believe that all worldly events are part of God's great scheme, that He loves all human beings of all nations equally, that He is perfectly impartial and has no favourites: this I consider as *the* great and never to be disputed comfort. That nation A is better than nation B, however backward B may be, I do not think. Second, I comfort myself with respect to the action of our Government, in thinking they were not able to do anything else; it was so ordained and had to be fulfilled. I wish myself that God had favoured us, and ruled for us to have had advantages over other nations, but again I do not wish it; for, if He favoured nations, He would favour individuals. We try to look after ourselves, *coûte que coûte*, and often deviate from the straight path. Nothing justifies trickery such as our Governments have followed: it is the ignoring of God. I am sorry for your flesh, my flesh would like it otherwise; but I cannot help thinking our Government is one of expedients."

Let not those who read this book be swift to make him "an offender for a word," but, looking into their own hearts, see if they do not find an echo to much that is presented in the following pages. "How forcible are right words!" (Job vi. 25.) True it is that many deem books of little importance, to be lightly taken up, no study vouchsafed, no lasting impression received. I would ask a more serious attention. May the thoughts be pondered over, and, so far as they coincide with God's truths, sink into the heart!

And now let me acknowledge the many expressions of sorrow that have come from all quarters, I may say from every civilized land, claiming to mourn with us as for a common loss.

Here also let me gratefully record that, among the first messages of sympathy which came to me, was a letter which our gracious Queen (ever in sympathy with the sorrows of her subjects) was pleased to write with her own hand. Her Majesty has been graciously pleased to allow this letter, and another with which I was afterwards honoured, to appear in this volume.

Let me return thanks to all those whose sympathy and kindness, so freely shown, did all that *human* means could do to lessen the bitter blow and loss; to those whose prayers and thoughts were unceasingly with my brother from the time of his leaving England in January, 1884, until the end; and to the public press which, joining in the sympathy of individuals, stood by him so loyally to the last.

In return for all this kindness and affection, let me offer my most heartfelt thanks and gratitude.

M. A. GORDON.

SOUTHAMPTON,
February, 1888.

LETTERS FROM HER MAJESTY THE QUEEN

TO

MISS GORDON.

OSBORNE, 17 Feb. 1885.

DEAR MISS GORDON,

How shall I write to you, or how shall I attempt to express *what I feel!* To *think* of your dear, noble, heroic Brother, who served his Country and his Queen so truly, so heroically, with a self-sacrifice so edifying to the World, not having been rescued. That the promises of support were not fulfilled—which I so frequently and constantly pressed on those who asked him to go—is to me *grief inexpressible!* indeed, it has made me ill! My heart bleeds for you, his Sister, who have gone through so many anxieties on his account, and who loved the dear Brother as he deserved to be. You are all so good and trustful, and have such strong faith, that you will be sustained even now, when *real* absolute evidence of your dear Brother's death does not exist—but I fear there cannot be much doubt of it. Some day I hope to see you again, to tell you all I cannot express. My daughter Beatrice, who has felt quite as I do, wishes me to express her deepest sympathy with you. I hear so many expressions of sorrow and sympathy from *abroad:* from my eldest daughter, the Crown Princess, and from my Cousin, the King of the Belgians,—the very warmest. Would you express to your other Sisters and your elder Brother my true sympathy, and what I do so keenly feel, the *stain* left upon England for your dear Brother's cruel, though heroic, fate!

Ever,
Dear MISS GORDON,
Yours sincerely and sympathizingly
V. R. I.

WINDSOR CASTLE,
March 16, 1885.

DEAR MISS GORDON,

It is most kind and good of you to give me this precious Bible,[1] and I only hope that you are not depriving yourself and family of such a treasure, if you have no other. May I ask you, during how many years your dear heroic Brother had it with him ? I shall have a case made for it with an inscription, and place it in the Library here, with your letter and the touching extract from his last to you. I have ordered, as you know, a Marble Bust of your dear Brother to be placed in the Corridor here, where so many Busts and Pictures of our greatest Generals and Statesmen are, and hope that you will see it before it is finished, to give your opinion as to the likeness.

Believe me always, yours very sincerely,

VICTORIA R. I.

[1] The Bible here referred to was one used by my Brother for many years, and was his constant companion when at Gravesend, Galatz, and during his first sojourn in the Soudan ; it was then so worn out that he gave it to me. Hearing that the Queen would like to see it, I forwarded it to Windsor Castle, and subsequently offered it to Her Majesty, who was graciously pleased to accept it. The Bible is now placed in the South Corridor in the private apartments, enclosed in an enamel and crystal case, called the "St. George's Casket," where it lies open on a white satin cushion, with a marble bust of General Gordon on a pedestal beside it.

GENERAL GORDON'S LETTERS
TO HIS SISTER.

PEMBROKE, 1854.—My dear Augusta, write another note like the last, when you have time, as I hope I have turned over a new leaf, and I should like you to give me some hope of being received.

. . . . . I got your very kind letter to-day, and am very much obliged to you for it. I have not had time to look out the texts, but will do so to-morrow. I am lucky in having a very religious captain of the 11th of the name of Drew; he has on the mantelpiece of his room the *Priceless Diamond*, which I read before yours arrived. I intend sending to you, as soon as possible, a book called *The Remains of the Rev. R. McCheyne*, which I am sure you will be delighted with. I told Drew to go to Mr. Molyneux; and he did so, and of course was highly pleased. I cannot write much in favour of our pastor, he is a worldly man, and does not live up to his preaching; but I have got Scott's *Commentaries*. I remember well when you used to get them in numbers, and I used to laugh at them; but, thank God, it is different with me now. I feel much happier and more contented than I used to do. I did not like Pembroke, but now I would not wish for any prettier place.

I have got a horse and gig, and Drew and myself drive all about the country. I hope my dear father and mother think of eternal things; can I do or say anything to either to do good? When you get my book, read the "Castaway."

You know I never was confirmed.[1] When I was a cadet, I thought it was a useless sin, as I did not intend to alter (not that it was in my power to be converted when *I* chose). I, however, took my first sacrament on Easter day,[2] and have communed ever since.

I am sure I do not wonder at the time you spent in your room, and the eagerness with which you catch at useful books—no novels or worldly books come up to the *Sermons* of McCheyne or the *Commentaries* of Scott. I am a great deal in the air, as my fort is nine miles off and I have to go down pretty often. It is a great blessing for me that in my profession I can be intimate with whom I like, and have not the same trials among my brother officers as those in a line regiment have. I ought not to say this, for "where sin aboundeth, grace aboundeth more fully;" but I am such a miserable wretch, that I should be sure to be led away. Dearest Augusta, pray for me, I beg of you.

TAKU FORTS, 15 *March*, 1862.—The climate, work, and everything here suits me, and I am thankful to say I am happy both in mind and body. I have had a slight attack of small-pox—it is not necessary to tell my mother this, as it will trouble her. I am glad to say that this disease has brought me back to my Saviour, and I trust in future to be a better Christian than I have been hitherto.

GRAVESEND, 12 *June*, 1866.—I cannot help sending you one of Molyneux's sermons. I picked it out by what the world would call an accident, but by us it must be considered His Providence; it deals so aptly with the subject we had been talking of. We are so hampered by our

---

[1] Nor was he ever confirmed.   [2] 16 April, 1854.

carnal nature that it is not easy to speak as one should. I omitted one point I was anxious to mention, namely, the whole secret of our trouble is want of love to God. If we have it to Him, we shall find it impossible not to have it to others. I can say, for my part, that backbiting and envy were my delight, and even now often lead me astray, but, by dint of perseverance in prayer, God has given me the mastery to a *great degree;* I did not *wish to give it up,* so I besought Him to give me *that wish;* He did so, and then I had the promise of His fulfilment. I am sure this is our besetting sin; once overcome it, and there will be no cloud between God and ourselves. God is love—not *full* of love, but love itself. The law is love; possessed of love, we shall find our other temptations fall from us like scales. We are all dreadfully prone to evil-speaking, but God is all-powerful against it; it is opposed to His nature, so He hates it. I pray for those I most envy, and the feeling leaves me at once.

I have had too much talking again and am now shut up for a few days; the result arrived at is, "It is not of him that runneth, but of God that showeth mercy" (Rom. ix. 16). We require to cast our care in *all* matters on Him. The great object of all our lives should be what our Saviour always spoke of as of inestimable value, even in His last hours, and again when He was leaving earth, namely, *peace internally,* let the world be as boisterous as it liked.

I am sorry to hear Miss B—— is ill; but I do not pray for restoration so much as for both the sufferer and those around to feel that they are in the hands of Infinite Love, who will never leave or forsake.

Man's happiness consists in present peace even in the midst of the greatest trials, and in more than hope of a glorious future. It comes by trust in the Lord Jesus Christ, by realizing that His atonement, as Head, suffices for the members of His body, and cannot be cancelled by any acts or affected by any merit of theirs, and that it is a finished work for the past as well as for the future. This being the foundation of peaceful happiness, it is experienced according as the sovereignty of God is acknowledged *in everything*, even our sins. He has said, " I will preserve thee from all evil." Does He do so in your opinion ? It is certain He does so as far as He is concerned, and you are bound to believe Him or make " Him a liar." He will give, if you ask ; you ask and do not think He gives, thus making Him out a liar.

Any deceit is a lie and injures His omniscience; it is aimed at His sovereignty : if done to a fellow-man, it would be humbugging him. Let our endeavours at least make us trust God as much as we would trust man. If we had a powerful friend ever near us, we would often ask his help and trust him ; is not God in that relation to us? Is anything too small or too great for Him? Therefore in all things make known your wants to Him, and trust Him to relieve them ; He never leaves or forsakes. Do not try planning and praying and then planning again ; it is not honouring to God. *Do not lean at all on your own understanding.* Your heart will call you a fool ; but let it call you what it likes, it has often deceived you and is desperately wicked. If doubt should arise in your mind as to what to do in any matter, think which of the two courses will best show forth God's glory, and follow it ; generally this will be the course most contrary to your own wishes. Supposing you have been led to leave the issue of any event to God, and afterwards begin to doubt if you are not called upon to do something to aid it, resist the temptation. All things are possible with God. Do not express your doubts ; pray to God to help your unbelief every time it arises ; remember we have power over our words, if we have not over our thoughts, and to prevent the tongue sinning is the first step towards the checking of the thoughts, which will soon follow. Act up to your religion, and then you will enjoy it.

14 *October,* 1866.—I think you will be blessed in sending
Rosas[1] the Testament. Mark the passages we dwell on,
namely, "Come unto Me;" and there are many others that
give peace to a mind that is, like a troubled sea, never at
rest. I am sure of one thing: great sinners, who have been
stopped in their career of sin by unforeseen circumstances
(not unforeseen by God), are very susceptible, and often
receive God's pardon with more humility than those who
have not so deeply broken His law. To them "much has
been forgiven," and generally, when they love, they love
much. "As in water face answereth to face, so the heart of
man to man" (Prov. xxvii. 19). It is grace alone that makes
us differ. Much thought over this does good; we see
ourselves reflected in every one else, and thus can realize
what great things God has done for us. I trust in God,
whose ways are not ours; we should always remember that
His glory should be more in our minds than our selfish
desire to feel happy or comfortable. It is selfish to wish
that God should hurry for your benefit; if we only wished
for the advancement of His glory we might perhaps be
impatient, but it is seldom for that we groan.

19 *October,* 1866.—Look on your heart as a harp with ten
thousand strings, very tender and delicate naturally, now out
of harmony, now in harmony; the devil or one of his agents,
by God's permission, strikes a string; let it respond by
sounding either God's praise or by calling His help. No
one ever speaks or writes to us without striking a string; so
look out, relying on Him without whom we can do nothing.
No such thing as *chance,* every emotion felt is for the great
object, His glory. No string is struck in exactly the same
way again. One of my strings is always being played on;
it is a favourite one, but, thank God, I can sometimes make
it sound His praise. I think it is a delightful illustration.

---

[1] Ex-President of the Argentine Republic.

A harp is affected by the weather, we can only keep ourselves in tune by remaining close to God.

25 *October*, 1866.—Every thought that enters our mind is for our good, even those which come from Satan. He who cannot lie says, "*All* things work together for good." What a comfort to feel that our temptations and sins are all working for good. All that is hateful and that distresses us is from the flesh, *i. e.* from our natural man, which dies at our death; while everything that is good is from the indwelling of the Holy Ghost. Only from the realization of this truth can we produce fruit, the more the realization the greater the amount of fruit. Much is contained in this prayer: "Lord, show forth Thyself in me, take my faculties and walk in me." Recognize all things as sent from Him, and be constant in the prayer that He should reveal Himself.

27 *November*, 1866.—We have all our ups and downs; my visitors have tried me in some ways, but all for the best. They make us feel how very weak we are, and that there is no such thing as storing up good thoughts. The manna had to be gathered daily; and so it is with grace. All that we gain by time is *experience—i. e.* to know where to go, to give up any thoughts of finding satisfaction in past goodness, to see that there is only one place we can get filled from—the Fountain—to give up thoughts of what we have been in times past, and to bow down to the decision of God that we should be tried—the result of all this being a most earnest wish to be at rest and free from all these troubles.

I can say after a month's little trials that the result has been to show my utter weakness; but, at the same time, I have this knowledge: that let me be strong or weak, it is the same, it is neither being the one nor the other that will carry me through the great day, and that makes up for all feelings of annoyance. I can only say that I truly wish to enter into my rest.

We are all invalids · but thank God are being cured,

though perhaps we know it not. Christ's Church is His body, now scattered; seen by Moses on the Mount in the patterns of the tabernacle; seen by David in the patterns of the temple; seen by Christ in the temple at Jerusalem. Flesh of His flesh, bone of His bone, we were with Him in Sinai, with Him when David saw the temple, with Him on Calvary, and now with Him in Heaven; we were destroyed with Him at Calvary, and in three days were built up again ("He spake of the Temple of His body"). What a thought! "If any man will do His will, he shall know of the doctrine" (John vii. 17). What a delightful verse! It means this: that just as much as we give up to our Lord, so much the more shall we understand; just as much as we live up to the light He has given us, so much the more light shall we receive.

——, 1867.[1]—To write of the varied scenery one has passed through on a railway journey is unprofitable, and so would be any account of what has been my course of life since we left one another. The longest day comes to an end, and, thanks be to God, the bright morning will soon come. We have not time to look back as yet, He carries us on through all and will never leave us. A passenger is carried in a steamer. He may or may not believe the steamer is proceeding on its course to the appointed haven, but he progresses irrespective of his belief or unbelief of the fact; and thus it is with God's ways. He is carrying out His work, however little we may be aware of it, or however unlike the course pursued is to that which we, in our perverted understanding, would choose. It would be no use to tell you of what you have so often seen in the way of exhibitions. This differs naught from the one of 1851. And you will soon see greater and greater wonders, such as human eye has not seen nor ear heard, and will see them

[1] After his return from the Paris Exhibition, where he was one of the jurors.

without pain, trouble, or weariness, or the corruption of our
poor fallen natures, without any alloy of sorrow, where all
around will be happy and at peace for ever; when the aged
will be young again and the sick at heart and body will be
made glad, and where, far surpassing any earthly melody,
we shall hear that new song, aye, and sing it too, when He
who was "despised and rejected of men," "the Man of
sorrows," "shall see of the travail of His soul and be satisfied." What a comforting thought it is that our Lord will
be satisfied, that He will feel that His work has been fully
accomplished to His satisfaction, that there is no drawback
to His joy! Shall we indeed see Him, and that near, and
shall not our thoughts be often on Him? Unless we keep
that hope before us, how can we be supported through the
routine of life here? But with that hope, and the knowledge
that He is *in* us and we *in* Him (irrespective of whether we
may believe this fact which God announces to us, 1 John
iv. 15), every single petty circumstance is of the utmost
import. Life is invested with a new charm, and death
exists no longer. Why be distressed at the departure to
inestimable happiness of those we love? Who would desire
to delay their home-going? Our only desire should be to
follow them at once. Our Lord has made death our friend
and deliverer from our poor fading bodies, the clogs of our
souls. He will support us through our last moments (Isaiah
xliii. 2).

Try earnestly to know the indwelling of God, and pray
to be taught it. What I say with all humility is, *that there
is a revelation made* about which there can be no doubt,
the sense of which always remains. If you have not this
knowledge, what I say will stir you up to seek it. The
covenant is the same throughout; the breach of the covenant or agreement is the preferring of anything to God.
He was our God and we His children in Christ before the
world began (Eph. i. 4). To take anything as our *chief* joy

is sin; and in this all the moral law is contained, for if we love God we cannot desire anything forbidden in the Ten Commandments. "Love is the fulfilling of the law" (Romans xiii. 10).

The Bible, by His revelation, is most absorbing; it seems so clear when He teaches. The flesh cannot receive the things of the Spirit; the spiritual soul never argues, it is only the carnal mind that does so.

3 *May*, 1867.—I am sure of one thing, we lose the very sweetest times by rejecting wilfully what God sends us: in avoiding people and disagreeable things. God says, "*I* will preserve thee from all evil." "*I* will preserve thy going out and coming in, from this time forth." "There shall no evil befall you." And yet we refuse to believe this for even a second, and go on plotting and praying for more communion with Him; and the moment He begins to work, we fly from Him. I want to realize this more than I do, it is evidently the reason of our deadness; there can be no confidence where there is distrust. If we think we are bound to look after ourselves, if we think these strong expressions are only figurative, or dependent on any particular frame of mind, they are useless to us. Unless we take them in their strength, we shall crawl along all our days.

I shall be very glad to see you when you can come. I wish you were here. I hear my mother is thinking of coming up to town. It will do her good, and you had better come here and see your brother.

There is a nice paragraph in the *Unchanging Love of God*, to the effect that the knowledge of sin is not acquired of ourselves or of our spiritual enemies, for by their consent we should never know it till we die. This is to the intent that, if the devil had his way, we should live perfectly moral lives, free from malice, &c., &c., and thus be lulled into a state of security. We are *born* corrupt, and, if the devil had his way, we should be kept in ignorance of it; our permitted transgressions show us our state; it is the root that is evil, and evil must be its emanations, yet we feel much more oppressed by the outward sin than by the inward corruption.

16 *May*, 1867.—I have had, and continue to have, the most exquisite delight in the Bible beyond any past experience I ever felt. All that dead time when I read without interest, merely because I ought to do so, is now repaid me, and God brings the passages back to memory with the power of the Spirit. "The Holy Ghost shall teach you all things, and bring all things to your remembrance" (John xiv. 26).

We have no conception or idea of what God will show us, if we persevere in seeking Him ; and it is He who puts this wish in our hearts. All I can say to you is : Persevere ; avoid the world and its poor wretched little talk about others ; never mind being thought stupid ; look on everything with regard to the great day, and trust Him implicitly. He says, "I will preserve thee from all evil. I will preserve thy going out and thy coming in, from this time forth and even for evermore" (Psalm cxxi. 7, 8). If you take these words and keep them in mind you cannot be moved ; for, whatever circumstances you may fall into, be quite assured that He is preserving you from all evil.

28 *May*, 1867.—The secret of reading the Bible is, abiding in Him who is "the way, the truth, and the life." "Ye need not that any man teach you." "I will instruct and teach thee in the way that thou shalt go, I will guide thee with mine eye." "Love not the world," for it passes away. "Pray without ceasing." If we keep these words in mind, we shall find the very greatest peace.

He, the mighty God, means what He says when He promises to teach us ; the more we trust Him the more we honour Him. I have felt a little of late of rejoicing in trials, and trust I may feel more. I mean really being glad at annoyances, inasmuch as they work experience and hope. This is a very great gift to obtain from God, but it is little to what He will give us if we persevere.

Of all epistles the living epistle is the most striking and easily read by all. Man sows seed, working hard to culti- vate the ground for the same, but he cannot produce a leaf of the herb. We use prayer and ask for what we think we want, but do nothing towards attaining anything. The herb springs up whether the man is anxious or not, "So is the kingdom of God, as if a man should cast seed into the ground ; and should sleep, and rise night and day, and the seed should spring and grow up, he knoweth not how" (Mark iv. 26, 27).

15 *June,* 1867.—We grow in grace whether we are aware of it or not, and are powerless to produce good or resist evil ; and not only are so now, but are so (however closely we may be living to God) as long as we are in the flesh. It is the knowledge of our weakness (and that can be known only by experience) which induces us to trust in His strength ; even that induction is His gift, He makes us willing. No one word can avail, unless the Spirit of God opens it to the heart. How very little one ought to indulge in converse on these matters, indeed how useless it is to do so, when we have Him not altogether in our thoughts. It is by far the longest road to learn from others, the shortest road is to learn from God ; and yet we are so proud that, knowing this, we try and use our most imperfect knowledge. The experience which God has given me tells me, in retire- ment, that this is the case ; yet, alas, how little effect this has when I meet others !

24 *June,* 1867.—We are placed on earth in order to suffer like our Lord, not to enjoy life, except in doing His will ; He will give us this frame of mind. It is not attained at once, but is a growth, the slower the more sure and the sturdier. It is meant, when He says we must forsake *all*

that we have to be His disciples; and it is only when we
do so that we realize that we have given up nothing in
comparison to what He has given us in certain possession.

Do not think that any are free of the cross, or that one
is heavier than the others; we all have them, He never
tries us beyond our strength. I feel often I am learning,
through much pain and bitterness of heart; the mortification
of the flesh will never be a pleasant operation; as crucifixion
was a slow process, so is our slow death of the flesh. It
makes us yearn for the complete deliverance, and yet not
to yearn for it, for we have the feeling that, compared to the
glory that shall be revealed in us, the sufferings of the
present time are not comparable. " Our light affliction,
which is but for a moment, worketh for us a far more
exceeding and eternal weight of glory."

21 *July*, 1867.—I hope —— will realize the truth, or
rather I trust God will open his eyes to see it. We all
have veils over our spiritual understandings; some of us
have them thicker than others, we are *quite blind* till we get
the veil removed. The veil is the flesh, it is never entirely
removed while we live in the world; it is only made trans-
parent by *living in the Spirit*, or *mortifying the flesh*, which
are similar things. We all want to live in the *Spirit* and in
the *flesh* also; this is impossible, thence the struggle. The
more we apprehend that the death of the flesh is the life of
the Spirit, the more we shall realize His presence. Death
of the flesh is painful, but absolutely necessary, for, as we
mortify the flesh, so shall we grow in the Spirit; we must
feed on our flesh as it were.

The pip of an apple is surrounded by the soft pulp, which,
when it decays, affords rich mould to the young sprouting
pip. Thus the germ is fed in us, and thus we go on germinating ourselves to the end of time. The young receive
the truth much more readily than the old. I hope God will
give light to some here.

The flesh is ruined and never improves. A due knowledge, through God's grace, of that truth prevents pride,
and enables us to look on any ebullition of another as not
emanating from him, but from the evil one, thus disarming
our feelings of any resentment; for who would be angry
with a maniac? And such, more or less, we all are—for we
are not in our true senses; if we were, we should care little
for the things of time, but wholly for the things of eternity.
There are still to be cast out dumb devils and violent devils,
and devils who say, " Depart from us, for we desire not the
knowledge of thy ways" (Job xxi. 14).

The word we speak is nothing, our emotions are often
more acted on by a look than by the sound of a word.
The influence is in the Spirit, and not in the sound which
passes away, while the effect on the hearer's spirit remains.
God speaks in us, but does not use a fleshly voice to make
Himself known to us; if we live much in the flesh, we shall
not hear His voice, unless by trials and afflictions; but, if
we live in the Spirit, we shall (according to the degree we
do so) hear His voice minutely and always.

Think over this subject. The sound of the voice has no
effect on our spirits; it is some invisible influence which
affects us, which influence could act without the sound, if
it pleased God. This thought makes one happy after having
spoken to any one on this subject; for it matters very little
what we may say, if our spirits are in unison with God; and
when we speak for His glory, it is not our argument which
will convince, for all the host of heaven could not tell that
secret or convince one man of the truth. When we speak
to any one, we have first God leading us to do so and
speaking from us; while, at the same time, He testifies in
the person spoken to just so much as His infinite wisdom
is pleased at that time that they should receive.

Keep in view 1 John iv. 15; it has in few words the
great secret of the new life. I have known many who have

lately come to the truth and peace by asking God to manifest the power of it.   As we remember it, we live happily;
every time we feel cold or apathetic it arises from not
realizing the truth, and God alone can keep that realization
before us.

31 *July*, 1867.—I have had very nice thoughts on 1 John
iv. 15—" Whosoever shall confess that Jesus is the Son of
God, God dwelleth in him, and he in God."   I think it is
the key to much of the Scripture.   I am more than ever
convinced that the secret of happiness and holiness is in
the indwelling of God.   The same truth is shown in many
other verses, but the above, to my mind, shows it more
clearly.   Let a man seek the teaching of the Holy Spirit on
such verses, and he will grow much in grace.   As we believe
that text, so we shall realize the presence of God in our
hearts, and, having Him there, we have as a sequence
holiness and love.   He alone can make us believe the
truth and keep it in mind.

10 *August*, 1867.—Make Him your guide ; you do not
want any other.   He has said, " I will teach you all things ";
and, depend on it, you will find it the shortest course to
pursue.

You say you have little time to read ; you have from six
to eight every morning.   I own it is not pleasant to flesh
and blood ; but, if this trouble is much, the corresponding
growth in grace is far greater.   We must not deceive ourselves ; we have plenty and plenty of time during the day
for ourselves.   If we aspire to walk in the power of the new
life, we must cast away all hindrances, and it must cost
something we really value.

We aspire to a closer and lasting communion with the
living God, which is a high aspiration and needs much
striving and many falls.   Many appear, from some wise
reason, content with a lower desire, and are satisfied with
distant communion and less striving.   Would we wish to be

like them? I say not. Let us have the heavier apparent cross (which is in reality the lightest one, if we could see it) and the higher aspiration, and, thanks be to God, He has given it to us, and, having done so, will carry out the work in us, which from beginning to end is of Him. Do not think that all who aspire to close communion arrive at the same, without parting with the eye of their personal comfort in many things. It is, as self is given up, so a man is holy. I believe Jesus is the Son of God. I believe, very feebly perhaps, that what God says is true, *i. e.* that God dwells in me, and I trade on that till I feel the power of it, viz. if God dwells in me, I can ask Him anything; and therefore I will ask Him to bless every one.

I own it is dull when we do not feel much in common with those we pray for, but after a time it will grow into love, and at any rate it is honouring to God and keeps us from thinking of things of no import; it also tends to make us less selfish. Take the Holy Spirit for your teacher, and you will never want another word from man on questions of doctrine. You will say what connection has the verse 1 John iv. 15 with holiness. Holiness is compounded of the fruit of the Spirit, and therefore, if you have the Spirit, you will certainly without trouble produce the fruit of the same. It is seldom that we find people interested in the matter; the truth is, either that the fact of God dwelling in us is accepted with joy, or else looked on as a dream, instead of its being the very keystone of all peace and comfort. Few will think of the fact.

Addresses in vague terms from the pulpit do not arrest attention; it is only by direct attack in simple plain words; and to do that, we must use a boldness not of our own but of the Holy Spirit in whose name we would speak. Let us strive to make those around us know *that* truth, and the way to do so is to live in it ourselves, for "if ye *abide* in me ye shall ask what ye will and it shall be done." What a

wonderful fact it is, and what new life it gives to all to
whom the Lord reveals His presence !

12 *August*, 1867.—I feel my remark about getting time
by rising at 6 A.M. was hard on you.   Peace is a fruit of the
Spirit, and is obtained only by the indwelling of the Spirit;
therefore the more we realize the truth of God's indwelling,
the more this peace will be produced—this realization is the
gift of God.   The indwelling of the Spirit makes the Christian
faith different from all other religions.   Meditate much on
the fruit of the Spirit (Gal. v. 22, 23), and with God's blessing you will soon have done with dark times, which all arise
from our thinking good of ourselves, or rather in our thinking
we are improving.

It is just as God manifests Himself to us, so we shall
walk.   It is through crosses that we live; let us have. few
crosses and we shall starve and be cold, let us have plenty
of crosses and we shall thrive.   We must feed on our own
flesh, and, as we feed on it, so we shall grow in proportion.
God has revealed the truth of the indwelling to me through
Galatians v. 19-21.   By these verses we can see that everything hateful and which distresses us is from the flesh, *i. e.*
from our natural man, who dies at our death, and not before,
while everything good and which pleases us is from the Holy
Ghost dwelling in us, and from that alone.   Therefore, as
we realize His dwelling in us, so shall we live in the Spirit,
and He will produce the fruit of the same in us.   What man
tries to do is to produce the fruit apart from the Spirit, and
thence his falls and unequal walk.   All is contained in this
prayer, "Lord, show forth Thyself in me, take my faculties
and walk in me."

I cannot say too much as to the necessity of avoiding the
trial of making the flesh conversant with the things of the
Spirit; the flesh must be thrown off, the old man must be
given up before we enter Canaan.

It is to my mind much easier to go into great trouble and

exertion, than it is to walk after the Spirit. What great self-denial it is to allow a trivial remark, perhaps not quite right, to pass by uncorrected; yet we give much more credit to ourselves for speaking to unbelievers, and relate to our fellow pilgrims the circumstance with unction, although the former self-denial is far greater to most people.

Of late, the truth seems more and more clear day by day : our promised possession is God Himself, and we have the earnest of that inheritance in His dwelling in our hearts. It will be something stupendous when we realize it, most assuredly no flesh could stand the revelation. I never expect to find the views God has given me accepted by all; if true, they will prosper, if not, let them perish.

Analysis of feeling is a work we often fail in, but, if we search our hearts carefully, we should find how all emanates from selfish motives, and would show to others a different spring from that which really works in them. It is strange how often the true spring which works is seen by outsiders perhaps, when hidden or dimly seen by ourselves.

MANCHESTER, 21 *September*, 1867.—Your heart would bleed to see the poor people here, though they say there is no distress such as there was some time ago : they are indeed like sheep having no shepherd, but, thank God, though they look forlorn, they have a watchful and pitying Eye over them. It does so painfully affect me, and I do trust will make me think less of self and more of these poor people. Little idea have the rich of other counties of the scenes in these parts. It does so make me long for that great day when He will come and put all things straight. How long, O Lord, how long !

I have but little time to write by this post, so will say no more than that I have less confidence in the flesh than ever, thank God, though it is a painful experience and makes one long for the time when this our earthly tabernacle shall be dissolved ; but may His will be done. If there is sin and

C

misery, there is One who over-rules all things for good; we must be patient.

The poor scuttlers here, male and female, fill me with sorrow. They wear wooden clogs, a sort of *sabot*, and make such a noise. Good-bye, and may God manifest Himself in all His power to all of you, and make you to rejoice with joy unspeakable.

If we think of it, the only thing which makes the religion of our Lord Jesus Christ differ from that of every other religion or profession is this very indwelling of God the Holy Ghost in our bodies; we can do *nothing* good; Christ says, "*Without Me* ye can do nothing;" you are dead in trespasses and sins, you are corpses, and must have life put in you, and that life is God Himself, who dwells in us and shows us the things of Christ.

GRAVESEND, 11 *May*, 1869.—I have been very remiss in writing of late, for the "Archers have wounded me sorely" in worldly matters. They have gone away, I am glad to say, and I am the better for their visit. A country lad of our Lord, a Hebrew, fourteen years old, has fallen to me, and I hope to get him on the Survey.

A few words on Free-will. Eve's sin was disobedience, and came through her believing the devil more than God; it was want of faith; this is the cause of all sin and of all heaviness of heart. Faith is the gift of God; can any have this, unless it be given by God? According to my realization of a future, so do I disregard the things of time; if any one lives for the things of this world, it is because he has no apprehension of the things of futurity, no faith in them. Faith is a fruit of the Spirit, and unless it is given us we cannot have it. God gives us the wish, and thence our prayer for it. If He gives the wish, it is virtually the earnest of the gift, which will come in due time.

I humbly believe our life is to learn our nothingness and His being everything; when we agree with Him that we are nothing and are not astonished at our evil nature breaking forth, when we are willing for the last to be first, when we are willing to be the least in Heaven, that every one we know should be higher than ourselves, then, I think, our lesson is learnt. If we are annoyed at any disparaging remark or conduct of our fellows, it is because we are not yet fully aware of our being nothing.

As the seed, *which must die* (see John xii. 24 and 1 Corinthians xv. 36), carries the future tree in itself, so we may carry our resurrection-body in us. It is the dying of the seed which feeds the growth of the tree which springs from it. This dying or corruption goes on from worse to worse till the end of our lives. The antagonism of the world to Christ was the antagonism of the flesh to the Spirit made visible; the same persecution that He went through visibly was precisely of the nature our souls go through from our bodies and in the outward world. In the degree that we are in the Spirit and look on things from God's point of view, so shall we be judged by those who judge from man's point of view and who live to the world.

A man who knows not the secret, who has not the in-dwelling of God revealed to him, is like this—⟮ Body / Soul ⟯

He takes the promises and curses as addressed to him as one man, and will not hear of there being any birth before his natural birth, or any existence except with the body he is in, he is more or less dim on all subjects. The man to whom the secret (the indwelling of God) is revealed is like

this— 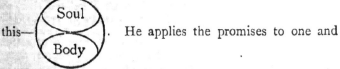 . He applies the promises to one and

the curses to the other, if disobedient, which he must

be, except the soul is enabled by God to rule. He then
sees he is not of this world; for when he speaks of himself
he quite disregards the body his soul lives in, which is
earthy. Thence come disputes between men; this one
speaks of a different self from the other, and both are right
after their apprehension. Our Lord was the Spirit made
flesh, but was not received by the flesh of this world, because
He testified to its utter worthlessness. If He had preached
good living and attendance on human ordinances, He would
not have been persecuted. His condemnation of the world
was not to be borne with.

"I am the Vine; ye are the branches." The branches
spring *out* of the vine, are one with it, are, in fact, the
medium by which it produces its fruit. We are *out* of
Christ, and are the medium by which He glorifies God the
Father by His production in us of much fruit: it is His
work, not ours. The branches are in the vine before they
are seen; their life is as long as the vine's; they date their
existence from the same time. If therefore Christ is eternal,
so are His members in both ways, future and past.

A body has many members, but it is one body. Each
member has its given position; some have one degree of
sensitiveness, and some have another, such as the nails and
hair. These are as necessary to the beauty of the body as
the other members are. A body without hair or nails, eyebrows and eyelashes, is unsightly. So with Christ, His
body is made up of us, who have each our different degree
of sensibility corresponding to our position in His body;
as in a body lying down and rising up, the head rises first,
then the other members to the feet, so I believe that, as
Christ the Head has risen, so also have those of His people
who correspond to the upper members of His body; and
so shall we rise when our corresponding position rises.
Only the beloved of God and blessed by Him enter
Heaven—none but the righteous, the unspotted, the

undefiled.   Only Christ and His body can fulfil these
conditions.

No human law allows of a substitute for an offender
against its enactments.   If a man steals or kills another, it
could never be urged that justice was satisfied if a stranger
should suffer the penalty which falls on the culprit.   He
who committed the fault must suffer for that fault.   If
before a judge an offender pleaded that his head had done
the deed, the plea would never be admitted, his whole body
would have to suffer; and so it is with our redemption.
Unless I, in every respect, am one with Him who suffered,
so that all His holiness is mine and all my sins are His,
justice would not have been met.   *I* sinned and *I* suffered
the penalty (1 Peter iv. 13).   A suffering head implies
suffering members.

The Head and the body (the limbs or members) are
Christ and the believer.   This is the secret of the Lord; it
solves all mystery.   It is the keystone of our existence,
redemption, and acceptance; and I humbly believe it is
utterly impossible to account for the Atonement in any
other way.   Man is saved by grace or favour through belief
in Jesus Christ, and that not of himself.   This belief or
faith is the gift of God, not won by works lest he should
boast (Eph. ii. 9).   Man cannot have the things of another
unless they are given to him, neither can he have faith, or
belief, unless it be given him by God; and without this gift
it is impossible to please Him (Heb. xi. 6).   According to
the degree a man has this gift, he overcomes the world and
subdues his body.

God gives unto each according to His will the measure of
faith differing one from another, corresponding to their
position in the Body of Christ.   "The testimony of Jesus
is the spirit of prophecy" (Rev. xix. 10).

I humbly believe our Lord's words, "Be not faithless," &c.,
were divine orders, like "Rise, take up thy bed," &c.;

"Stretch forth thy hand," &c.; and His remark, "Blessed are those," &c., to mean, happy are those to whom God has been pleased to give a greater measure of faith. The born of God believe they never, never sin; indeed, they "cannot sin because born of God" (1 John iii. 9). They overcome the world; do not belong to it, even as Jesus did not, though in it. Except you die, you cannot see this Kingdom; flesh will not inherit it, for it profits nothing; it is grass which withereth. You are composed of many members: some children of obedience, sinless and believing, born of God; some children of disobedience, unbelieving and sinful. The latter will be cut off, left in the wilderness, and do not enter into rest. Only a remnant is saved. They are the Israel of God, the Children of Promise to whom all the promises are given; they have union with God in Christ, by the same Spirit dwelling in them as in Him; they are His sheep and hear His voice, are elect or chosen, and cannot be deceived; they can pass through the sea or grave unscathed, while the others essaying to do so will perish; they can walk through the furnace, while those who put them there perish. Before a new *creation* there must be a *death*. Without shedding of blood there is no remission of sin; the blood is the natural life; without death there is no entrance into Heaven.

He shall separate the wheat from the chaff, the grain from that which surrounds it, the children of obedience *in us* from the children of disobedience. As the wheat and chaff are one seed, so the spiritual and carnal man are one seed. "He will gather His wheat into the garner, but He will burn up the chaff with unquenchable fire" (Matt. iii. 12).

The seed is sown; it grows, the wheat and chaff together. They are inseparable till the harvest is come; and, like the kernel of a nut, they become more detached as the grain ripens. The seed is *in* or encompassed by the chaff. Chaff is always chaff, as wheat is always wheat. It is worthy of

remark that both the wheat and chaff are required to make
the perfect fruit.

This illustration will, like all His words, bear the strictest
looking into ; it will not fail in the smallest particular. You
notice Jesus blesses one part of the seed and curses the
other part; so with us, the new man, which is God in us, is
placed in His garner; the old nature, the chaff, is to be
burnt up with "unquenchable fire." "The wicked doth
compass about the righteous" (Hab. i. 4). The soul of man
is the germ, his body is the husk, the sprout is the new body
made out of the old body by the soul. As long as the
sprout remains under ground, it is fed by the husk's absorption ; as soon as it appears above ground, it absorbs for
itself air and light.

October, 1869.—I cannot say what very quiet, relying
comfort there is in doing everything quite openly and irrespective of the consequences. We are weak and uncomfortable when we act for man's view of things ; it is humbugging
God in reality, not man, and as surely as we do that we shall
reap the reward. The things may be comparatively small,
but a very immense principle is involved in them. It is most
wonderful what power and strength are given to us by living
for God's view and not man's. I do many things which are
wrong, and I can say truly that, thanks to God, I am comforted in all the troubles, because I do not conceal them
from Him. He is my·Master, and to Him alone am I
accountable. If I own in my heart that I am culpable, I
have such comfort that I do not care what my fellow man
says. We are most awful liars, every one of us, utterly false ;
it is no use mincing it. "Trust in the Lord with all thine
heart, and lean not on your own understanding."

A lie is told either to gain something or to conceal something. By telling it the person trusts more to what he may
say having an effect on the person he addresses, than he
does to the fact that God knows what is in his heart and can

actuate as He wills the heart of the hearer. He reasons thus: "There is no God ; I am quite free, and it is in my power to say this or that." It is, as it were, as if there were three persons present, A, B, and C. A tells B something before C, as if C were not there, not thinking that C, without being heard audibly, can speak to B the answer to give.

It is fear sometimes on the part of the liar [1]; he fears his fellow more than God, and thinks God is so weak as not to be able to help him, if he did tell the exact fact. It really is unbelief or distrust which induces all lies, either spoken or acted.

Supposing a child tells you a lie, how do you act? Punish him severely is the recipe of the world. Will that prevent him from telling another? No, it will make him more careful for fear of punishment, but it will not touch the root of the matter; it will not tend to make him trust in God's power to get him out of a scrape. Then how should we act? I believe it would be better if we told him that we knew of the fact (if we did), and that we pardoned it, because it was already pardoned by God ; that we felt with him in his troubles, as liable to be in the same ourselves, and encouraged him to look above man to God. In the case of men, we may not be able to speak thus, but the feeling should be in our hearts. We ought to punish, if power be in our hands, with that feeling ruling in us. If we are told a thing and cannot ascertain its truth for a certainty, we ought to act as if we believed it ; as far as that particular action is concerned, we may be deceived, but it is better to let off many guilty, than to punish one who is innocent.

And to you who act lies, or prevaricate, or use evasions, and then comfort yourself, or try to do so, by making out what you said was not quite a lie, that it was the truth, but

---

[1] "If it be well weighed, to say that a man lieth is as much as to say that he is brave towards God, and a coward towards men " (MONTAIGNE). "For a lie faces God, and shrinks from man " (BACON).

not *all* the truth, Reason says you are simpletons. Why, all your petty stratagems are known, and, if they take effect, it is only that it is tacitly allowed to be so for a time. If you tell the truth, you have infinite power *supporting you ;* but, if not, you have infinite power *against you.* The children of kings should be above all deceit, for they have a mighty and a jealous Protector. We go to other gods—Baal, &c. —when we lie ; we rely on other than God. We may for a time seem to humbug men, but not God. It is indeed worldly silliness to be deceitful. Who can stand against the honest, " I did it, and I am sorry it has vexed you ? " Who is then the highest, the judge or the culprit ? The latter may say in his heart, " A Higher than thou hath forgiven me, and I care not what thou, His subject, may do." Even if he put the law in force against you, it will be but a feather's weight. How mean and humbled is he who does the reverse, even if he is let off by the judge—even if he is successful in his lie. Oh ! be open in all your ways. It is a girdle around your loins, strengthening you in all your wayfarings.

Do not ignore the Third Person's presence. Where there are two gathered together for whatever purpose, there is He also, ready to help to the uttermost, and more than willing. Let people tell lies of you, He will blunt the shafts. Do not be a hypocrite, and pretend to be better than you are : you are utterly bad, corrupt, and every imagination of your heart is evil continually. A blackamoor might as soon become white, or a leopard change its spots, as *you* do good. Anything said against you is infinitely less than ought to be said, and, if it is any comfort to you, know that all men are alike, even as face answereth to face in water. Happy indeed are you, if you know your corruption and weakness, for then His strength is made perfect.

Do you want to be loved, respected, and trusted ? Then ignore the likes and dislikes of man in regard to your actions : do to them as you would have them do to you, leave their love for God, taking Him only; you will find that, as you do so, men will like you; they may despise some things in you, but they will lean on you and trust you, and He will give you the spirit of comforting them. But try to please men and ignore God, you will fail miserably and get nothing but disappointment.

The ninety-first Psalm is a mountain of strength to all believers, as is also the twentieth verse of the thirty-first Psalm.

If a man speaks well of me, divide it by millions and then it will be millions of times too favourable. If a man speaks evil of me, multiply it by millions and it will be millions of times too favourable. Man is disguised, as far as his neighbour is concerned; this disguise is his outward goodness. Some have it in a slight measure torn off in this life, and are judged accordingly by those whose disguise of goodness is more intact; the revelation of the evil by this partial tearing off is but the manifestation of what exists. Whether the disguise is torn or intact, the interior and true state (known to God quite clearly) is the same corrupt thing; the eye of the Spirit discerns through the disguise.

Who could bear to have this disguise quite rent off, and the evil exposed to the eyes of the world? How would the world receive me, if they knew what I really was and what God knows that I am at this minute? Yet, how hardly I judge another whose disguise, slightly rent, shows a little of the corruption I know exists in me.[1] Nothing evil was ever said of any man which was not true, his worst enemies could not say a thousandth part of the evil that is in him.

Job can bear loss of friends, children, and worldly prosperity; but when given over for trial to Satan, who brings out in him the black leprosy, "he cursed his day, for the thing he greatly feared came on him" (Job iii. 25). A

---

[1] "O wretched man that I am! who shall deliver me from the body of this death?" (Romans vii. 24.)

spiritually-minded man may by God's grace be able to support with submission the loss of all earthly joys and comforts, but let him be tried by Satan's demonstrating the corruptness of his flesh, which is the same thing; let him fall into sin, though he may feel safe (even as Job was, for God restricted Satan's devices to Job's body and told him to *save his life*), yet he will be inclined to curse his day and partially murmur against God. Where is there any one who could bear to fall into those terrible sins *in act*, which exist most certainly in man in thought, and which thoughts a spiritually-minded man is well aware are known to God? Yet, why this shrinking? It is virtually only showing to man outwardly what God sees us to be inwardly. To avoid it is to love "the praise of man more than the praise of God." Yet who could endure it? · Who could bear to be known as God knows us? When all is quiet, our friends agree that "in the flesh dwelleth no good thing"; but if a fall takes place, they belie by their acts what they have said in words, and they are surprised, showing that they do not *really* believe it practically, but only theoretically. There is a great difference between theory and practice, between the acceptance of a truth in words and in deeds; we need personal practical experience to accept in deeds.

23 *July,* 1870.—I am glad you are quiet: "enough for the day is its evil." He that is dead has ceased from sin. When we die we are born again. Our bodies did not die in Eden; our souls did, and therefore are born again when God speaks the word in this life.

The shedding of blood is figurative of death, for "the blood is the life," and the shedding of it is the giving up of life. If our Lord had not shed His blood, He could not have entered the kingdom of death to break its bonds, for as He had no sin in His body, there were no elements of death in it. As we anticipate death by self-mortification or self-denial, so we shed our blood or natural life, and so far only do we feel the remission of sin.   As we are selfish, to that degree shall we be without that assurance.

The people who have sons or husbands in the war [Franco-Prussian] have their attention drawn to God, now that sorrow has come on them.   They know He directs the bullet, and that He alone rules; all men believe this in their hearts, so they call on Him.   In their need they search themselves and subdue their evil natures, as He gives them strength, thus shedding their life,—self-mortification,—and realizing the assurance of the remission of sins, not by their abstention from sin, but from the trust He gives which causes them to abstain from it.   The war, when looked on with respect to individual families, is not worse than every-day life (there are many suffering mentally much more than these men suffer).   All these things are beautiful and glorious in the extreme.   They come from the *Rest of God* into which we enter, when we cease to think for ourselves; when we cease from our own works, and let Him unroll the scroll, knowing that, as the day, so our strength shall be, and that all things will work together for good.

Good-bye, my dear Augusta.   It is by the above reflections, after being well-read in the Bible, that we get peace; not so much in reading, as in chewing the cud over what is read, and with the golden rule measuring the events of this life, which thus is made an interesting scheme.   Saul was not a bad man in the eyes of the world; David was.   Why was one perfect in God's sight, and the other rejected? Because one leaned on God, and, though he often fell, he was helped up; but Saul leaned on himself and had no support when he fell.

10 *November*, 1870.—If you dissected facts, you would never be disturbed.   What people do is for the best, and designed by Divine wisdom for some object far beyond our ken; we may suggest respecting futurity, but should not do so dogmatically, but with an " I think in my obscured state "

that this or that course will be the best. We often try and convince others to our way of thinking from sheer wish to rule, and often in our heart of hearts we do not care a jot beyond the conversion to our wishes of those we try to influence : the sequel is of no consequence.

It is often a trial to me to find others so obstinate on things that by man may be said to be undoubtedly foolish. For instance, A.,[1] whose neck had been bad but had healed up beautifully, and who was going on well, when his mother goes and gets him a place at ten shillings a week. This caused him to have his meals at all hours and to be out at night, and now his neck is getting bad again, and I feel a little annoyed; but, when I investigate the annoyance, I think I am more put out by not having my advice taken than because the boy's neck is bad. We must look above ourselves to rest in peace; we must get into God's crucible to have our motives analyzed. The world may say this is selfish, but it is not so, if we pray for those we are interested in. In nine cases out of ten, our motives will not bear the Scriptural anatomist's knife.

G. is another case. He never came to say good-bye to me, neither did he go to you, but God thought it better; so I rest (thank Him) quiet, and do not say I will not bother myself about any more lads, as I feel inclined to do. How often has God done much for me, and I have utterly and contemptuously forgotten to thank Him? Content with what we have means complete and perfect union with God, never to be attained altogether while in the flesh. It has to be learned. Paul says, "I have learned to be content," a long life lesson.

28 *December,* 1870.—Humanly speaking, this is not a time to marry when so much sorrow and trouble are about in the world; but perhaps there is no more sorrow than there always is. I expect we shall see some such *dénouement*

[1] A boy General Gordon was interested in at Gravesend.

as this at the end, that what appeared times of great physical suffering were times of less sorrow mentally. I expect we shall see there the exact contrary to what we see now. I was reading, "The Lord is *good to all.* His tender mercies are *over all His works;*" so He must be good to all the poor shivering wretches, and He must be showing them tender mercies. It is incomprehensible, but must be true; so I comfort myself, as far as my faith will allow me. I believe that, did we know a tithe of what God has for all of us, the inhabitants of the world would run to death. I expect the future must be, as it is said, quite past man's understanding. "Eye hath not seen, nor ear heard, neither have entered into the heart of man, the things which God hath prepared for them that love Him" (1 Corinthians ii. 9).

Looking at our Lord's life as our example, we do not see any disturbance in His mind at the vast number of afflicted people who came to Him. It is said He had "compassion" on them; but there is no surprise mentioned at the existence of these ills. We do not find Him in any way taking the part of the poor against the rich individually. He pointed out the fallacy of the pious rich in thinking they fulfilled the law while they neglected their brethren.

The whole of our Lord's life, taken in respect to our duties in our own spheres, is very useful and comforting. I believe it is a great task and beyond our natural strength, to so far overcome ourselves as not to be put out by injustices done to ourselves or to others; in this teaching we enter into God's own position, who so often sees such injustices done by man to his fellow, and who is so often misrepresented Himself.

I think our life is summed up in patient waiting and in being content with the evil of the day. Night soon comes, and with it comes rest.

30 *December*, 1870.—I more than ever believe in the

soul-and-body doctrine. In the seventh chapter of Romans
it is said, " The law hath dominion over a man as long as
he liveth," therefore it hath no dominion over him after he
dies; also it is said, " He that is dead is freed from sin "
(Romans vi. 7), so that both the law and sin are non-
existent after death. I shall, D.V., try and write some more
of the thoughts that strike me. I see, thank God, so many
passages which deepen this impression. There is no work
going on, and I fear therefore much distress; but from my
knowledge of the East I expect our Lord saw very much,
and yet He made no remark.

I read, from the pouring-out of the ointment by the
woman and the objection of the disciples to the waste
(Matthew xxvi.), that often things may be done by ourselves
and others which look like neglect of the poor, but that our
judgment is not right in these matters. This your interesting
fable [1] illustrates. It is very much to my liking.

We too often look on things in the abstract, and do not
understand that far higher issues are at stake.

The key to the knowledge of God is the sensible perception of His indwelling. Before He gives the feeling, He

---

[1] The fable referred to is as follows :—"Our worthy forefathers have
left us the following fable in verse: Hans Priem was admitted into
Paradise on the express condition that he was not to indulge a habit he
had acquired of censuring and criticizing whatever came under his notice.
Accordingly, on seeing two angels carrying a beam crossways along the
road and knocking against every object they met, he said nothing. In
like manner, observing other two drawing water from a fountain and
pouring it into a cask with holes in the bottom, he was surprised, but
held his peace. Many more things of the same kind occurred, but he
was silent, though surprised. At last, however, he saw a cart stuck fast
in the mire, with one pair of horses yoked before and another pair behind, and the carter giving the whip to both simultaneously. This being
his own vocation, it was more than Hans could do to refrain from
criticizing it ; and the consequence was he was turned out of Paradise
by two angels. Before the door closed behind him, however, he looked
back, and perceived the horses were winged and had succeeded in drawing
the cart out of the mire into the air. Nor can there be any doubt that
in the cases of the beam and cask there were equally good reasons for
what was done" (SCRIVER : *Gotthold's Emblems*).

lives in us; but He only makes Himself known when we feel it, and thenceforth we see His deep things. The more we leave the world the more we know of Him. We, our true selves, are veiled in a sheath or body. Daniel says, "My soul is troubled in my sheath" (chapter vii. 15, margin); and, like our clothes, that sheath is a perishable thing, which day by day He shows us is only a temporary garment, to be put off, as we put off our clothes to go to sleep (the type of death). Every night we, in a manner, die to the world; and who can say but that the best time of their lives is spent in sleep? And so it will be, when we put off these poor garments and rise to everlasting day; not waiting, as some think, till the resurrection of these garments, but passing from death to life at once. God was Abraham's God. Abraham, thousands of years after he had thrown off his earthly sheath, was living to Him, and we really enter life when we close our eyes to this poor world.

Endeavour to realize the completeness of salvation to *all* men; know that God rules all things, even evil. Weigh the characters of the worst of men and women. What do we know of the influences to which they may have been subjected, influences which it was not in their own power to avoid, such as their birth, their bringing up, &c. &c. ? Think for yourself, if you had your will, would you not be free from malice and all the evil that affects you as a mortal? Then think of others as having the same desire. God sees it is better for us to have these trials, that we may know that we are not in our home, that we may groan for the happier world that looms beyond the tomb. We may rest assured that *God loves us, loves us all*, infinitely. Would He wish any to perish? How could He wish it? And, if He wishes it not, who is to stand in His way? We know not these things now, for we see through a veil, but that veil will be rent, and then we shall know Him and His love as He knows us. Join no sect, though there may be truth in all.

Be of the true army of Christ, wear His uniform, *Love:*
" By this, and by no other sign, shall men know that ye are
My disciples."

THE PRISONERS OF THE LORD.[1]

He that believeth that a man, by name Jesus, a carpenter,
who was put to death as a malefactor and blasphemer by his
countrymen eighteen hundred years ago, and who, when in
the world, was almost universally despised, is the Christ and
Saviour and the Son of God, is born from above, is born of
God, not of blood, nor of the will of the flesh, nor of the
will of man (John i. 13) (the flesh believes in what it sees ; it
can catch hold of a rope when drowning, but its belief is only
so far as its actual vision extends). He then that believes in
Jesus is directly born of God, emanates from Him, is begotten
of Him, and necessarily has everlasting life. It is his birth
that gives him that belief in Jesus, and he who is thus born
" doth not commit sin," for " His seed remaineth in him and
he cannot sin " (1 John iii. 9) because of his birth. If then
any one believes in Jesus, that belief emanates from a spiritual
being *in* him, a spiritual man or existence, which is as directly
a son of God, as the body that he inhabits is the son of the
father who begets him. " That which is born of the flesh is
flesh, and that which is born of the Spirit is spirit " (John
iii. 6). There is a spiritual body, and there is a natural or
earthly body ; the one born of God, and the other born of
man ; the one delighting in the law of God, and the other
in the law of sin ; the one blessed and an heir of God, with
a kingdom prepared for him ; the other cursed, corruptible,
and which cannot inherit the kingdom. Begotten with the
word of truth, by God's own will, " to an inheritance incorruptible, undefiled, and that fadeth not away " (1 Peter i. 4, 5).

[1] The following papers were written in Gravesend and sent to me as
letters, though without dates. I have thought it best to place them
together, as they were all written about the same time.

Children of God, ye are kept by the power of God, "ready to be revealed" with the Lord Jesus Christ, when He appears in His glory. Ye are His words, pure as silver tried in the furnace of earth, purified seven times. The flesh you inhabit is "as grass, its glory as the flower of grass; the grass withereth and the flower thereof fadeth, but the word of the Lord endureth for ever" (1 Peter i. 24, 25). All that the flesh admires is doomed, therefore heed not the admiration of men; "that which is highly esteemed among men is abomination in the sight of God" (Luke xvi. 15). It is only the flesh that loves the world. By the "flesh" I understand the carnal mind, the natural man, which as a substance is as useless as the dust it is and to which it must return. "All that is in the world, the lust of the flesh, the lust of the eyes, and the pride of life" (1 John ii. 16), will pass away. The difference between you and your flesh is manifest: *ye* are the "offspring of God" (Acts xvii. 29). *The flesh* is the offspring of the devil; *ye* cannot sin, it cannot help sinning, for it is of the devil; it does the deeds of its father the devil, and his lusts it will do (John viii. 44). It cannot bear God's words or understand them; "they are foolishness unto him" (1 Corinthians ii. 14), because it is not *of* God. "He that is of God heareth God's words: ye therefore hear them not, because ye are not of God" (John viii. 47). *It* is not of God, though it may claim Him as its Father. Children of the light, as heirs of God, ye were under bondage, and "observe days and months and times and years" (Galatians iv. 10). But now, because ye are sons, God hath sent forth the Spirit of His Son into you; ye know, or rather are known of God, and are free from your tutelage; for the creature itself, though now corruptible and made subject to vanity, is yet to be delivered from the bondage of corruption into the glorious liberty of the soul, of the manifestation of the sons of God. "For this purpose the Son of God was manifested that He might destroy the works of the devil" (1 John iii. 8) (*i. e.* to take away the sins of our bodies) and to deliver those bodies "who through fear of death were all their lifetime subject to bondage" (Hebrews ii. 15).

The righteous will alone enter Heaven; without are all those who work iniquity; therefore nothing of the natural man of the flesh can enter, for *its* works are manifest.

The world is a vast prison-house; we are under hard keepers, with hard rules, in cells solitary and lonely, looking for a release. What have we not to put up with from our masters? By the waters of earthly joy and plenty to the world's inhabitants (our flesh), but by the waters of lonely afflictions to our souls, we sit down and weep when we remember our home, from which death, like a narrow stream, divides us. Yea, we hang our harps upon the willows in the midst thereof, for they that oppress us require of us mirth, saying, "Sing us one of the songs of Zion" (Psalm cxxxvii.). How, oh how, shall we sing the song of the Lamb in a strange land, in the (to us) waste, howling wilderness, in the land of strangers? Oh, for that home where "the wicked cease from troubling and the weary be at rest" (Job iii. 17); where the good fight will have been fought, the dusty course finished, and the crown of life given; when our eyes will behold the only One who ever knew our sorrows and trials, and who has been with us in them all, soothing and comforting our weary souls! No new friend to be made there, but an old, old friend! Are you weary now? So was He. Are you sad? So was He. Are you despised? So was He. Is your love repelled, and does the world not care for you? Neither did it for Him. He was unutterably weary, sad, and lonely, "a man of sorrows and acquainted with grief"; and shall we repine at our trials, which are but for a moment? We are nearing home day by day. No dark river but divided waters are before us; and *then* let the dust take *its* portion—dust it is, and dust we leave it. "I heard a voice from heaven saying

unto me, Write, Blessed are the dead which die in the
Lord ; Yea, saith the Spirit, that they may rest from their
labours" (Revelation xiv. 13)—rest from troubles, rest from
works of weariness, from sorrow, from tears, from hunger
and thirst, and sad sights of poor decaying bodies, and
sighing hearts, who find no peace in their prisons, from wars
and strifes and hard words and judgments.

It is a long weary journey, but we are well on the way of
it. The yearly milestones quickly slip by, and as our day
so will our strength be. Perhaps before another milestone
is reached the wayfarer may be in that glorious home by the
side of the River of Life, where there is no more curse,
neither crying nor sorrow—at rest for ever, with that kind
and well-known Friend. The sand is flowing out of the
glass day and night, night and day, grain by grain : shake
it not, you have a work here—to suffer even as He
suffered.

MARK IV. 13.

"Know ye not this parable? how then will ye know all parables?"

In this parable a field for seed is represented having a
path through it. A wayside part of it is stony and rocky,
and destitute of moisture ; another part has thorny bushes
in it which hide the ground from the sun ; and another part
is good ground, but varying in quality. A sower goes forth,
and scatters his seed over the field. Some falls on the path,
is picked up by the birds and trodden down by passers by ;
some falls on the rocky soil, which, retaining the heat of the
sun and being covered by a thin layer of earth, soon pushes
the seed into vegetation, and, as the roots find no moisture
when they strike downwards, they soon wither away under
the scorching rays of the sun. Some falls among the thorns,
which spring up with it and choke it, so that it produces
no fruit. And some falls on good ground, varying in goodness, and brings forth some thirty, some sixty, and some an

hundred fold. It finds here depth for its roots and moisture, and grows *slowly,* as much out of sight as above the
surface.

The sower is the Son of Man, the Messiah, the Christ ;
"the seed is the word of God" (Luke viii. 11), the words
of the Kingdom. He sows where He will, He knows the
ground. It is His seed which produces fruit when in union
with the ground it is sown into. The sowing of the seed
changes not the quality of the soil. The wayside is still
the wayside, the rocky is still sterile, and the thorny still
thorny. The seed will only fructify in the good soil, though
in the rocky and thorny soils there may be appearances of
a crop. The sower is the only one who could improve the
soil, which is passive in itself. The seed that fell by the
wayside is immediately taken away by Satan ; there is no
appearance of any crop. The seed that fell on stony places
springs up rapidly, but is soon scorched by the heat of tribulation, affliction, and persecution. " It had no root," however promising its appearance may have been. The seed
that fell among thorns (which could have been eradicated
only by the Sower) gets choked by them—viz., the cares of
this world, and the deceitfulness of riches—and becomes
unfruitful. The seed sown on good ground, having root
and moisture, brings forth fruit with patience, unhindered
by thorns, birds, lack of moisture, or by little depth of soil.
The unproductive soils are "those *which are without.*" The
productive soils are those who believe in Jesus—the disciples.
The flesh is unproductive ; the soul is productive under the
influence of the Holy Ghost.

To some "it *is given* to know the mysteries of the kingdom
of heaven," and to others "this knowledge is *not given*"
(Matthew xiii. 11). The soul, in union with Christ by the
Holy Ghost, produces the fruit of the Spirit—"love, joy,
peace, long-suffering, gentleness, goodness, faith, meekness,
temperance" (Galatians v. 22, 23). The flesh, not being in

such union, is not influenced by the Holy Ghost and produces no fruit, but is influenced by the wicked one, by the
cares of this world, the deceitfulness of riches, and the
pleasures of this life.   Now the things which scorch up the
flesh and make it wither owing to want of root (union with
Christ) cause the *soul* to fructify on account of its having
that root (that union with Christ).   "The earth which
bringeth forth herbs meet for them by whom it is dressed,
receiveth blessing from God: but that which beareth thorns
and briers is nigh unto cursing; whose end is to be burned"
(Hebrews vi. 7, 8).   The curse of the earth was that it was
to bring forth thorns and thistles, and that curse was the
crown of our Lord.   On the good ground or heart the effect
of the seed sown is lasting, and produces fruit, though of
slow growth.   It draws its nourishment from an unseen root;
it is *braced* by *persecution* and *affliction*, and is free from the
cares of the world and its pleasures.

We can see the *history* of the Bible, and may understand it, but we
forget that we are blind to its secret mysteries, unless God shows them
to us; our Saviour says, "Unto you it is *given.*"   Only the Spirit *in*
man finds God.

SPIRITUAL BLINDNESS.

"He that saith he is in the light, and hateth his brother, is in darkness even until now.   He that loveth his brother abideth in the light.'
—1 John ii. 9, 10.

If the blind lead the blind, the result must be obvious.
"Whosoever hateth his brother is a murderer" (1 John iii.
15), he abideth in death.   Christ removes the blindness by
means the world does not like.   Laodicea thinks she can
see, but is blind (Revelation iii. 17).   The fallacy of the
blind is that they can see, and feel it most irritating to be
termed blind.   The world does not like a man to make clay
and to spread it over the eyes of another.   It looks for-
biddingly at the man who has so little pride as to submit to

such humiliating means; it would itself sooner remain blind than undergo it. The Pharisees want *signs;* they can see if there is anything to see; their eyes are wide open; as far as they are concerned they are complete. The Publicans want *eyes;* they dimly discern something and feel they are wanting in the means of discerning more clearly what that something is; feebly they feel that, if they only had the telescope, there is plenty to see. The ones will teach you everything and are angry if you will not be taught by them, though their teaching gives no comfort. The others want to be taught, and do not look so much at the teacher, as they do to the comfort they get from his teaching. The Pharisee is generous; he will impart all his knowledge. The Publican is selfish; he gets what he can and ruminates over it, feeling he can impart nothing.

1 KINGS XIX. 9, 13.

"What doest thou here, Elijah?"

Why art thou away from the battle-field before the battle is over? Thou hast expected a change in what is unchangeable, a clean thing from an unclean, an Ethiopian to change his skin and a leopard his spots, a lasting effect to be produced on the flesh by witnessing a supernatural event. The flesh is evil and corrupt, and nothing that may be shown to it will change it into goodness or incorruption. The flesh hates and fears supernatural sights. Adam and Eve hid away from God. The place where Jacob saw God was dreadful to him. Israel heard His voice and desired to hear it no more. Gideon and Manoah both expected death from seeing God. Isaiah was "undone" because he had seen God, and Peter would have the Lord depart from him. "Depart from us," says the flesh, "we desire not the knowledge of Thy ways. What is the Almighty that we should

serve Him? and what profit should we have if we pray unto
Him?" (Job xxi. 14, 15). The flesh is as "stubble before
the wind and as chaff that the storm carrieth away;" it shall
lie down in the dust, and the worms shall cover it; it shall
be brought to the grave and remain in the tomb, the clods
of the valley shall be sweet to it (Job xxi. 18-33). The
mighty of the earth only for a moment are silenced by the
most stupendous sights. The manifestation of God on
Sinai was followed by the making of the golden calf (they
like a god who will not interfere with them), and the whole
of the miracles in Egypt were soon forgotten. Jehovah was
the true God for only a short time after the sacrifice at
Mount Carmel, when God showed Himself, or after Samuel
had called for lightning in summer. If a man rose from the
dead (Luke xvi. 31) it would produce only a momentary
silence, not any change in the flesh. The flesh worships
idols of silver and gold, its praise is the praise of men, its
fears are for what men say. "Cursed is the man who
maketh flesh his arm" (Jeremiah xvii. 5).

The flesh would keep out of sight all things which tend
to show that it is mortal; if there is disease, it is the fault
of the sufferer; if there is poverty, it is the improvidence of
those who are poor. As far as the judgment of this world
is concerned, God does *not* rule, however much His rule
may be acknowledged *in words.* "This and that could have
been avoided, if this or that had been done;" the world's
preachers and the world's religion of forms and ceremonies
are hard and cold with no life in them, nothing to cheer or
comfort the broken-hearted. Explain, O preachers, how it
is that we ask and do not get comfort, that your cold services
cheer not. Is it not because ye speak to the flesh which is
at enmity to all that is spiritual and must die (joy is only
from the spirit)? It is as a troubled sea which cannot rest,
whose waters cast up mire and dirt; there is no rest for it
this side the grave. You preach death as an enemy instead

of a friend and liberator. You speak of Heaven, but belie your words, by making your home here. Be as uncharitable as you like, but attend my church or chapel regularly.

There was no fear of Herod being reproved by the high priest for his breach of the law, though you must not carry your bed on a Sunday. Does your vast system of ceremonies, meetings, and services tend to lessen sin in the world? It may make men conceal it. Where would you find more hardness to a fallen one than you would in a congregation of worshippers of the Church of this day? Surely this hardness is of the devil, and they who show it know not God. If you gave your bodies to be burned it would not make up for the absence of this quality of mercy, *which is spiritual.* Why this surfeit of religion without heart on Sundays, and unkindness, cheating, and over-reaching in the week days? O Pharisees of this day, ye are tenfold more self-righteous than the Pharisees of old. They had one community and held together; while ye are many, and each one's hand is against the other. Poor shepherds! happy is it that there is a Shepherd who does know and care for His sheep. We should be in poor case, if we fell into your hands!

"YE ARE MY WITNESSES."—Is. xliii. 10.

I humbly believe the witness of Jesus is as if a man in any assembly were to stand up and say: " I have found in my pocket a warrant by which I am convinced I am the heir of an estate. Do you all search in your pockets and see if you have the same, and, if you have, be sure you *are* heirs of estates." So any man can address his fellow-men, and say: "Look and see if you believe in Jesus; if you do, God lives in you." As in the example nothing that the speaker could say could put the warrant of heirship in his hearers' pockets, so nothing that any man can say can make his hearers believe in Jesus. The spirit in man addressing his fellows speaks to pieces of silver or pieces of clay; his speech cannot metamorphose one into the other; it is only the silver which can be affected by his words. The joy he feels in finding a hearer agree with him is similar to that felt when, amidst a crowd of strangers inimical to one, a friend is found of the same degree and country as one's self.

·As in a cosmopolitan assembly a man seeks his own countrymen, so the child of God seeks the other children of God. His effort is not to *make* children of God, but to look for them and to encourage them to look to their heirships for themselves. Christ in His Word speaks to believers and to believers only; Paul's epistles are to the Church, he has no message to those without. Man judges belief after the flesh, which profiteth nothing at all. Christ died uselessly, if the flesh profiteth; by its works none are justified. The offence of the Cross consists in the preaching of the doctrine that man is justified or accepted in Christ, irrespective of his acts; the world wants to have a say with God in the matter.

FLESH AND SPIRIT.—BODY AND SOUL.

Our Lord having stated that "the flesh profiteth nothing" (John vi. 63), it is important to discern between it and the spirit. Now, God tells us distinctly what are the works of this flesh which profiteth nothing. They are manifest. "Adultery, fornication, uncleanness, lasciviousness, idolatry, witchcraft, hatred, variance, *emulation* [laudable after the world's ideas], wrath, strife, seditions, heresies, envyings, murders, drunkenness, revellings, and such like" (Galatians v. 19-21). The flesh cannot inherit the Kingdom of God, against which it is at enmity. In it is "no good thing" (Romans vii. 18). These works are the results of its corruption; it serves the law of sin; what is born of it is flesh.

It is not "subject to the law of God, neither indeed can be" (Romans viii. 7). None in the flesh can please God. "That which is born of the flesh is flesh; and that which is born of the Spirit is spirit" (John iii. 6). (Every one of the above-mentioned sins emanate from a root, the condemned flesh which must die and be sown before it can be quickened; the creature must be sown in corruption, dishonour, and weakness, before it can be raised in incorruption, and glory, and power; the creature will then be released from the bondage of corruption to the "glorious liberty of the children of God.") If the flesh profiteth nothing, then neither do its works. To profit nothing signifies to make no difference, either one way or the other; therefore whether a man is guilty of the above works or not is immaterial to his ultimate welfare or salvation. And now we see the breadth of God's law: *there is not a being in the earth who is not guilty in God's sight of every one of these works, for with God the thought is the deed.*

There are seen in the world persons guilty of some of these works, which militate against the law and well-being of society; and such are therefore outcasts from that society which seeks to make the world a better home and condemns those works which would incommode it; but society takes little heed of those works which do not materially interfere with its comfort and well-being. This is right so far as acts are concerned, but it should extend also to the sins of the heart. Society is the creature, and the creature knows only the flesh which has to be restrained outwardly by the law.

Dives says, to dress meanly would be peculiar, not to wear false hair of dead people would be to make my daughter conspicuous. If Dives' daughters could by any means obtain wings, they would not care for this peculiarity, but would be proud of them. Few of us are above the question of dress, but we seldom feel the same bashfulness in wearing goodly apparel that we do in wearing mean apparel.

We are all lepers. Some have their leprosy covered with silk, some with tattered rags; take off the silk and take off the rags, there are the lepers! Cover the face, and cry "Unclean, unclean!" The leper in rags shows more to the fleshly eye of his leprosy than the leper in silk. Adam, Noah, Moses, David, Solomon, Daniel, John the Baptist, Peter, Paul, Herod, eminent divines, bishops, kings, all are lepers in the flesh; after the flesh you will not inherit. "Flesh and blood cannot inherit the kingdom of God" (1 Corinthians xv. 50). From a corrupt tree corrupt fruits necessarily are produced.

Leprosy is of all sorts. I know it does not show so much in one who is quite occupied as in one who is idle; hence my ardent wish to be employed some way or another, and thus be more free from temptations. I know therefore you will let me leave you for employment. I fear settling on my lees, I fear waxing fat, I fear my God, and this fear at times makes me deeply sad. Perhaps, as my God has given me great gifts in His secrets, so He has given me a rebellious body to humble me. A query arises: if *works* are immaterial as far as salvation is concerned, and if I am guilty of them in thought, I am no more guilty if I commit sin than I was before. Such would be the result of these truths, if we followed human reasoning; but here we have to deal with One who is all powerful, all loving, and who works in us to hate the garment spotted with the flesh, and in our souls to hate these sins or works. Quickened by union with Him, the flesh, and consequently its works, have to contend with an Almighty foe; and it must little by little decrease in strength, as Christ in us waxes older and older.

"Now there was long war between the house of Saul and the house of David; but David waxed stronger and stronger, and the house of Saul waxed weaker and weaker" (2 Samuel

iii. 1). Victory is assured to the soul; flesh is mortal, it
has its term, its seventy years rule of tyranny and sorrow.
Every day brings this tyranny nearer to an end; it is grass
soon to wither, its goodliness to fade, but the words of God
incarnated in it will abide. Flesh can believe only what it
sees, it is therefore condemned; it cannot enter the gates of
Heaven, though they are never shut, "for there shall in no
wise enter anything that defileth," it must rest without with
"dogs, murderers, sorcerers," &c. &c. But those who enter
have their names written in "the Book of life, of the Lamb
slain from the foundation of the world" (Revelation xiii. 8).
Words of God proceeding from His mouth, they shall not
return unto Him void, they shall accomplish that which He
pleaseth (Isaiah lv. 11). Born of God, from above, they
sin not, neither can they sin; their birth is the day of the
death of the flesh ("This day have I begotten thee").

For a small moment had the Lord forsaken them, but
with great mercies hath He gathered them; in a little wrath
He hid His face from them, but with everlasting kindness
will He have mercy on them (Isaiah liv. 8). "O thou
afflicted, tossed with tempest and not comforted" (Isaiah
liv. 11), great shall be thy peace. The "holy ones" will
not see corruption, they leave a land—in which they are
strangers and sojourners, where they have no abiding cities,
but live in frail tents; in the day the drought consumed
them, and by night the frost—for a city in which there are
many mansions, houses made without hands (2 Corinthians
v. 1), eternal in the heavens, a holy city, New Jerusalem,
having "no need of the sun, neither of the moon, to shine
in it: for the glory of God did lighten it, and the Lamb is
the light thereof" (Revelation xxi. 23). In those frail tents
they had groaned for those houses from Heaven, desiring to
be free from the bondage of corruption.

"And who are these who have come out of so great
tribulation?" Those who have everlasting life: not of this

world, not of the flesh, though they have been *in* the world
and *in* the flesh.   They are inhabitants of another kingdom,
to which they are appointed and which was prepared for
them before the worlds began, a kingdom that cannot be
moved and that will have no end.   They owe no allegiance
but to their King (the King of kings and Lord of lords,
rejected by this world); they (the prisoners of the Lord,
His hidden ones, of whom the world was not worthy) were
sought for and released by their Head from the iron furnace.
The joys of this earth have no allurements for them, are not
their portion, and cannot satisfy them.   Dimly at first and
by degrees they have seen the light, often obscured by their
veils; they have been led on by little and little to see
another kingdom, and that kingdom's King in the Man of
Sorrows.

Though feeble in age, stature, and understanding, in spite
of the carnal reason of their bodies, they are insensibly
drawn to Him closer and closer, till they *know their oneness
with Him*, till they have revealed to them that they are He
and He is they, no longer twain but *one*.   A crown of glory
and a royal diadem are they in the hand of their God (Isaiah
lxii. 3), and He is the crown of glory and diadem of beauty
to them (Isaiah xxviii. 5), His jewels refined in the furnace
of affliction.   Their joy and the joy of their King is mutual;
before ever a star was made He loved them with an everlasting love, a love knowing no ending and having no
beginning; over them their King rejoices with singing, their
days of mourning are ended, their sun will never more go
down nor their moon withdraw itself, for the Lord is their
everlasting light (Isaiah lx. 19, 20).

They have left that inheritance, defiled, corruptible, that
fadeth away; they have escaped from that city of Jerusalem
in bondage, to Jerusalem the free.   While in the frail habita-
tions of this earth, they had known of those mansions above;
they felt they had no resting place here; they knew that

above their dwelling-places were existing, even while they wandered in that desert land, that waste howling wilderness, in tents of flesh; they had no thought of taking those "vile bodies" into those realms of peace. The perishable stones of the temple of their body, as a community and as individuals, they see must be thrown down, that God may build His temple of living stones, not wrought by hand; the Lord God and the Lamb will be their temple (Revelation xxi. 22), and they will be His temple (1 Corinthians iii. 17) and His city, they in Him and He in them, one name for the Lord who dwells in it and for the city, "the Lord our righteousness."

Strange combination: one body and soul, dust and spirit, mortal and immortal, accursed of God and blessed of God, unbelieving and believing! These have struggled on, the waves and the billows have gone over them, they had cleaved to the dust yet they had been always safe, when they had been passing through the water of affliction He had been with them, and the rivers had not overflowed them, neither when they walked through the fire of temptation had they been burned. The Lord was their shield, their hedge about them, and now they will hunger no more after righteousness nor thirst after the living God (Psalm xlii. 2). Neither shall the sun smite them by day, for the Lamb will feed them and lead them to the fountains of living waters, and their God will wipe away all tears from their eyes.

A royal race of priests and kings, unknown by the world, in bitter bondage; they claim a higher lineage than man can give. When there were no depths, before the mountains and hills were settled, they were brought forth; when their King prepared the heavens and set a compass on the deep, there were they by Him daily His delight (Proverbs viii. 24, 25, 30). Fall down, oh ye mighty of the earth, ye kings and warriors and priests, and hide yourselves from the face

of Him, who comes with all His people. He was hungry
and thirsty and you passed Him by. Little did you think,
in the days of your pride, you had turned the Royal Race
from your doors; and in treading them down, you trod
down the King of kings. " Inasmuch as ye did it not to
one of the least of these, ye did it not to Me " (Matthew
xxv. 45).

Though the eyes of that Eagle Race may be weak, and
the clouds in which they are enveloped be of thick darkness, in a little while that will be rent and they will be
manifested as God's children. In that day, ye high ones
and ye kings of the earth, ye lofty and haughty ones shall
be made low, the moon shall be confounded and the sun
ashamed, when the Lord cometh with His ancients. " Comfort ye, comfort ye, my people! saith your God " (Isaiah
xl. 1). Your warfare will soon be accomplished ; though it
tarry, wait for it. " Enter thou into thy chambers and shut
thy doors about thee : hide thyself as it were for a little
moment until the indignation be overpast, for, behold, the
Lord cometh out of His place to punish the inhabitants of
the earth " (Isaiah xxvi. 20, 21), not those of the heavens ;
" And in that day, lo this is our God, we have waited for
Him." " The pleasure of the Lord shall prosper in his
hand ; He shall see of the travail of his soul and be satisfied." He will have reaped their fruit and He will be
satisfied. Oh, how long, how long, O Lord, must we wait
for Thee ? Day by day, we thank Thee, we near our home,
our tents grow threadbare and can be seen through, our
" flesh is as grass, and all the glory of man as the flower of
grass." The grass will soon wither, its flower soon fall
away, but we, Thy Words, will endure for ever.

Looking humbly on this dispensation, our human reason
assents to the wisdom of God's ways. How could we know
Him in so many circumstances and trials as we do now,
unless thus incarnated ? To hear of the work in a coal

mine, however well told, could not give us a particle of an idea of what the work there really is. To know that truly we must work out a year there, but a lifetime to know the bitterness of that labour, of hard masters, of heat and cold and dirt in the delicate fibres of our skin, of the sorrows of those around, bereaved of support by sudden catastrophes. Who can tell this but one who has lived through it? And who could tell the horrors of sin and the love of God, but these who have borne the fleshly mantle? We know indeed, but in part; but that part is sufficient, for our teacher is God, and He will teach us thoroughly. We have a lesson to learn, that having *nothing* with Him will suffice our wants, while possessing *everything* without Him is a waste and void. When we have learnt *that*, our course is finished and the race will be over. Press forward, servant of the Lord. Be patient until the coming of the Lord.

MATTHEW V.

Christ's disciples only are addressed. They are those who believe in Him; the flesh does not believe in anything but what it sees, "In it dwelleth no good thing." His word is not in *it*, it is not poor in *spirit*, it does not mourn if it has the things of this life, neither is it meek, nor does it hunger and thirst for a holier state, for the Living God; it would be content with bread and the kingdom of this world; it is not pure, or merciful, nor is it persecuted for righteousness' sake, it dislikes being hated, and is inclined to retaliate, it is not the salt of the earth, nor its light amidst a crooked and perverse generation. The righteousness of the Scribes and Pharisees, which is for the view of men, must be that of the flesh, the righteousness of the soul must exceed this, for it is for the view of God. From the "garment's" point of view, everything that does not agree with it is evil. From the spirit's point of view, nothing is evil, for all things work together for good.

E

There dwells in every human being two natures, the carnal and the spiritual. Christ's atonement gave that power to the spiritual which enabled it to become conqueror. In some, during their earthly existence, there is such a development that it is *evident* that they are "born again"; whilst in others their life here is so full of sin and wicked works that neither to themselves nor to others do they show signs of a new birth, but death—the carnal creature being destroyed and the spiritual remaining—gives them an entrance into heaven and an eternal abiding in the presence of God.

"As in water face answereth to face, so the heart of man to man" (Proverbs xxvii. 19), and "He fashioneth their hearts alike" (Psalm xxxiii. 15). We must allow all men come from Adam and are not different one from another in God's sight, however mysterious this may seem. I accept it, and do not consider myself better than any other being breathing. I believe there is a spiritual child of God in every one, which is his true self, and was with us in Christ before the world began, and will be with us in the eternal future.

THE TWO KINGDOMS.

The world contains the people of two kingdoms, acknowledging two separate kings and two separate systems of government. The one is an everlasting, undefiled, and incorruptible kingdom; the other is mortal, defiled, and corruptible. Christ is the King of the Kingdom of God, and the Devil, anti-Christ, is the king of the kingdom of the earth. "My kingdom is not of this world" (John xviii. 36). The Kingdom of God is a spiritual kingdom; that of the earth is an earthly or fleshly kingdom. The people of God are united by spiritual union to their King; the people of the earth are united by fleshly ties to their king. The people of God are hidden from the eyes of the people of the earth, owing to their union being spiritual. The people of the earth only look on things seen and created, which are temporal; while the people of God look on things not seen and uncreated, which are eternal. The one people look to this world as their home; their efforts are to ameliorate it, and render it more of a resting-place— thence all temperance and similar societies. If all disease, pain, sorrow, and care were removed, they would desire no other home; and even though these are not removed, yet their desire is still for this world, in which all their joys and pleasures are found. The other people look on this world as a wilderness, in which they are sojourners and pilgrims. To them the removal of all pain, disease, sorrow, and care would still make it no home. They have no abiding city here, but are strangers. "They seek a country . . . a better, that is, a heavenly country," for they are not of this world (Hebrews xi. 14, 16). To the one, death is the end of all their hopes; to the other, death is the gate of everlasting life. One king will be in all the glory of the flesh, a man to be admired; the other King came in the lowest form of the flesh, a man to be despised. The one will have power over the treasures of gold and silver and the precious things of this world; the other had nothing in this world, not even a place where to lay His head. The one will rule all flesh; the other was forsaken by all men. The one will rule by the wisdom and reason of the flesh; the other rules by the indwelling of the Holy Spirit, which is incomprehensible and foolishness to the flesh. There is a "wisdom of God" and a "fleshly wisdom" (2 Corinthians i. 12). The one people proclaim God to be glorified by their acts; the other proclaim God glorified by the Holy Ghost's spiritual working in them, in virtue of their union with Christ. The one cling to outward forms and ceremonies as essential, and to outward displays of godliness, to circumcision, or cleansing of the

E 2

flesh, to be seen of man, whose praise is more sought for
than that of God. "They loved the praise of men more
than the praise of God" (John xii. 43). The other look
on outward forms and ceremonies as non-essential to
inward spiritual purity; to the mortification, death, and
burial of the flesh as a thing utterly corrupt; and to be
seen of God, whose praise is to be more sought for than
that of man. The one look to their works to make them
children of God; and the other look on themselves as
children of God by grace, and therefore they do the works.
The one look to be saved at last; the other look on
themselves as saved already. The one exclaim against
murder, drunkenness, lasciviousness, and stealing, but are
guilty of uncharitableness, malice, &c., inward sins. The
other people look on the "inward sins" as being as bad
as those outwardly committed. The one people hold the
other in captivity, making them conform to their rules and
their views.

As in the world there are two peoples, so in *each*
individual there are two principles—the flesh and the
spirit—the one holding the other in bondage—one born
of man, the other born of God; one mortal and sinful,
the other immortal and righteous; one of the earth, earthy,
the other of heaven, heavenly; one loving the praise of
man, the other loving the praise of God.

The Assyrian and the Israelite, the one holding the other
in captivity by the power given by God, will be eventually
judged by Him; their destruction will be sudden. The
captives are not to rebel; their captivity is only temporal,
and will be broken by another power at a decreed time.
The destruction of the flesh is the release of the soul; the
one serves the law of God, the other the law of sin.

As in Babylon many captive Israelites forgot their origin
(Nehemiah xiii. 23, 24), and looked on themselves as
Assyrians, so in the world many children of God forget their

origin, and contend for the things of this world; and, while animated by spiritual impulses, are still struggling for the amelioration of this flesh, not clearly seeing its doom.

The duty of the children of God under the bondage of the children of this world is to wait till God delivers them from the same, for it is He who gives the power to make them captive. That bondage to forms and ceremonies and to the things of this world cannot be broken by their means, such as by austerities or seclusion from the world; it must be by the power of God, and must be patiently waited and prayed for. Inwardly, when the soul accepts the gross wickedness of the body as a bondage under which it has been subjected for a time (and after which that body will be judged), then it is in its proper condition. Oppressed, it prays for redemption; it sees the necessity for the destruction of the flesh, and rejoices as it wears out day by day. As in the Old Testament the Assyrian held the Israelite in bondage for seventy years (Jeremiah xxv. 11), so will the body hold the soul in bondage three score and ten years— the age of man (Psalm xc. 10).

LUKE III. 3.

A man unknown to the outward world preaches the necessity of change or returning, if sins are to be remitted or put away. John preached the *inward cleansing* of the fleshly mind, the Pharisees preached the *outward cleansing* of the flesh. Jesus preached the *death* of the fleshly mind, and that the *flesh* was utterly corrupt. The Pharisees preached that man had power to be holy; their idea of holiness was outward show and ceremony, and was gauged by the praise of man. John preached that man had power to be holy; his idea of holiness was that it was inward: he testified that his ministry was only a precursor to one of a higher description, the cleansing effects of which would be as superior to his as fire is to water.

John's idea was the reform of abuses; to him the world was capable of amelioration.   Jesus's doctrine was the utter corruption of the world, the hopelessness of anything good being derived from it; He preached the condemned state of it, and exhorted man to look beyond it for succour.   His kingdom was "not of this world" (John xviii. 36).   He did not belong to it, neither do His people, though *in* it.   "They are not of the world, even as I am not of the world" (John xvii. 16).   When John ceases his preaching (which the world will bear to a certain point, and with which Pharisees will also agree as far as discussing the question of the purifying of the flesh with him) then Jesus begins.   He declares that, as man, the flesh cannot inherit (become holy), but must be buried in Jordan, and raised again, the heavens opening, and the Holy Ghost descending in power, and God acknowledging the risen as His Son in whom He is well pleased (Luke iii. 21, 22).   So we may be publicans or Pharisees according to our bringing up, either quite given up to the devil and greedily following iniquity, without the pretence of godliness, or else attending forms and ceremonies, and coming up to the world's standard of goodness, whited sepulchres standing on our own merit, "*holier than thou*" who art not attending as many services as we are, judging others as extreme who go further in forms or realities than we do; calling all right who agree with us, and all wrong who do not; asking questions in order to justify our walk, irrespective of any desire to know the truth, which is rejected when against us, and accepted if against others and for us.   But whether publicans or pharisees we are not satisfied, and are led to John in the wilderness, who points to a higher ministry, his own being only transitory.   Here we have to wait, looking for this "mightier" one, God giving us the hope of it, and with the hope a desire to be rid of our iniquities, which are too heavy to be borne. We wait for His time, and, when the flesh is buried in corruption and no hope left, a voice calls us forth to know ourselves children of God, temples of God, and the heavens are opened never to close again. In the power of this resurrection life we, or, rather *God in us*, can do all things. We no longer belong to this world, our yearnings are for our thrones, our crowns and sceptres, and day by day, as Jesus is developed *in us*, shall we more and more apprehend our divine descent. That descent will be questioned by the devil and by man, according as we proclaim it; for the opened heavens, the voice, and the descent or anointing will be only known to the recipient by his spiritual eyes.

If you are the son or daughter of God, how is it you are in any want? You ought to be able to command. We answer, we are heirs who have not come to our inheritance, our life is not supported by the things of this life, but by God's presence. He will, when He thinks fit, relieve the temporal wants of our " sheaths " (Daniel vii. 15, margin). Those who live wholly for the pleasures of this world may receive them ; but we look for higher glories than this world can give, and cannot be content with transitory, fading joys. God has put us in a position of trial, and the having His presence with us will restrain us from tempting Him on the strength of His love. We have full conviction of His love without these tests. We proclaim our divine descent and our mission in our families, and are first accepted, and then rejected because of our relation to them after the flesh (Matt. xiii. 57).

" Why is this not known to us, as well as to you? outwardly there is no difference between us " is the question. " Because God has chosen to reveal Himself to me. He does what He likes, irrespective of man or man's choice " is the answer. " Favouritism," is the cry, " I cannot tolerate it. If such be the case I would rather not be a Christian.

I do not mind the outwardly good being saved, but I cannot
tolerate the saving of the outwardly bad. I cannot agree to
the fact of a man, who has led an ungodly life all his days,
having the same position as myself, who, for many years, at
great inconvenience, have attended many prayer-meetings
and services and ordinances. I have glorified God by this,
and that man has dishonoured Him by not attending His
services. I have toiled all day; he has not toiled at all. I
have not resisted God; he has. I ought to be saved, for I
am better than he. I do not like this, for it will bring my
merits down to that of every one else, and I have a lurking
feeling that God sees something in me above the common
herd of men."

LUKE V.

The expounders of the Scriptures, the professed expositors
of God's Word and Will, the self-righteous come down to
judge. Satisfied with themselves, they give their opinion
on this new doctrine. Ignorant people bring a helpless
man, and disregarding conventional forms let him down by
the roof. The Lord announces to him the forgiveness of
his sins, thus claiming a prerogative of God and thereby
raising the question of His Divinity, which is at once disputed by the self-satisfied expositors; for if He was God,
and yet a poor man, whose learning was not from their
teaching (whence knew He letters, having never learned?),
they ought to give up their learning and accept His doctrine
and position. The Lord calls their attention to the fact
that to raise up a helpless man was a harder matter *in their
human estimation* than to pronounce the forgiveness of sins,
and therefore, if only God could do the one, so it could
only be God who could do the other. In doing this He
asserted His Divinity. The scribes were silenced but not
convinced. Angry at their discomfiture, they were outraged

that the followers of the Lord (whom they did not dare to face openly) should prefer the company of publicans and sinners and people of all sorts, who openly did evil, to their outwardly immaculate society. They thought this evil in their *hearts*, which, not being seen of men, they did not reckon as evil at all.

The Lord takes His followers' part. His mission is to the sick, not to the well, to those who have not the slightest doubt of their sins, not to the self-satisfied.

The scribes now try another mode of attack. They take offence at the non-fasting and non-making of prayers by His followers. "We fast and make prayers," they say, "and even John's followers, with whom you claim to have some affinity, agree with us in that particular. Why do not your followers do the same? You must be wrong here." The Lord replied that there can be no mixture between His doctrine, that of salvation without works, and theirs, which was that of salvation by works pure and simple, or John's that of works and belief in a future Redeemer. The Lord's doctrine was the Gospel, or salvation by belief in Him alone, irrespective of works, and was one *out* of the flesh, not *in* it, as was that of the Pharisees and of John the Baptist.

The self-righteous attack the followers of the Lord again. " It is not lawful to take the ears of corn on the Sabbath " (Luke vi. 1). "We must defend the outworks, for, if the Sunday is not observed in trifles, it will not be observed in greater things. The sheep, &c., will not be brought to the Temple; we shall lose our temporalities; we shall lose the credit to be gained by outward observance of the strictest sort." Never mind what the thoughts may be about, man cannot see them, so they are unimportant. The Lord repulses their attack by showing that, as God, He could at times permit the ceremonial law to be suspended.

The Sabbath question has too much in it to be allowed to be passed over thus. The next Sabbath the self-righteous are on the watch, feeling sure something gracious would be done. Their watchfulness against an innocent man was not seen by man, and therefore in their view there was in this no infraction of the Sabbath which they were so jealous about. Their advice is asked in the matter of the healing of the withered hand (Luke vi. 9), but they will not give it: the question of the lawfulness of the act, or whether the sufferer was healed or not, are quite secondary, the primary object being the trapping of the Lord, so that they might accuse Him, and destroy one who did not bow to their views and had no opinion of their sanctity, and who, they felt, could read their inmost hearts.

John in prison, before his departure, doubts the fact of Jesus being the Christ, perhaps through his hearing of these infractions (to human eyes) of the law by the Lord, and He sends to ask (Luke vii. 19). The Lord answers by calling John's attention to the execution of miracles, which God alone could work, and which miracles fulfilled the prophecies concerning the Christ. He then terms John "the greatest born of woman," as keeping the law after the flesh, but proclaims the least born of God and believing on Him alone for salvation as greater than he. The publicans and sinners agreed to this testimony, acknowledging the necessity of a change of life, which John preached, while the Pharisees rejected it, not considering a change of life necessary; which led to the Lord's remarking to them that they were not satisfied with John because he was stricter in keeping the law than they liked to be, and consequently put him down as having a devil; neither were they satisfied with Him because He did not practise those austerities, saying He was a wine-bibber and a friend of publicans and sinners. Also in this generation man says, "So-and-so is all right; he goes to church or chapel, and prayer-meetings without number; and So-and-so is all wrong, he never attends those meetings" (the mark of Christ's disciples is a matter of no import). If you say, " I believe So-and-so will be saved because of his strict devotions," they will not have it, for it is justification by works; if you say, " So-and-so will be saved because he believes in Jesus, and that irrespective of his works," they will not have it, for it is licentious teaching; the one is too strict, and the other too lax. " I have mourned, and you will not weep: I have piped, and you will not dance."

The Lord dines with one of the Pharisees (Luke vii. 36), who is displeased because "a woman which was a sinner" drew near to Jesus, and settles the matter in his heart by setting down the Lord as an ordinary man who could not discern her heart; but he found that the secrets of his heart were known, and, had he light to see his debts, he would have found that they were as heavy as those of the woman, who had to some extent realized the magnitude of hers.

Why are the prayers of men apparently unanswered? There is no doubt that to our reason our prayers, even for laudable subjects, are very often unheeded or delayed in their answers, that the benefit is unperceived; and yet we must believe that God, who has so encouraged us to pray, and who says, "Ask and ye shall receive," is true to His Word, and that therefore the prayer of man *is* answered. I think all prayer for temporalities must be made in subjection to God's will, with this reservation—if it falls in with His great scheme. The person who prays must be ready to have his request denied, if it runs counter to God's rule, which is dictated by infinite wisdom.

A prayer for temporalities, couched in terms, " Let it cost what it will, grant me this," would not be in a spirit acceptable to God; such a prayer would emanate more from the carnal than the spiritual nature, and to the carnal nature God has made no promises, for He is at enmity with it. A prayer also of this nature would necessarily be dictated by self-will, the granting of it would be for the gratification of the flesh, bodily comfort, or worldly glory. If a prayer for temporalities is offered up in a spirit of subjection to God's rule, and not dictated with a view to carnal purposes, then I think it is answered or not according as it falls in with God's general scheme. With respect to prayer made for spiritual blessings, I imagine they are always answered, though in ways we do not understand; a man prays for more spiritual knowledge, and he is thrown into greater tribulation than ever,[1] the reason being that the evil he is clothed in must be more and more destroyed before he can have more light; he must know his worthlessness before he can know the truth; he must be more humble and abased and feel more and more of his emptiness before being filled.

As all prayer to God must be actuated and prompted by God, I confess I do not understand how it is that prayers for temporal benefits are not more often granted, if asked in submission to His will. We are encouraged to pray even for temporalities, and yet we do not receive; may it not be because, "Ye ask amiss that ye may consume it on your lusts"? It requires a very close analysis to detect whether we would consume it on our lusts and pleasures, if certain requests were granted us, such as deliverance from pain, from adversities of body and estate.

This question is the great stumbling-block to unbelievers, and I wish I could see the true answer, for certainly there is one to be eventually revealed. I speak of heart prayers, not mouth prayers of those who pour out words without thinking of their import—"Make me humble-minded,"

[1] "I asked the Lord that I might grow
In faith, and love and ev'ry grace,
Might more of His salvation know,
And seek more earnestly His face.

"'Twas He who taught me thus to pray,
And He I know has answered prayer;
But it has been in such a way
As almost drove me to despair."

Olney Hymns.

when the speaker is ready to take offence the next moment, and perhaps is, at that very time, thinking over some grievance from his neighbour. These prayers from the mouth are never even expected to be answered, for you never see nor hear of the spokesman looking for the result.

Prayer is spiritual labour, and brings food to the soul; we try to feed our souls on the serpent's meat (Isaiah lxv. 25).

"In the sweat of thy face shalt thou eat bread." This applies to the soul as well as to the body; after labouring we bring forth fruit to God.

How often, after one has been reading and seeming to understand what one has read, the conscience has felt tender, and one has declared, "I will not do this or that, for I protest I have seen its foolishness: I have seen by my conscience how wrong it is, and how detrimental to me," and a few moments after all is forgotten, memory has failed.

How can we remedy this state of affairs? How is it our lives are not better? When we know all these things, how is it we do them not? It is from ignorance, *i. e.* want of understanding. It was through ignorance the Lord of Glory was crucified (Acts iii. 17). "Father, forgive them; they know not what they do." "Those that kill you will think they do God service, because they know not the Father." "None of the princes knew; for had they known it, they would not have crucified the Lord of Glory" (1 Corinthians ii. 8). "They do always err in their hearts, for they do not know My ways." Therefore I say all sin is owing to ignorance.

Psalm cxix. is full of sayings respecting the necessity of an enlightened understanding in order to keep the commandments of God and to purify the heart. Christ says, in Proverbs viii. 14, "*I* am understanding." Again,

"Get wisdom, get understanding" (Proverbs iv. 5). "Man that is in honour and understandeth not is like the beasts that perish" (Psalm xlix. 12). Therefore I maintain that to purify the heart, which is the seat of the affections, the understanding must be opened, and thus, with conscience and memory made tender and renewed, the will is worked on, and the affections die to the world; and inasmuch as they (the affections) must fix on something or remain dead, they rise again to fix on things unseen.

How is it that so many stop short? Their affections die outwardly to carnal things, but they secretly lust after them, and do not rise to heavenly things, but turn off to politics, business, pleasures—anything in fact which will distract them. As these things are lawful, the will agrees with the affections and the sequent life follows. A life, to end—how? A life that even now is not a happy one, for the conscience is always upbraiding and saying "All is vanity." These stick in the wilderness, having lost Egypt and being unwilling to cross Jordan. I say that, to enable the affections to be purified, it is essentially necessary to understand the deep things of God. Affections will not leave a seen for an unseen thing, unless a hope is given of attaining that which is unseen. Christ Himself needed a hope to be set before Him ere He despised the shame of the Cross (Hebrews xii. 2). Remember that in speaking of understanding, of conscience, of memory, I speak of faculties which make up the soul which was breathed from God, and is of God: that soul which was buried by the erring of its case or body, but which is renewed in Christ and quickened by God's Holy Spirit. The soul, in virtue of its Quickener, quickens the body in its will and affections, when once the latter are dead to the world. But what is generally the case is that the quickening action of the soul ends in the will, and the affections are, in a way, more *coerced* than changed; they care no more for the things of this world, but neither do they care for the things of eternity; they long for dissolution, for, though they may scarcely relish the idea, they are in the state described by Paul, when he said, "Wretched man that I am," or else, as I have said, they go out after politics, business, pleasures, &c. God often hedges up their success in these directions, and then they are turned on themselves, and often die altogether, and rise to fix themselves on things unseen. How often this is the case with old statesmen. A man who is dead has no affections, nor has he a will; nothing will tempt him, he has ceased from sin. The heart, the seat of the affections, is the citadel head-quarters either of Satan or of God: it was once God's head-quarters, then Satan's, and must be God's again. It surrendered to Satan willingly, it must receive God willingly.

What is lust? It is the desire of the affections for things seen or present, for present gratification. What is love? It is the desire of the affections for future as well as present gratification. Lust is selfish. Love is unselfish. Lust seeks the beautiful as seen. Love seeks the beautiful as unseen. Lust is satisfied in gratification of self. Love is insatiable in its desires. Lust is for things apart from God. Love is for things in union with God.

No visible manifestation of God would awaken or enlighten the understanding, and through it work on the will.

The Jews required a sign from God, for to them Christ crucified was a stumbling-block. The Greeks sought wisdom, for to them Christ crucified was foolishness, because "the natural man receiveth not the things of the Spirit of God: for they are foolishness unto him: neither can he know them, because they are spiritually discerned." "The Spirit searcheth all things, yea, the deep things of God."

What is the moral of all this? Seek the opening of the understanding by the reading of the Scriptures, the softening of the conscience, and the revival of the memory by prayer. This being done, the understanding, memory, and conscience work on the will, which coerces the affections, causes them to die, *i. e.* to care no more for the world, to rise and fix themselves on heavenly things: then peace will soon reign, we shall enter His rest, cease from our own works, and live a resurrection life.

GALATZ,[1] 21 *December*, 1871.—In the view of the events of the Bible being represented in us, I think there is a great connection between John and Elijah. They were both of the same principle, and were both forerunners of great changes in God's work. It is these keynotes which open out the Scripture to us. As Elijah is the corresponding type of John, so the events which follow Elijah's time till the coming of our Lord typify the events which follow John's time till the end. These things are so very intricately and wonderfully interwoven that I cannot with my carnal reason follow them out, but I have the innate feeling that they are so. If God had so ruled that I or any one else had lived a life very near Jesus, denying self and living only for His glory and praise, the veil would be thinner, and all would be made clear by the Light of the World; as it is, it is not clear, but will be so when we put off the flesh. Thank God! we can look beyond this world, and I do look forward to death as a great boon. Meantime we must be patient, and believe all things are going well. Read *Proverbial Philosophy*, it has many deep truths in it.

"Ye shall hear of wars and rumours of wars; see that ye be not troubled." We are not of this world, but of an everlasting kingdom. "Come out of her, my people," says our God. Let us then, as far as He gives us power, try and bring these things to the minds of those troubled about

---

[1] After being six years employed at Gravesend upon the defences of the Thames, General Gordon was sent as English Commissioner to Galatz, at the mouth of the Danube.

them, try and point out that His wisdom is working, and that we cannot expect peace here. Enough for the day is its evil.[1] Let us lift up those who mourn to look beyond the grave and this world to that home where there will be no sorrow. Let us pray for the whole of humanity, and rest, knowing He is working *good to all in everything He does.*

2 *August,* 1873.—I hope you will soon get more and more case-hardened to the rubs of life; you know Who sends them.

A great thing with merchants is to make a good invest-ment, and so we ought to act with God; if we venture little we shall gain little, and the reverse if we venture much. It is true that after a time one gets quite accustomed to trust God, to get experience that He is trustworthy; but if we do not try Him, we shall never know it. How full the world is of religious talk, and how little is known of truly trusting Him! It is a gift; but we ought to exercise it so as to strengthen it. The events of life have less to do with us than we imagine; you may say this or that, but its effect will depend on God; whatever we say is overruled by Him. We need eagle's wings to bear all our little and great trials.

BERLIN, 12 *October,* 1873.—Getting quiet does one good; it is impossible to hear God's voice in a whirl of visits. You must be more or less in the desert, to use the scales of the Sanctuary, to see and weigh the true value of things and sayings.

What a comfort you will feel when the Gate of Life is

[1] General Gordon frequently quoted this verse, or part of it :—

"Oh! ask not thou, How shall I bear
The burden of to-morrow?
Sufficient for the day its care,
Its evil, and its sorrow;
God imparteth by the way
Strength sufficient for the day."

He had a copy of this hung up in his bedroom at Rockstone Place, Southampton.

F

opened for you; it is quite impossible, when disturbed by
worldly thoughts, to feel that He is "not a God of the
dead, but of the living." One cannot, when thus disturbed,
but feel that at the death of those we love something goes
to the cemetery; but it is not so: the dross, the worn-out
coat, is cast off. I think the promises to the widows,
orphans, and poor are to those who are so in *spirit*.

The prophets are voices in us remonstrating and getting
often killed by fleshly thoughts, getting cast out as "being
no prophets." Exactly as the world is the battle-field of
nations and individuals, so is our body.

I hope you will more chew the cud of the Scriptures; they
afford an inward nourishment which few enjoy; I would say,
read them much, but chew them more. A vast population
of thoughts, good and bad, are born and die in us daily,
bringing forth multitudes in their turn.

I hope you will think of the "knowledge of the truth" as
a thing not to be forced. As I said before, it is as if we
were approaching an island (which exists in all its details
whether we see it or not); some see clearer than others, all
in their degree. It is possible to approach and appreciate
details quickly or slowly, but the end in either case is to see
clearly.

Kiss my dear mother, and do not fret for me. I have,
thank God, all comfort, peace, and happy reminiscence with
the knowledge that the Comforter is with you all; that He
is able, willing, unselfish, and kind, and that He will keep
you all till you reach the land where the "sun never sets,"
and where you will see Him, and know why "Jesus wept"
at Lazarus's grave. Feed by the living pastures; they will
fatten you.

GALATZ, 31 *October*, 1873.—You cannot tell, my dear
Augusta, how I am wounded by sword-fish in the shape of
people wanting money; it is really quite a trial (sent I
believe) for me, and I am such a donkey. The only advan-

tage in marriage is, it would prevent these true extravagances. By keeping my watch at your time,. I feel enabled to know what you are doing. It will be a sore trial for you to see my dear mother leave her worn-out shell, but you will feel that God takes her to Himself. My dear mother has spent a useful, hard-working life, and a happy one; it seems as if it is for you she is kept.

All mental discomfort comes from our minds being in divergence from God's; when the two are agreed no warfare occurs, for they work together, and man's mind accepts God's rule, but reason tells us that disagreement must bring conflicts. He will have His way, and would have us accept all events with the knowledge that He is love, whatever and however contradictory those events may be to our comprehension of Him. It is frequently repeated in Scripture that we are virtually dead to the events of this world, and therefore can have nothing to do with them. It is extraordinary to think He places our spiritual nature *in* the flesh, with the view of separating it *from* the flesh; all the events of this life, willingly or unwillingly, tend to the death of the flesh; life is a continual crucifixion, whether we know it or not; the less the conflict, the more the peace.

9 *November*, 1873.[1]—The basis of all peace of mind, and what must be obtained before we get that peace, is a cessation of the conflict of two wills—His and ours. It is difficult to talk on worldly subjects to people who do not trace everything to God; we glide into discussing the ways and means, and we ourselves forget how futile those ways and means are—hence the necessity of being more alone. If we want martyrdom, state this doctrine, and people will cease to regard us except as fanatics; it is so very hurtful to all our

---

[1] In September, 1873, General Gordon was asked, through Nubar Pasha, if he would accept office under the Khedive—Ismael—in the Soudan; the following letter was written whilst waiting to know whether the British Government would give him permission to accept.

pride to have Him intruded into our affairs. "We agree to all that, but must act ourselves." After a long discussion we find, when the people have gone, how foolish it has been; we all want our independence; we would serve Him at stated times and leave Him at all others. Even really religious people are more or less infidels, and it is only when some great calamity strikes them that they will in any way recognize His hand; their every-day happiness consists in every-day things, and they are more or less distressed if they have not peace in these. .

A person takes an interest in the poor and makes himself a benefactor to them : he sets one up in business, and is greatly disheartened by finding ingratitude and failure in his effort: he ought to expect it. For some wise design God turns events one way or another, whether man likes it or not, as a man driving a horse turns it to right or left without consideration as to whether the horse likes that way or not. To be happy, a man must be like a well-broken, willing horse, ready for anything. Events will go as God likes. It is hard to accept the position; the only solace is, it is not for long. If I go to Egypt or not is uncertain; I hope He has given me the strength not to care one way or the other; twenty years are soon gone, and when over it will matter little whether I went or not.

When religious people reason with you and say what a deal of good you could do, it is an atheistical saying, though they do not mean it. Humanly we may feel compassion, but spiritually we should feel how events are ruled. Once possess this blessing of accepting *all things* from God's ruling, and a man will have little need of others; he suffices for himself; each person gathered his own manna, and it fed him. I know no one who will accept this view except yourself, and no one to whom one can write it who will altogether relish it. One's reason supports this view, as to the base of peace—namely, acceptance of all the events of

the world as coming directly from God; not a mere acceptance, but a *willing* one, however outrageous some things
appear to human judgment. God has allowed slavery to go
on for so many years; born in the people, it needs more
than an expedition to eradicate it; open out the country,
and it will fall of itself. I am averse to the loss of a single
life, and will endeavour to prevent any happening *if I go.*
I have a Bank, and on that I can draw; He is richer than
the Khedive, and knows more of the country than any one;
I will trust Him to help me out of money or any other
difficulties.

TULTCHA, 17 *November*, 1873.—I believe if the Soudan
was settled, the Khedive would prevent the slave trade;
but he does not see his way to do so till he can move about
the country. My ideas are to open it out by getting the
steamers on to the lakes, by which time I should know the
promoters of the slave trade and could ask the Khedive to
seize them. I have been more or less acted on by sharks,
who want to go with me for money. I have told them that,
if it is in my power to employ them, they must belong to
the A class—*i. e.* those who come for the occupation and
interest it may give them, and who are content if they are
fairly reimbursed their expenses; not the B class, who go
for the salary only and who want to make a good thing
of it.

My object is to show the Khedive and his people that
gold and silver idols are not worshipped by all the world.
They are very powerful gods, but not so powerful as our
God; so, if I refuse a large sum, you—and I am responsible
to you alone—will not be angry at my doing so. From
whom does all the money come? From poor miserable
creatures who are ground down to produce it. Of course,
these ideas are outrageous. "Pillage the Egyptians!" is
still the cry.

I am quite prepared not to go, and should not think it

unkind of God if He prevents it, for He must know what is best. The twisting of men carries out some particular object of God, and we should cheerfully agree now to what we will agree hereafter when we know all things.

Keep me from writing and talking, and then I am humanly safe. As a rule, Christians are really more inconsistent than "worldlings." They talk truths, and do not act on them. They allow that "God is the God of the widows and orphans," yet they look in trouble to the gods of silver and gold: either He can help altogether, or not at all. He will not be served in conjunction with idols of any sort. Kings and Chronicles are full of the deliverances He wrought against all human calculations, when trusted in alone, and of the calamities that fell on those who mixed their trust in Him with a trust in other gods. His "eyes run to and fro throughout the whole earth, to show Himself strong in the behalf of them whose heart is perfect towards Him" (2 Chronicles xvi. 9).

PARIS, 29 *January*, 1874.—I am happy and peaceful, and feel more and more that, get into what trouble I may, God will take me out of it. He will keep him in " perfect peace, whose mind is stayed on Him." " Stayed " means "anchored."

I remember that God has at all times worked by weak and small means. All history shows this to be His mode, and so I believe if He will He may work by me.

SUAKIN, 26 *February*, 1874.—I wear Engineer undress, with fez. It is very fine in its effect ! I still think it is all a joke, and shall not realize matters till I get up. I have no title, but, as in China, keep my own. Of course I am " His Excellency "—of nothing. The German servant was threatened with death if he called me thus.

KARTOUM, 20 *March*, 1874.—It was odd near here to see large flocks of my Tultcha storks assembled on the islets, ready for their flight to Turkey, where they arrive at a regular time in April. You know they build on the houses there, and are tame; here they are very wild. I dare say I have seen some of them before, and here they were walking about among the crocodiles 2000 miles away. These things are suggestive. Birds are like thoughts: when the dark times of winter come in other lands, the birds go to Egypt. When we get spiritually dull and cold, our thoughts go to the things of the flesh. It is also remarkable that Egypt should be such a hot-bed of slavery; it was fond of slaves in Pharaoh's time, and it is so now.

There is inestimable comfort in leaning on God to get you out of all difficulties; no one knows the true comfort of religion who lacks this. He to whom God gives it is free indeed; he has to account to One who knows the intent of every act, and, whether it is wise or foolish, He will comfort him in his difficulties.

I do not like to miss a mail to you. I hope you are well and plodding through the wilderness in comfort, avoiding the thorns as well as you can, and not being astonished at getting a dig or two now and then. No news to tell you. The rats are dreadful at night, "circusing" about everywhere, and I fear that the older ones eat the younger members of their families, for there are great outcries at night, with lamentations and woe, and I found part of a young rat eaten by an older one, and the remnant left for my benefit—a delicate attention!

GONDOKORO, 21 *December*, 1874.—What comfort one gets in all worries by looking to higher things! The true comprehension of our union, as members of Christ's body, to Him, our Head, will enable us to comprehend the Atonement, and our perfect justification and sanctification by virtue of that union. As we were innocent of transgression in Adam (whence our corrupt nature sprang), so had we naught to do with our redemption. Christ chose us ere the world began, and, with full pre-knowledge of all the errors and sins of our corrupt nature, made us members of His body.

What a weak gospel is now preached! Not tidings of great joy, but "If you do well, you will be received; if not, you will be rejected. This is the law." They say, "Oh! but you must repent." How do they know that every sinner does not repent and long for freedom from his sins, whilst perhaps the righteous of this world hug themselves that they are not like their neighbours? If they were so tempted, could they say they would stand? Let them keep a week's journal by God's Word, and they could only say, "God be merciful to me, a sinner." And yet probably, though they may strive the next week, they will find the same story and the same result.

Study the union of the Head and its members. Merits you have none. You are received only because God willed you should be a member of His Son's body, and anything you could bring, even if you had any merits, would be but to detract from His sacrifice. If it were possible for you to work out your righteousness, then righteousness could be by the law; but we are told, and have the inward conviction, that it is impossible, and that it is the ministration of death. It is true that the "soul that sinneth shall die," but the soul that emanated from God cannot sin (1 John iii. 9). Death fulfils the law on our sinful bodies, but Christ, the Head, broke the bondage of the tomb and showed the life beyond.

Nicodemus said, "How can a man be born when he is old?" Jesus said in answer, "Except a man be born of water and of the Spirit he cannot enter into the Kingdom of God." A new birth to a living being implies a previous death. Read all that interview and you will see Nicodemus thought of the improvement of the flesh and its entry without death into eternal life. Our Saviour spoke of the death of the flesh and the new birth from the grave, typified by water, *i. e.* the resurrection. "That which is born of the flesh is flesh." "Flesh and blood cannot inherit."

What an extraordinary and mysterious thing that there should be such difficulties with these sources of the Nile! It seems wonderful! Make what arrangements you will, and yet you will find it blocked time after time. It must have some spiritual meaning.

Do what you can, plan and arrange, but with the memo. to be always well remembered, not to build on such plans in such a way as to be hurt by their fall or failure; then, come weal or woe, you stand fast and overcome the world. Remember that all you do is comparatively nothing at all; your efforts will be modelled in a way you never dreamt of. Each of us builds his little bit, and that little bit is as important as anything done by the present generation, and yet how despicable it often seems.

Imagine the intricacy of the government of the world, the detail required for each person, each work, each rag of humanity, and judge of His wisdom who can never make the least mistake and who is still and tranquil in the turmoil of it all. Exist in the world, do your part, but do not entangle yourself with it, so that when you leave it you will have no wrench; that is true life. It is quite impossible any one can be happy, or even tranquil, unless he accepts that God rules every little item of our daily life, permitting evil and turning it to our good.

Want of money is a great sore, and yet, to have enough, it only requires that we lower our flag a little. Does a new carpet really make you a jot the happier, and do any one of your friends care an atom whether your carpet is good or not? People think that they do, but it is a great mistake; others are far too much engaged with their own affairs to give your carpet a thought.

There, I have written enough for to-day, and will go and "worrit" the Arabs! but with the remembrance that, looking deeply, it is very little real import if they do what I tell them or not—not that I tell them *that.*

I have a beautiful meerschaum mouthpiece, brought from Marno for Mr. Hansall,[1] who, happily for me, does not smoke. It is a splendid bit, and I have accepted it ! Do you know date-stones will give fruit-bearing trees or shrubs three years after planting?

LARDO, 25 *June*, 1875.—No steamers as yet; most trying to the flesh, as the river is so very high. I can believe He is looking how one bears the trial. Sometimes I forget Him and am furious at the delay ; sometimes I think, Would I have it otherwise? It greatly depends on whether I find anything to do or not. The worst thing is the utter want of occupation; if I had my Concordance and Text-book I would try the mystic nature of the Nile.

It appears Berber is the sixth cataract, if we do not count Beddin, which can hardly be called one (perhaps there may be more ahead). After the sixth cataract you may say rest comes, the seventh day ; it really is marvellous, for it is this bit of road only that has for so many years prevented the solution of the Nile mystery.

I like the " jaw-bone " of Samson ; one would never think of using such a thing, neither would one think of one's strength being in one's hair, as his was. I like distinct colours, black and white. I like decision, and I have seen it much wanted up here ; they (the soldiers) hang on me as a dead weight and need a push to remove them. (What you have undergone with my pushing at you with questions on religious matters you will never forget !)

27 *June*, 1875.—"Shall there be evil in a city, and the Lord hath not done it?" (Amos iii. 6.) "I make peace,

---

[1] Mr. Hansall was for many years Austrian consul at Kartoum, and acted in that capacity till he was slain on the fall of the town in January, 1885. He is mentioned several times in General Gordon's "Journals at Kartoum."

and create evil: I the Lord do all these things" (Isaiah
xlv. 7). These verses contain the great mystery, and are
the stumbling-block to very many—the co-existence of God,
holy, righteous, and full of love, and of evil. How are
these attributes (which none deny) to be reconciled with the
sufferings and sorrows of evil? It seems impossible that
any can contend that God is not supreme, infinite in power,
or that anything can exist without Him. He is the Alpha
and the Omega. "Beside me there is no God." It is
therefore impossible to believe that evil is a separate and
independent principle or power existing in despite of God's
will. We may not be able, with our limited knowledge and
understanding, to reconcile this co-existence and the sub-
ordinancy of evil to God, and therefore fail to investigate
the matter; or we may on the other hand believe that God
permits evil for purposes which we may not be able to
understand.

All the actual events of this life on which we are so intent
are *in themselves* of not the least import. "The things
which are seen are temporal; but the things which are not
seen are eternal." I believe that man consists of a "vessel
unto honour" enshrined in a "vessel unto dishonour"—
the one unseen and "eternal," the other seen and
"temporal." It is not of "him that willeth," nor of "him
that runneth."

The vessel, temporal and fragile, in which the vessel
eternal and enduring is enshrined, "profiteth nothing,"
"cannot inherit the kingdom of God"; "that which is
born of the flesh is flesh, and that which is born of the
Spirit is spirit": the one corruptible, the other eternal.

Although the similitude may seem (as it is) quite unworthy
of the subject, I believe this world is as a stage, on which
the manager allots certain parts to certain individuals, who
go through those various parts and resume their original
positions. The part of one may be that of a king, the part

of another that of a servant, as the manager wills. The actors put off their clothes as a man puts off his body. It is written that "by the church the manifold wisdom of God" might be known to principalities and powers in heavenly places (Ephesians iii. 10).

I believe the evil in each of us is put off at our leaving the stage of this world, as the actor puts off his clothes, leaving the true and eternally existing portion of us with the experience of God, which we could not otherwise have acquired. He, "Jesus," will reconcile *all* things unto Himself, heavenly or earthly, and be All in All.

With the knowledge which the spirit must have when freed from the body, the existence in it of the "works of the flesh" (Gal. v. 19) would be impossible. They are essentially works of the flesh, temporal and corruptible. The "fruit of the Spirit" further mentioned is quite compatible with spiritual life.

The moral I draw from the above is that my earthly shrine is ordained to certain evil works, and my spiritual shrine is ordained to certain good works; that neither in one case nor the other can I alter the decree. The sentiment which should actuate me is that I should endeavour, as I know not the future, to coerce the former and foster the latter; to despise the flesh as only a temporary existence, and to exalt the spirit; to set my affections on "things above," inasmuch as I should be *dead* to the *things below;* to have nothing in this world to divide my affections or make me cling to it : as far as these sentiments are felt, to that degree will they render a man happy. A divided heart must be misery. "How long halt ye between two opinions?" Decide whom you will serve, God or Baal. Remember that Baal is of many forms—money in the bank, pride of place, carriages, the things of this life, a good name for being a Christian, &c. &c.

The god a man serves is the one to whom he goes in

trouble for relief, who he believes can help him.   Men send
to other gods for help if they think, as they often do, that
the true God neglects them, or if He does not help them
in their own way.

You find many on their way to inquire of the god of
Ekron (2 Kings i. 3).   All of us go sometimes, but it is of
no use; they are mere idols of gold, silver, or stone, who
cannot help even themselves.   If we judge of our worship
of God by our reliance on Him, we are more or less atheistic.
The behaviour of others towards us is regarded quite apart
from any consideration of His existence ever entering our
minds.   We would serve Him and the other gods as well,
but He will not have a divided worship.   At Jerusalem
high places were made and other gods were adopted, but
it is believed that the people never thought of neglecting
the worship of Jehovah; they only added to it.   God would
have us believe and consider Him existing, though not seen.
Sacraments, churchgoing, good works, &c. &c., are all other
gods, as far as they are trusted in.

What comfort these thoughts give !   They overcome the
world; they take away from me any pride about the new
route; they—or rather *God*, not the thoughts, as that would
be putting them as gods with Him—would enable me to
bear the disappointment if the Nile is not navigable to
Makadé, and in this delay to feel it is He, not I, who is
working, and that He would work it out as it pleased Him,
whether I were here or not.   Though the subject is to *me*
of the greatest interest, yet in reality it is of the smallest
import.   Having these views, and given His support, how
can one feel hurt?   Whether the opinion of man be either
favourable or not, it can matter little.

The positive gain in this world by being given these views
is immense, even in temporal matters: not to fear man is
often told us, "Be strong," &c. (Joshua i. 9).   I feel that
the matter is in God's hands.   He may take my spirit when

He wills; He may use me for years to come in these lands; or He may take me to-night. Certainly celibacy is a great boon; I feel my presence is not necessary. Though endued with a love of life, and instinctively endeavouring to keep in health, I am given to feel that the happiness of the future must be preferable to this life. As one gets older, one feels that really death separates us very little from those we care for, for they are all approaching it also. Few fathers and sons, as they grow in years, care or think much for one another; their ideas, pursuits, and life separate them from community of feeling, their standpoints of view are far different.

It is remarkable with what different dispositions we are endowed, and how long it is before God breaks us in and makes us feel we are children. Yet all must be broken in, though the full accomplishment may be on a death-bed. All shall say: "The Lord, He is God; the Lord, He is God." We believe that the gods of Ekron are allowed to help sometimes; but it is not they, for "there was no voice, nor any that answered," and they do not exist; man is allowed to think so, but afterwards finds out his error. Nations, as men, seek their gods in armies, &c., which will surely fail them.

I should like much to hear the oratorio *Elijah*, and to see a tableau of the scene at Carmel: "I, even I only, remain a prophet of the Lord," "and the people answered him not a word." After a great conflict (in which you are nothing) expect an attack from Jezebel. Elijah showed his mortality in flying from it so soon as the day after; " I, even I only, am left." Imagine what God must be, to manage all the things of creation to perfection, the thoughts of each heart, the words and acts of each created being, or insect; it is a stupendous idea; and all that management without any exertion, in perfect calmness and peace ! Then think that neither death, nor life, nor powers, nor principalities shall separate us from His love. Can a soul be divided into two? Neither can you be separated from God, though, for the moment, we are temporarily veiled in flesh, and thus separated; as the flesh dies, we are to that degree joined to Him.

"Love not the world;" why? Because "all that is in the world—the lust of the flesh, the lust of the eyes, and the pride of life—passeth away." "I thank Thee and praise Thee, O Thou God of my fathers, who hast made known what we desired to know; but as for me, the secret is not revealed for any wisdom that I have more than any living" (Daniel ii. 23 and 30). I feel that I wish it to be God's will that the river may be navigable to the lake, and *that* for the Khedive's sake, who has been at such expense and has been so kind to me—but the Lord of the whole earth, shall not He do right? I do trust Him, that if it is navigable He will save me from being puffed up. He has given me to wish that nothing should come between Him and me, that no weight should clog me to the earth. I would realize that "I am not of this world," that I desire a better country and the city of the living God, and where the former things are passed away (Revelation xxi., xxii.).

The great point of which we must be convinced is that of our *nonentity,* and of God's *entirety.* Some of us acknowledge in words, but practically deny our nonentity. All we do, more or less, we would count as something in the work, and of all lessons this is the most difficult to learn, for it is only by repeated failures we get experience and really know we are nothing. A lurking feeling exists in us that, though no doubt God has done much, we have ourselves done a little. God will not have this; He will be *all,* as He truly is; if it were otherwise, He would not be the Supreme, for there would be other powers, independent of Him.

We are all inclined to say in our prosperity: "Is not this great Babylon that I have built by the might of my power,

and for the honour of my majesty?" and I will build me
greater barns and take more ease.   Nothing could be more
distasteful to the world than the doctrine that we deserve
no credit whatsoever ; its acceptation by any one quite
destroys all the pleasures of building castles in the air, for
while they are being built we keep thinking how little we
shall have to do with them.   Read Daniel v. 18, &c.·

I do not think in words any one doubts God's complete
supremacy over evil ; if we, or the children of God in us,
are ordained to perform certain good works, it would follow
that we, or the children of the devil in us, are ordained to
perform certain evil works (1 Peter ii. 8, Jude 4).

In our combined state of children of God and children
of the devil we are one, and yet we are two entirely
separate : we, as the children of God, are *in* the world, but
not *of* the world, the "remnant" (Zephaniah iii. 13).   We
do not know what is ordained, and therefore are told to
pray.   God ordains us to pray, and our prayers are always
heard, though we do not think so.   Our Lord prayed for
the cup to pass from Him.   He was heard, and strengthened
by an angel.   If we pray in any emergency for relief, even
though the impending calamity may come on us, yet strength
to bear it is given, which comes to the same thing.   The
dissection of the children cannot be made now by us : it is
like the tares and wheat in each of us; we are so entirely
mixed that we cannot distinguish them in ourselves.   (You
know that the tare and the wheat plants are exactly alike as
to the form of the leaf.)

The Psalms are the utterances of the children of God in
us.   We have no right to avoid the reading of the judgments against the wicked, for they apply to each one of us
in our present union.   "What if God, willing to shew His
wrath, and to make His power known, endured with much
long-suffering the vessels of wrath fitted [made up] to destruction?" (Romans ix. 22.)   "He hath made all things for

Himself; yea, even the wicked for the day of evil"
(Proverbs xvi. 4). We must be called out of the world to
know these truths: *i. e.* we must be separated from the
children of evil in us. The Word of God is the sword
which divides. As long as the children of God in us are
mixed up with the children of the devil, nothing is known;
they are led out into the wilderness, owing to the judgments
on their companions (the children of the devil), and then
He makes Himself known.

To the whole united man this is a period of great suffering. The children of God suffer in the wilderness, and the
children of the devil in us suffer before the departure of the
former takes place. During our lives we are under certain
rules, some good, some evil. As the ruler is, so are the
people, except always a remnant who are faithful. So in us
evil reigns one day, and good may reign the next. The
children of God desire that the king should be of them;
the children of the devil that he should be of them; but it
is God who ordains who should rule.

The whole subject is of the deepest interest. We are
much more important than we have any idea of. Nothing
is trivial that is unseen; it is only the material things of life
that are of no import.

Evil has its source in unbelief; if unbelief was destroyed
so would evil be; it is the unique offence and sin. Unbelief
is an ignoring of God, because the flesh does not see Him.
(It was always a sign from heaven the Jews wanted.) Unbelief is brother to distrust, to hard thoughts and judgments.
Unbelief will cease when He makes Himself known : it will
disappear, and so will the children of unbelief in us, even as
darkness disappears before light. "Unto the upright there
ariseth light in the darkness."

Belief makes man of no account at all; unbelief engenders
pride, for it gives him attributes of independence. *He* will
do something *himself; he* will give something to God; God

G

and *he* will work together ; *he* is necessary to God for this or that work.   So speaks the flesh, which cannot know God.

The harvest or death is the complete dissection of the two opposite natures in us: one, corruptible, inherits corruption ; the other, incorruptible, inherits incorruption.   A partial separation can be made during life.   The Lord may give light to discern.   The servants said, when an enemy had sown the tares, "Wilt thou then that we go and gather them up?" which would imply that they could discern to some degree, but not enough to insure the safety of the wheat (Matthew xiii. 28, 29).

The whole field of wheat may ripen at once, or in parts. If it is ripe at once, the separation of the tares may take place at once; if it ripens in parts, then those parts are reaped and separated from the tares.   So in man, he may die to the world while still living, and be given to discern the evil portion in him to a certain degree ; or he may live on in the world and not discern the evil portion from the good till he dies actually.   In both cases the same result is attained : both are eventually given to discern the evil from the good (the gathering of the tares and wheat; *i. e.* the harvest was to be performed by angels).   Who are to be destroyed in everlasting fire?   The enemies of the Lord. Who are His and our enemies?   Our sins, our iniquities, and our transgressions.

In our favourite parable, the Pharisee and the Publican, the Pharisee claimed individuality, although he owned it was from God.   The Publican makes no pretensions ; *he* had nothing to say, or plead, or give to God.

I wonder what part in us typifies these negro nations— "the heathen are His inheritance."   One wonders what agency will be used to bring them into the fold.   They are so intimately connected with the Nile, which has so much to do with the power of Egypt, and again Egypt with Israel, that they must have some action in us.   I imagine they must

be connected with our animal desires and appetites. By its
inundations, the Nile, to Egypt, was the source of food as
well as of power; the negro's sole idea is that of food, and
they hold cows as the most desired acquisition they can
have. They have no ambition; their feuds are always for
food, never for conquest; their unique requirement is rain
for their crops. They are what may be termed good; they
have no vices, at any rate prominent ones. Egypt has
always enslaved them; they minister to her, are her servants,
but they rise to no eminence in that land.

The geographical position of Egypt and Assyria in relation
to the Holy Land, and the geographical position of *these*
lands in relation to Egypt, would show some curious connection, had we the spirit to discern it. The Nile nearly
destroyed Moses (the law). It is an odd river; it has presented the greatest obstacles to the knowledge of its source
for nearly 2000 years, and now perhaps this may be made
known by merely the taking up of a steamer, with no great
trouble. Many nations have tried to fathom the difficulty;
it may be that Egypt will be given the solution. No interest
equal to that shown towards the Nile is felt respecting any
other river in the world. Egypt cannot exist without slaves,
and yet the slave is his master's master in Egypt. We, after
the flesh, are the masters of our appetites, but they in reality
rule us, for we cannot well control them. Other nations
would have Egypt (the flesh) give up those who minister to
her wants; but she cannot do without them; they are
essential to her existence.

9 *July*, 1875.—We are an odd mixture; for instance,
those men [1] were ordained to suffer by to-day's accident, and
yet I cannot help pointing out to the others that it was their
own fault, and that, if they do not take care, the same may
happen to them. Oh dear, what sorrows! and yet " He

---

[1] Two men who were much injured when firing a gun, and of which
injuries one afterwards died.

doth not willingly afflict the children of men." It is these
apparent contradictions that our reason cannot solve. Truly
the joys of the next world must be great to repay the sufferings
of this!

The Nile is not going to be torn open as easily as one
thought. I acknowledge I should feel a sort of regret had
I to leave this before opening the river to the *lakes;* but this
feeling would soon pass; for I should know it to be God's
will, and in accordance with His general design in these
parts, that I should not complete the work; it would be like
getting paint on your dress, or a cold in your head, an unavoidable occurrence, though the flesh would say afterwards,
" Why go near the paint? " or " Why not wear goloshes? "
Wretched religion, without life, without rest, with no nutri-
ment in it at all, is that which looks on events as avoidable; yet I believe all have more or less developed in their
inner hearts some sort of belief that things good and bad
are inevitable. Sound or unsound, religious or irreligious,
none have earned the penny or anything like it; ostrich-like,
we cling to a lurking hope that the rags (in which we outwardly profess to have no faith) will be found *not altogether*
worthless; but we must leave this hope and be utterly down
in our own estimation before we enter the heavenly realms.
The divine balance is a far different one from our own; it
rejects at once anything but the pure metal. Happy are
those who, even in an infinitely small degree, are given to
make use of it in the affairs of this world, for then they
appear in quite a new light.

I think I have a knack of being able to forestall
storms, and take in sail, generally speaking being close-
rigged, with no rope hanging over the side. It is a quick
operation.

Two miles south of KERRI, 5 *August,* 1875.—How odd
it is that we judge one another as though each one of us
was consistent! " Why, yesterday you said so and so, and

now you say the reverse." It is quite possible for a person
to have been sincere in his expressions on both occasions;
a man may say to-day, "I will not remain another year,"
and mean it, and yet to-morrow talk of staying three or four
years, and mean that also.

How little all these things will appear when on one's
death-bed! Certainly, looking at the apparently unnecessary amount of trouble one has, this life has infinitely more
in it than we think for; there is some deep and wonderful
design in all these trying obstacles which come in one's way
—it is agreeable to think thus and to be forearmed against
evil tidings. Why men appear so stupid, and so misconceive
their apparently plain orders, can only be explained by supposing them to be acted on by some unknown agency for
some specific objects. I consider we have not the least
ground for supposing our clever thoughts are from ourselves,
and, in spite of my feelings, I think we are in reality only
spectators of the unrolling of the record of events.

The *sound* people!—what satisfaction does their religion
give them? Their Father in heaven—what a distance they
keep from Him! No nearness of acquaintance, if they
disavow His working in *every* event of this life. "God is
not in all their thoughts."

MOOGIE, 29 *August*, 1875.—I think that, happen what
will, a husband ought to take his wife and children with
him wherever he goes, and trust God with the results; the
separation is unnatural, and shows how little we trust God.
It is not the climate, it is not the fever, but it is He who
snaps the thread, for wise purposes of His own. Bridge the
grave this side of it, and these very temporary separations
will lose their sting.

Look what a struggle B—— had to make his boys good.
I remember how they came in to say their prayers, and
they read out in a loud voice the fifty-ninth Psalm, both
pronouncing each syllable at the same moment. Look at

verses 6, 7, and 14. It almost caused one to laugh at their
parrot precision. Could they have answered who were their
enemies? "A man's foes are those of his own household"
—i. e. *himself.*

LABORÉ, 4 *October*, 1875.—The veil with which our flesh
(the cuticle) wraps our spiritual nature is wonderful, so that
we cannot discern right from wrong. We are a heathen
nation, in spite of our profession, with a large number of
idols, gold, silver, and clay; we are all worshippers at the
shrines and believe secretly in the power of these idols. I
think God will scatter them *in each of us* ere we leave this
world, and make us to see their impotency. Happy are
those who by suffering learn this early.

If I had sons, I certainly would teach them a little of
most trades, amongst others, boot-making. You have no
idea how feeble one feels not knowing these things. People
in our position of life must see the time has gone past for
sinecure posts; that their sons, or grandsons at any rate,
must be prepared for the colonies. What a number of
useless boys there are, who cannot even write a good hand
(I can't, I know). I had a signal failure with my repairs
on my boots to-day. A little carpentering, black- and tin-
smithing, shoe-making and tailoring, would be a real gift to
a young man; he would be prouder of himself, feeling,
"Let the worst come to the worst, I am not useless." I
declare I feel for the poor little chaps of the future, if we
give the A B C education we do now. Large schools are,
to most boys, not an advantage, but the reverse. What
earthly use will the Latin, Greek, or algebra be to thousands
who have learnt, and probably forgotten, them?

Looking at many one knows, they never need have learnt
more than reading, writing, arithmetic, history, and geo-
graphy. A disastrous war would close the army, except to
strong men who were soldiers only. It seems cowardly to
say it, but I am glad I was born when I was. I imagine six

months would give a boy a good insight into all trades sufficient to let him carry on any one with ease if he chose to
pursue it in after years.

Variety is pleasing! Got away from mosquitoes to find
sand-flies and harvest-bugs instead. However, they are
quiet by day, and here there are no flies with irritating feet.
There must be some wonderful mystery about this life.
Why should these countries be so full of annoyances to
man? Why should even the alighting of a fly, *his foot-
prints*, cause such irritation to the skin? It must be for
some good object eventually to be made known to us. I
have cleared up the mystery of the palm. When *young* its
whole stem is covered with cacti sort of leaves, but when it
gets a certain height all these fall off, and the stem is as
clean as a mast. Linant told me a queer story of the white
ant. He says the queen is a sort of slug, white, and as
thick as your little finger; that she lies encased in a chamber
in the centre of the nest with four portals; that in this
chamber is a small black ant, which is the male and which
does no work, but is always with her majesty; the other
ants bring down their collections of food, and, passing
through the queen's chamber, put it in the magazines;
that there are soldier ants, red fellows, who also do nothing.
I have seen these red ants in the same nest as the common
white ones, and shall try and investigate the subject. Are
these ants the same as the Indian ones? If so, their
history must be known.

FASHELIE, 3 *November*, 1875.—It is odd people who are
false fear falseness in others; people who are jealous fear
jealousy, and so on. I judge from myself. We have a
very good map of the world in ourselves, and by careful
study of it can read others. I know it is a reproach: "You
judge others by yourself;" but that does not to me alter
the facts, though we ought to add a great deal of charity
with the judgment.

I have the garrisons small on purpose to make them keep
awake; and it has its effect, for they are all in a fearful
fright along the line.   I cannot help feeling somewhat of a
malicious enjoyment of their sufferings.   If I personally am
at any station, even if there are thirty or forty men there,
the sentries all go to sleep in comfort.   Not so in my
absence; every one is awake I expect.   Having nothing to
do—or rather not doing anything, though there is plenty to
be done—they sit and talk over the terrors of their position,
until they tremble again.   I never in the course of my life
saw such wretched creatures dignified by the name of
soldiers.   Fortunately, though I can do the work of the
province without an interpreter, I cannot speak to the men
except by my looks, or tell them my opinion in words,
though my letters are pretty strong.

FATIKO, 3 *January*, 1876.—When, D.V., I get home I
do not dine out.   My reminiscences of these lands will not
be more pleasant to me than the China ones.   What I shall
have done will be what I have done.   Men think giving
dinners is conferring a favour on you.   I look on these
constant invitations to dinner as a positive infliction.   You
cannot go and see a man without his pressing you to dine
with him, where you are certain to say something you regret.
Why not give their dinners to those who need them?   This
is against the rule, not to fly people; but I do fly people,
however much I like them, who make me tell lies to avoid
their feasts.   I believe there are people who cannot do
without these things.   Many husbands and wives are bored
to death with each other's society, and want new faces and
new ideas; it is a different thing with one's brothers and
sisters; they know you are a " tuppenny " and full of faults,
and do not pick at you like strangers.

You may think I am cantankerous; so I am, but it is on
principle.   I will not cater to this world's appetites, nor be
drawn into its coteries and squabbles.   What have we in

common? They think men deserve credit for this or that. I do not think so. Am I to agree with them?

A man glories in some act he has performed, I say he has nothing to do with it; that God used him, as we use any instrument; that God could have worked with the smallest insect as well as with him, in spite of his pride and cleverness. Feeling this so strongly, I cannot help expressing it. Then the conversation goes to religious matters; and then you are either mad,[1] or you are unsound, or you are a fool. Though I do not consider those who do not agree with me are "swine," yet there is no doubt your pearls are not appreciated, and that many turn and rend you for placing those pearls before them instead of worldly turnips.

When one knows the little one does of oneself, and any one praises you, I, at any rate, have a rising, which is a suppressed "You lie." There are several nice bits in our Lord's life, when He replied with some unpalatable truth to those men who would follow Him, and would make much of Him, but afterwards they entirely changed their demeanour.

If these people were agreed with one that what the world says is but for a moment, then we could converse; but if one thinks the world's reputation of value, and the other thinks and knows by experience how false it is, how can you get on? "How can ye believe, which receive honour one of another?" (John v. 44.) "Who art thou, that thou shouldest be afraid of a man?" (Isaiah li. 12.) It is a great deal more trouble trying to wear the mask of conformity with the world than to throw it off; you can never wear it well enough to remain undetected long. To undergo martyrdom you have only to despise man's praise. What is more irritating to the world than to see a man take an independent course and do what he thinks is right? The

[1] "The spiritual man is mad" (Hosea ix. 7).

whole antagonism against our Lord was from His following God's way and not man's, and from His fearless exposure of the *sayings* without *doings* of the Pharisees. They washed their hands, why did not He? We all have it. "Oh, do not go out in the rain;" and if he *will* go we feel annoyed, not because he will get wet, but because our will is not followed. Every one must be alike and worship the same idol.

Why (it is God's will) will you keep caring for what the world says? Try, oh try to be no longer a slave to it. You can have little idea of the comfort of freedom from it—it is bliss. All this caring for what people will say is from pride. Hoist your flag, and abide by it; in an infinitely short time all secret things will be divulged; therefore, if you are misjudged, why trouble to put yourself right? You have no idea of what a lot of trouble it saves you. Give your advice, give your opinion on all subjects; if neither are approved, what does it signify? Roll your burden on Him and He will make straight your mistakes. He will put you right with those with whom you have set yourself wrong. The more you throw on Him the better pleased He is, and the stronger you will grow in your reliance.

Let me be called at this second, I fear nothing; for the world to come has better pleasures than this world has to give. Let me be called some time hence, till that time I am protected. Make your religion *more practical*, adventure a little in the matter; as some things harden by exposure, so does your faith increase by launching forth on it. Do you think God really wants your services? Could He not as easily work with an ant as with you? You are nothing, nothing whatever; we are all poor worms.

I am much better to-day, and look forward to the passage north; but, if not allowed to go, it will still be right. As for my burdens, I have rolled them off on my God. He will work, and will glorify Himself in His work. You will never learn to swim unless you throw yourself into the water, *i. e.* you will always have the "doles" unless you risk something in faith. Pray thus: "I am the clay, be Thou the Potter. Mould me as Thou wilt; heed not my cries, for Thou actest in infinite wisdom, but give me the conviction that all will work for good." You are a *barnacle* to the world and its judgments.

This is a horrid climate. I seldom, if ever, get a good sleep. It is a very great comfort to feel that God will rectify one's defects in this life, and make right all mistakes, also that He governs everything. Is it my present temperament, or is it truly the case that things go untowardly more in this land than anywhere else? You wrap up an article in paper, the paper is sure to tear, the string you least want to be broken is broken; every, *every* thing seems to go wrong. It may be my liver which makes me think this, but it has been the same with all travellers. Look at the burning of Schweinfurth's botanical collection. Oh! how I wish I had finished this work. I have yet two months of weariness; shall I get through it? God knows.

The mosquitoes are horrible here; the proboscis is formed like a bayonet, with a hinge at the bend; they turn it down for perforation and press on it with their head, muscles and chest. I am very susceptible of their bite or dig; the least touch of the "bayonet" makes a lump.

KERRI, 20 *April*, 1876.—I do not think religious books or sermons do harm; they present, if they are true, views of the truth as seen from certain standpoints, and taken as such are useful for those at those standpoints. Grace by works, if preached, will induce men to try the same; then they will see the futility of their efforts, and may thus learn grace without works. The preaching of John the Baptist was grace by works (to be followed by a mightier) and is useful to lead to God; it is not to be despised or thought to be wrong doctrine.

Till the word of God separates the spiritual from the carnal man, the proper allotment of Scripture texts cannot be made, for it is true the wicked will be utterly destroyed, and that only the righteous will enter the kingdom of God; it is the discernment of the allotting of the texts of the Scriptures which is the great stumbling-block, and which gains the name of fanciful ideas. The great principle is this: that which comes from God was, is, and will be ever *sinless;* that which comes from man was, is, and will be ever *sinful.* Now, what came from God in man was known before the world began; "their names were written in the Book of Life;" their existence is contemporaneous with the existence of their Spiritual head, "the Lamb slain from the foundation of the world," and is therefore eternal as He is. Their existence is as necessary to their Head as that Head is to them. He came to "seek *His own,*" who were for a while lost.

The principles of the "*unsound*" doctrine are these: *Firstly,* the pre-existence of the soul. *Secondly,* its sinlessness, except from its union with a fleshly body, in which it is incarnated, and for whose breaking of the law it is exculpated from blame by the atonement of its Head. *Thirdly,* its restitution to its pristine state in God, as pure as when it issued from Him into incarnation. To me nothing could be more infinite in wisdom than God's arrangements by which He teaches us Himself, without risk to our eternal welfare. I know no explanation which would so fully fill up the difficulties of the Bible.

"How long halt ye between two opinions? If the Lord be God, follow Him; but if Baal then follow him. And the people answered him not a word" (1 Kings xviii. 21). The same question is before us every day. Do we believe Jehovah to be the Almighty, namely, the ruler of all things, supreme in all, and against whose will no power can act; or, do we recognize Baal, namely, the various events, accidents, and circumstances of life, as acting *independently* of God, and *therefore* to be considered in the walk of life? How long halt ye between these opinions? The world says "worship both," but God says "thou shalt have no other God (*i. e.* ruler, creator, director in all things) but Me." When asked the above question, "the people answered him not." Why? Because they could not deny Jehovah was God, but it suited them better to serve Baal. The sacerdotal class have always abounded; they are allied with the temporal civil power, who need their aid to keep the people quiet. "By whose authority teachest thou these things?" is their cry; from them alone must come the authority.

LABORÉ, 29 *June*, 1876.—I have been, as usual, an ass! have spent 1080*l.* on —— and ——, and have been careless in my private accounts, and pitched away, in one way or another, 920*l.* Therefore out of 5000*l.* (two and a half years' pay) 2000*l.* has gone! and my reflection is, I could certify no one is more unfit to have money than I am, so you may just as well oblige your brother, and take that house! It is a *sine quâ non (i. e.* decided) that you accept it as a present from me. How the 920*l.* has gone I have not an idea; some one has got it, and that person or persons were destined to get it. It was but lent to me, and He who lent has given it to some one else and not told me. I have not, I know, spent it in merry-making; as soon as I can, you shall have the 500*l.* salvage from the wreck. I know it is not altogether right to be so careless; but I think, if God pleases, He can settle these accounts. If you have a friend of His might and wisdom, you cannot too much trust Him, and with His power it is no trouble to Him; therefore the closer your intimacy the better. I know these views are outrageous, but I would take His own invitation, to cast all my cares on Him, "for He careth for thee," and what I ask Him is not more than one would ask one's brother to do.

4 *July*, 1876.—Last night I thought over what we pray for—namely, direction in the courses we should pursue; and I think, provided your petition is made in sincerity and that you really wish to do His will and not your own, even if you do not daily renew that petition, I believe it is granted, and it is want of faith which prevents your enjoying the fruits. Therefore I think that all who have even once made that petition in *sincerity* may rest comfortable, with the trust that all that happened that day is His will, let it be good or bad, or let it be according to our reason or not. This jewel will comfort me for a long time. Though in its aspect it seems fresh, it is not so; it is only the application of the fact and truth that *all things* are ruled by Him and that He inspires and answers our prayer; it is, as it were, a clearer view of the island from the ship; it existed before, but now a portion more of the fog or veil is swept away. It may or may not strike you as a new view of an existing fact; that will depend on whether that particular portion of the fog or veil is lifted to you. The way these truths fit into one another corroborates my faith in them; did they differ, then I should fear; but as they are one and indivisible, I accept them at once. No doubt they may be for a time obscured, when one is carnal; the veil may come over them again, but it is only a temporary obscuration. When a man abuses these truths, the veil over the whole of them falls at once, and he no longer believes them, and then can no longer abuse them, for he falls under the law's direct action.

We are all approaching at different intervals our great existence—God. He has explained Himself to us as the Truth, Love, Wisdom, and Almighty; we accept these attributes in the abstract, but do not believe them heartily, on account of *apparent* contradictions. We are as it were blind, and by degrees He opens our eyes and enables us by dint of sore troubles to know Him little by little. We may not at once sincerely accept His statements, but eventually

He will show Himself, as He is, to each one of us. According to His pleasure, He reveals Himself in different degrees to different people, to some sooner, to some later. *To know Him* is the ultimate point of His vast design of creation both of this and all worlds. Man from his birth beholds a veil before him which shrouds the Godhead. If his lot is to be born in Christian lands, he has the attributes of the Godhead explained to him by the Word, both written and incarnated; but, though he may know by his intellect the truth of the Word, things are so contradictory in this life that the mystery still remains. By suffering and trials the veil is rent, and according to the extent of that rent his mind accepts sincerely that which he before had accepted by his intellect. The rent in the veil may often present inconsistencies to him which disappear on new rents being made, and he at length sees a harmonious whole.

To the black man the same shrouded Being reveals Himself, but we do not know in what manner; and perhaps the black man could not tell himself; but it is the same Godhead and has the same attributes, whether known or unknown. Watch the conflict of the flesh and the Spirit in peace, for the result is certain. "Stand ye still, and see the salvation of the Lord" (2 Chronicles, xx. 17). Every time the flesh is foiled by the Spirit, so often is a rent made in the veil, and we know more of God. Every time the reverse takes place, so often does the veil fall again. When the inevitable event—death—occurs, then the veil is rent altogether and no mystery remains. The flesh is finally vanquished by the Spirit, who is thus the conqueror of his life-long foe. I think the veil is thickened by the doctrines of men, and that to rend it is more difficult when these doctrines have been accepted and found inefficient. Had you not been imbued with them—had God not willed it in His wisdom—you would not have had such suffering in learning the truth.

I believe when we begin life we are far more capable of accepting those truths than afterwards; when we have imbibed man's doctrine we must unlearn and then learn again—a child has only to learn. It is easier for a Publican to accept those truths than a Pharisee. The Pharisee builds his house and uses man's doctrine; after a time he sees differently, and tries to dovetail his new views into his house. They will not fit in, and he says, " Why, I cannot pull down all my work and begin again ! " so he forces them in, and still they will not fit; then he takes down a little, and then a little more, but it is no good; he finds the foundation is at fault, thence great trials and troubles, till at last he has to pull all down. When he has done all that—why, the miracle of a new house on the true foundation appears before him, in which work he has not had to make an effort. The Publican has built and feels he can build nothing, but that all is done for him.

Why one should be a Pharisee and have all this toil and the other should be a Publican and have none, is the mystery of God's government. It is pain and grief to pull down a life's work and grub up even the foundations; but while you pull down each stone, God is building up your true house, so that in fact, whilst you are pulling down, you are in reality having your house built.

We often cling to one stone—to one doctrine of man— and cannot make up our minds to give it up. Every one says it is a good stone, and we like and cherish it, but, being useless, it must be weighed and rejected sooner or later, and we must suffer the scoffs of the other builders who are erecting similar structures. The world's master-builders will shrug their shoulders, and tell you that you will have no house at all, that you are mad and unsound in rejecting a stone which every one in the world values. " The greatest builders have used that stone, and thought it a good one," &c.

It may indeed be a good one, but in a wrong position, or

the foundation may be at fault. Men would make themselves a dwelling-place for eternity out of their works in this world; we need not so trouble ourselves, for we have one already made; theirs is transitory and to be seen, ours is eternal and invisible. If we use this truth carnally we shall doubt its truth, for so God guards His treasures. One is God's work, the other is man's. In us are the two natures, both building houses of their experiences, the materials being widely different; one builds on sand, the other on the rock; each nature thinks the other a fool. The architect of one is the world and the doctrines of man, and the Architect of the other is God.

I often think I should like to return and study these truths in quiet; but this is foolishness, for if I returned I might not know them. I feel sure that no study without trial is of avail; life must be lived to learn these truths. I believe, if a man knows his Bible fairly and then goes forth into the world, God will show him His works. The Jews learnt the Scripture by heart, and so I expect our Saviour did; He therefore had no need to study it. He applied its teachings to life and its trials.

But to go back to the "house." We must think what our Saviour meant by His type: a house is a place one returns to, where one is sheltered from storms, winds, and weather, where one keeps one's treasures, and where one looks for repose. The "religion" of a man is *his house,* built up of doctrines. He forms his idea of God and His working, and looks to that "religion" for shelter in all tribulation. When that "religion" or "house" is built of the doctrines of men, and when the builders try to *fit in* God's doctrine and cannot do so, they fall into a desperate state, and become atheistical and indifferent, give up all effort, so to say, and are, perhaps, at last driven into relinquishing their old ideas, pulling down the house they had built. You have often said, "Why is it there is so much

L   H

toil, and yet no comfort?" Because that toil has been erected on a false foundation, namely, man's work, and not Christ's free grace—we would *do* something. This is the main obstacle, however we may blind ourselves. Till we own futility, we are not on the true foundation, and everything we may build is therefore doomed to fall or fail us in the trials of life, which are the "winds." Our buildings give us no shelter.

I feel I have a mission here, not taken in its usual sense. The men like my justice, candour, my outbursts of temper, and see I am not a tyrant. . . . I dare say some of my letters have been boastful, but I know that my looking-glass (conscience) has remonstrated whenever they have been so. Some of my letters are written by one nature, some by the other, and so it will be to the end.

This conflict makes me terribly inconsistent in some affairs, both carnal and spiritual, which require a decision. Being in authority and responsible, action is necessary, while mercy should temper justice. In such matters as the line of march to take, the selection of a site for a station, measures to be taken against hostile tribes, I am able to decide firmly enough, but in questions like ——'s I feel the difficulty owing to the existence of my two natures. I want to be kind to him, and yet he puts me out by taking advantage of this kindness. I want to teach him things which, to my human understanding, it is dangerous for him not to know; and I fear I am not kind in my tuition : these things trouble me, or rather did so.

The more one acts from principle and not from feelings, the straighter is our course. No one can be perfectly honest, but the nearer one can be so the stronger one is, and the wish is accepted as the deed. To deceive when you have knowledge of the fact is a lie to all intents and purposes.[1]

DUFFLI, 10 *July*, 1876.—I went up the river in the ten-

[1] "The wilful suppression of truth is a lie" (Latin adage).

horse-power steamer to-day; the country is very pretty but very mournful. There certainly is some mystery about this Nile.

Thank God I am well, and so happy now I have resigned the government of the Province and put all the faults on my "Friend." He is able to bear them, and will use me as long as He pleases as His mouthpiece, and when He has done with me He will put me aside. "Casting all your care on Him; for He careth for you," has just come to my mind. I do not know if you will see this "*pearl*" at once, but I consider it a great stride in the knowledge of Him, and yet it is an *old truth*. I consider, now I am free from any responsibility about the Province or my staying or leaving, that He has taken the whole work off my hands and that I am on leave as it were. What a comfort it is! He offers to do the same for all; but many appear to say, "*No, I would rather do my own work*."

I thank God, I look for nothing on earth, and that, dull or gay, all is alike to me. I may wish it was more cheerful, as you wish it did not rain when you are going out, but it is a transitory wish. Since I had the "pearl," "He careth for thee," and as it were resigned the rule of the Province, I have had much comfort and peace, and if I had paid off all my "pensioners" I could say "*Nunc dimittis*" with Simeon without regret; it would only be a day or so before I saw you again.

I have had to pay 26*l.* for ——, as I could not put all his expenses on the Government. However, my dear Augusta, if God wills, this will be the last of my escapades in this direction, though I have now so little confidence in myself that it might happen I should do the same thing to-morrow again. This is a grand country for a man to know himself, to feel his impotency and learn God's power and mercy. Your body is so humbled and so feeble that you can no longer suffer it to reign supreme. I think you would like ——. He is a quiet young fellow, and modest. He was *never* boastful, and so now he has not to lower his colours. The safest course is to close-reef your ship, close the ports, have no ends of rope hanging out for people to catch hold of; or if you have, at any rate do not make these ropes fast to the ship, for in pulling them in they will retard the vessel; and carry your colours low down. People will say, "What a miserable craft!" but it will ride out the storms.

27 *August*, 1876.—What wretchedly poor notions we have of ourselves! The mass of men think that the purpose of their lives is plain, namely, to live comfortably, and they flatter themselves they not only know themselves but others. But what a complicated affair man truly is! In reality he knows nothing of *himself* even. We may pray in our ignorance that we may cease from ourselves, and ask and expect His government; but man for the most part has no higher idea than a vegetable, how to get through life without trouble.

MROOLI, **2** *September*, 1876.—The troops from Dubaga must, D.V., be back in three or four days, and then I shall be able to move, I hope. It must be for some good purpose one is compelled to wait; God never acts uselessly. I am destined at some future period to meet some event or some person whom I should not meet were I not delayed, and I would not alter it. Paul abode silent three years after his call—a long trial for an energetic mind; our Saviour was silent till thirty years of age; so was Elijah during the seven-years' famine. We are all apt, while on earth, to think our lives our own, and to follow our own likings. We do not realize we are only here to fulfil a certain work in a certain programme. We would make our nests here; but it is no use: we are compelled to move on and fulfil our tasks, whether we realize it or not.

To each is allotted a distinct work, to each a destined

goal; to some the seat at the right hand or left of the Saviour. (It was not His to give; it was already given—Matthew xx. 23. Again, Judas went to "*his own place*"—Acts i. 25.) It is difficult to the flesh to accept "Ye are dead, ye have naught to do with the world." How difficult for any one to be circumcised from the world, to be as indifferent to its pleasures, its sorrows, and its comforts as a corpse is! That is to know the resurrection.

The future world must be much more amusing, more enticing, more to be desired, than this world—putting aside its absence of sorrow and sin. The future world has been somehow painted to our mind as a place of continuous praise; and, though we may not say it, yet we cannot help feeling that this would prove monotonous. It cannot be thus; it must be a life of activity, for happiness is dependent on activity; death is cessation of movement; life is all movement. There are two rests, one of the grave, the other of freedom from harassing cares, *contretemps*, fears of evil, &c. &c.

I think, now, that, D.V., all the moving incidents of my career up here are at an end; you could cease sending my letters out. What is the use of jarring with the convictions of others? Why should I open my mind to those who cavil at my views and only learn them in order to judge me? All those apparently innocent queries, addressed as if with a wish for information—"Is it lawful to heal on the Sabbath day?" "Moses said this," &c., "Whose wife shall she be?"—are all repeated even in our day, and though the infirmity of our flesh prevents us the answer "Why tempt ye me?" yet something tells me these queries are traps and are not honestly asked, and the consequence is a chilled feeling.

Our Saviour did not seek, nor did He *avoid* these people; they sought Him, and, when they came to Him, He was with the publicans and sinners. This should be our course,

" Let them alone." There was nothing in common between Him and them; though as God He gave His life for them, He did not like them as man, after the flesh. They were the children of this world, in spite of all their sacrifices, their ceremonies and their sanctity as acknowledged by the world. "You should go to church" (at Jerusalem you should worship). The answer is, "God is a Spirit : those that worship Him must worship Him in spirit and in truth" —not at Jerusalem, nor in this mountain.

When men " wrestle " in prayer (for what has already been given them) it is like one man beseeching another to give him this or that, while, all the time he is making his supplication, he has all he asks for in his house, and either does not know it or else does not value the things given him. What man has to do is to realize that he *has had all* given him ; it is not a question of further gifts, but of power of appreciating what he already has. These *wrestling* prayers would be more applicable to a heathen idol than to our gracious God. The boxes are *all* in your house ; there are no more to come ; you have only to unpack them and see their contents, but you must make room for these contents by getting rid of the things of the world, for the two must not be mixed, and there is no room for both. To the degree you turn out the things of the world, the more you will know the contents of the boxes. All have the boxes, but some overlook them and leave them unpacked, and still keep on asking for them, till at last the things of this world are obliged to be turned out, and then they find they have all the time been possessors of priceless treasures.

KARTOUM, 29 *October*, 1876.—There are English sparrows here; it is quite a pleasure to see them. I have been terribly attacked here by cavalry (sand-flies), infantry (tortoises), and artillery (opal-coloured insects), and have suffered a good deal, especially from the artillery, whose attacks are something fearful. You feel the wounds for days; and yet there are not many in action, but ill-naturedly they attack much ground. I feel sure if you were wounded by an "opal" you would feel it for a week at least. The doctor who was with me says that in all these insects there are a couple of vesicles near the head, and, when they bite, these vesicles are compressed against the skin, and poison is injected; I think his theory is good. Mosquitoes and flies are absent.

4 *November*, 1876.—The seeing many people upsets me from my thoughts, and stirs up "Moab" terribly. I thought I should like coming home, and now I don't know whether I do or not. Talk of two natures in one! I have a hundred, and they none think alike and all want to rule. Whether it is the climate I cannot say, but I never know my own mind for two days consecutively. "You ought to know your own mind" is to me as if you said, "You ought to have red hair," or "You ought not to have the scarlet fever." One knows oneself better than any one else does, and I wish I was more decided, but alas! I cannot be so. I envy Gessi, who knows his own mind. I expect having had my blood at a high temperature day and night, from year's end to year's end, must have some effect on the temperament.

Looking back on the three years' vista, I have been much blessed in that long avenue. How many mosquitoes have I not killed on the nape of my neck! It saddens me to think of it. I have a dear little lioness not bigger than a small dog, which I am taking down with me till I can find a master for it. I have precious few *curios*. I cannot collect these things.[1]

---

[1] General Gordon came home to England, and decided on not returning to his command, but the receipt of the following telegram from the Khedive made him reverse his decision, and on the 31st of January, 1877, he again started for the Soudan :—

EN ROUTE FOR KASALA, 8 *April*, 1877.—The Arabs here are a fine lot. They are nearly chocolate-coloured. They, and indeed the mass of the inhabitants, wear their hair frizzed out at the top like a brush, then a series of curls hang down all round ; they never could get the frizzle part into any hat. They generally ride along with a boy perched up behind them, like a monkey. No camel will allow of any caresses, none are even patted ; they repel all overtures of friendship, and seem to be a cross-grained ill-natured face, hating man, and never looking in the least degree happy.

KATARIF, 22 *April*, 1877.—I got here to-day after a hot journey ; we did it in a very short time—150 miles in sixty hours. The great Sheikh of the Shukyriah says he will *never* forget it, the journey was so fast ! This travelling is what some people would call pleasure, but I do not so call it, and I have a year of it before me. Nothing can be more miserable, which is a comfort, for when one is down at the bottom you can go no lower. Ambition, oh what a thing thou art ! Nearly everything is broken ; pelting along on the camels ought eventually to shake one's organs out of their places. A few storks build on

" CAIRO, 17 Janvier, 1877.

"MON CHER GORDON PACHA,—Monsieur Vivian m'a communiqué la dépêche par laquelle vous le chargez de m'informer que les circonstances ne vous permettent pas de revenir en Égypte. Je ne pouvais m'attendre à cette nouvelle après l'entretien que j'ai eu avec vous à Abdin, entretien dans lequel je vous ai fait réaliser la nécessité qu'il y a pour enlever d'intérêt à achever l'œuvre que nous avons commencée ensemble, et je vous ai prié de revenir reprendre votre poste en Égypte. Nous nous sommes séparés en nous disant, ' Au revoir.'

"Je ne peux donc attribuer votre dépêche qu'à la première impression du contentement bien naturel que vous avez éprouvé en vous trouvant chez vous, et je me refuse à croire qu'un gentilhomme comme Gordon veut sous un prétexte quelconque reprendre la parole qu'il m'a donnée Je ne puis donc, mon cher Gordon, prendre en considération votre dépêche, et je vous attends, selon votre promesse.

" Votre affectionné,
" ISMAIL."

the huts here, but they are not like those on the Danube,
which have much more white about them and have only
their wings black ; these have also black heads and necks,
and a short black waistcoat with white pantaloons.

NEAR OBEID, CAPITAL OF KORDOFAN, 27 *May,* 1877.—
I nearly acted as Juggernaut to a little black naked boy
to-day. My camel had shaken out its nose-ring and ran
off with me; I could not stop it, and of course the little
black ran right under it; the camel did not tread on it,
though it was a miracle the child escaped being killed.
Nothing is so perverse as a camel; when it runs away it
will go anywhere. I am quite well. I do not think it fair
to tell even you what I have in hand; with the Abyssinian
business it was another matter, for it had a European
interest. Thank God, I have confidence He will and has
undertaken the government of the Province for me, and
only He can help me through; consequently I am not the
least disturbed, and feel every confidence of success, should
He will it. If He wills otherwise, surely His will should
be mine and yours. What comfort this is, is it not?
That is the way to use the revelations He has made to
us, otherwise where is the support in religion? It is no
vain promise, " Thou wilt keep him in perfect peace, whose
mind is stayed on Thee" (Isaiah xxvi. 3). In reality,
whatever happens will be a comfort to me, for, looking
at the work of years before me, life presents but little
attraction.

I am glad to say I am now more comfortable on the
camel, and am happier on the march than in towns with
all the ceremonies. The route here is a plain of sand and
bushes, quite uninteresting. I have been most wonderfully
blessed in my government, and hope my sojourn in these
lands may be a comfort to the poor people.

FOGGIA, 7 *June,* 1877.—The road is a flat and uninteresting one, and I have no anecdotes to tell you. Has

it ever struck you that, if man's birth and death are predetermined by God to happen at certain epochs, so every
intervening event must be also predetermined? Few are
atheistical enough to say either man's birth or death are
things of chance; and how can they therefore dispute that
the intervening events are not pre-ordained? In governing
these countries, I wish I could realize this truth more than
I do, so that I might cease from criticizing the actions of
others. I do not mean by this that if a man offends I am
to look over it, but I would wish to reprimand him in a
spirit of kindness, and not in the frame of mind that
comforts the flesh by the thought of "How much better
I should have acted in his place." The more I live in
this country, and the more God prospers me, the more I
despise myself and feel despicable; some of the *coups* I
have made, and which have been successful, have been
such flukes, or chances, as the world calls them, as to
astonish me quite as much as they have astonished others,
and I cannot feed myself with the thought of "How clever
I am," for impressed on my mind is the fact, "You know
you had no idea of what would happen on your so acting."

I will not inflict on you the history of my affairs or the
death-blow I think slavery has received. It would be a
long story, and you will know it more completely in the
future life. Praying for the people whom I am about to
visit gives me much strength, and it is wonderful *how
something seems already to have passed between us* when I
meet with a chief (for whom I have prayed) for the first
time. On this I base my hopes of a triumphal march to
Fascher; the chiefs cannot wish war, and can have little
hopes of success, seeing that, as I trust is the case, Fascher
has been relieved. I have really no troops with me, but
I have the Shekinah, and I do like trusting to Him and
not to man. Remember, unless He gave me the confidence and encouraged me to trust Him, I could not

feel it, so I consider in this confidence I have the earnest of success.

11 *June*, 1877.—I have certainly got into a slough with this Soudan, but looking at my Banker, my Commander-in-Chief, and my Administrator, it will be wonderful if I do not get out of it; had I not got this Almighty Power to back me, with His infinite wisdom, I do not know how I could even think of what is to be done.

OOMCHANGA, 25 *June*, 1877.—I have put down some thoughts which have risen up in me but are not yet evolved in much clearness.

It is remarkable that the woman Eve was not prohibited from touching the tree. Of all parts of the Scripture, next to our redemption, that of our fall is most worthy of study. If the Scriptures are not to be studied thus, then the various little glimpses of light given by our Lord and the Apostles were wrong. Melchisedec's father was not named, and with an object. Who ever would have thought the resurrection to be exemplified by the expression, "the God of Abraham!" and yet it was such a convincing argument that the questioners ceased to inquire further.

Those who study the religion of Egypt protest loudly that they were not idolaters. (Their mummies are their way of softening the effect of the inevitable decay of the flesh.) Their religion is a very intricate subject, but any man that has studied their history would laugh at the idea that they worshipped the mummied cats, &c. Of course, they would agree the common people might have done so, but they maintain, according to the papyri, that such was not the original religion.

It would also be a mistake to think that, though Egypt was used as a type of the flesh and of earthly power, it was a corrupted nation. The king, or Pharaoh, of Moses' time may have been stiff-necked, but this may not have applied to the people; and if history is true, this Pharaoh had, after the. flesh, reason to hate Joseph's people, for Joseph was prime minister to the Hykso Pharaohs, who were usurpers and did Egypt much harm.

Egypt was to the Israelites as our flesh is to our spiritual nature. Egypt gave asylum to Israel and to our Saviour, and with Israel it will be blessed (Isaiah xix. 23–25).

It is remarkable the rain does not fall there, rain being the type of the Holy Spirit. Egypt was not to be abhorred by Israel (Deuteronomy xxiii. 7). If clergymen, instead of those fearfully dull sermons, would only search the Scriptures and then throw these subjects of thought to us, we should be much better off.

What a terrible thing our education is ! In no time have services been so long as now-a-days. The Temple services must have been very short. It is a yoke that has been put on us little by little. I have read the Jewish ceremonial: it was at most two chapters and a few prayers. I really pity the clergy, who have to prepare such long and frequent exhortations.

EN ROUTE FOR TOASHA, 30 *June*, 1877.—I have been obliged to leave one of my servants behind at Oomchanga, he was too ill to come on. This is cruel, but I could not help it, for time presses for me on all sides. What a life it is, full of sorrows. I now think, ill as he was, I ought to have taken him with me; but then I was told the road was unsafe, and it was a query whether the fatigue might not have been worse for him; I might have waited for his recovery, but then there was the question of food for the troops at the station. In reality, I suppose if I delayed or not the issue would have been the same, as far as Darfur is concerned, for it is in His hands. We are torn in twain by our two natures, namely, our own judgment and our faith, and the result must be inconsistent work. How can it be otherwise? In appearance the Bible is inconsistent, and so must we be who fulfil it. The only consolation is to fall back on the text, "Trust in the Lord with all thine heart, and lean not unto thine own understanding" (Proverbs iii. 5). Do what comes into your heart; and trust He will make it right. Do you remember the passage in Bogatzky [1] for April 13th (omitted in recent editions as too strong)? It runs, "If we desire to feel less evil in us than God suffers us to have, this desire comes from pride or an impatient wish to be rid of the trouble of striving against it."

NEAR TOASHA, 2 *July*, 1877.—Since I sent away my drunken major-domo I have had a half-Maltese, half-Arab. He is the slowest of the slow, a perfect funeral, and he starves me. Some days I have no meat (there is little game, only a very occasional antelope). The only part I object to is the parade which takes place to bring in next to nothing: also the number of servants, saucepans, &c. It is very grand, I know, but I would sooner go quickly. When out in this way, I often wonder what the many applicants for posts would think of it. If it were not for the expense, I would try it merely to let them rid themselves of the idea that I do not have them because I am averse to Europeans; but 1st, I have no duty I can give them; 2nd, they would not be content with the country, &c.; and 3rd, they are far too expensive.

Adam was made outside the garden and was put into it, and Eve was taken from his side afterwards (see Genesis ii. 8, 21). My mind keeps on this subject very much. If Levi paid tithes in Abraham, our Saviour was present in Adam, and did what Adam did. God in due time incarnated Himself in a sinless body known by us as "Jesus." I think we are each of us incarnations of the Godhead, but we are in sinful bodies, whilst He, Jesus, was in a sinless body. However abrupt these remarks may be, they cannot be controverted, nor their deductions refuted, if one believes in the Scriptures. How few would believe that man had

[1] Bogatzky's *Golden Treasury.*

not been cursed. It was the *ground*, not man. Man was blessed (see Genesis i. 28). How few think what God's object in this world is, and how low they put it. Ephesians iii. 10 and other passages state that it is to make manifest to the powers in heavenly places the *manifold wisdom* of God. And this He does by His Church—His members. In proportion, this wisdom is as much shown forth by each member as it is pre-eminently manifested by the Head.

No conception took place in the garden (Genesis iv. 1). To know good and evil was the attribute of God. Man acquired this knowledge by the eating of the tree, but to One only was the power given to choose the good and refuse the evil (Isaiah vii. 15).

DARA, 17 *July*, 1877.—There are a number of texts in the Bible (Proverbs, &c.) which distinctly say a man's judgment is of the Lord. How can that be, if we direct our own judgment? It seems extraordinary that so very many put away these inconsistencies from them, and refuse to consider them. There is no doubt, till they are considered, no one can feel really comfortable. You will see that I have been "tossing up" again. I never do it if I can help it, or unless things are so balanced that I cannot see my way. (See Acts i. 26, about the choosing of Matthias.)

25 *July*, 1877.—Last night I found out that the white birds which roost in numbers on the trees near me are white egrets, of whose feathers the horse artillery officers' plumes are made ; it is, as you know, a stiff spray-like feather. I have not mentioned it, as I do not want the poor things to be killed. The birds are rather dirty just now owing to the rains, which make their plumes muddy.

My lot seems, by the GOVERNOR-GENERAL, to be to wait here doing nothing. I ought to have sufficient confidence in my Superior to be quiet under the trial, as it must be for the best that I am so placed. The road from Obeid to this is safe now, but the Mudir does not send on the letters ; so

we are kept quite in the dark, and I hear there are a host
of telegrams waiting for me. It is no use repining at this.
The puzzle will work itself out in due time; either I or
some person depending on my movements have not been
brought down to our bearings yet.

What a comparatively small sin was the murmuring of the
Israelites for water! What was it to them that they had
seen wonders, when their little ones were thirsty? It would
not make them less so; yet how hardly the pulpits judge
them. The most religious persons would cry out if deprived
of this essential in these hot deserts, and would complain at
their chief for leading them there.

Taking together all the offences committed in the wilderness, which prevented the entry into the Holy Land, they
were not to be compared with the sins of any one of us; and
taking those Israelites as a type of each of us, we see that
some were not meant to go into that land, but must perish.
And so it is with us and our members; it is hopeless to
persuade them, they must be coerced into obedience; they
are never altered, never improved. Man thinks the events
of this life are important; he cannot help it, but they are
nothing in comparison to his inward life. Supposing God's
treatment of all is equal, as it is, how is it some have important (so-called) duties, and some have a labourer's life,
without incident? I suppose each is equally important and
interesting to those powers who are to be instructed in God's
wisdom (Eph. iii. 10).

Duggam, 14 *August,* 1877.—The slave question gets
more and more troublesome; there have been some curious
scenes. I found a child whom I had seen yesterday with
its mother, left by her; it was a clear case of desertion.
However, I hope I have found a woman to look after it.
This little black creature was of no value, and no one cared
for it; even the mother felt it to be a bore.

En route to Shaka, 11 *September,* 1877.—I had at

Dara 2000 troops of only mediocre sort ; all were timid, the
fort bad, and I had not the least confidence of victory if it
came to war. I rode to the slaves' camp with fifty men and
saw their troops. I should estimate their number to be
about 4000. I told Zebehr's son and his chief to come to
Dara ; they came, and I told them I knew they meant to
revolt, that I would break them up ; but they should be
paid for their arms. They left me, and then wrote to give
in. Then came three days of doubts and fears. Half were
for attacking me, the other half for giving in. The result is
that I think they have all given in, and I am on my way to
Shaka, their head-quarters, with four camps.

I thank God He has given me strength to avoid all tricks ;
to tell them (the slave-dealers) that I would no longer allow
their goings on, and to speak to them truthfully. There
are some 6000 more slave-dealers in the interior who will
obey me now they have heard their chiefs have given in.

You may imagine what a difficulty there is in dealing with
all these armed men. I have separated them here and
there, and in course of time will rid myself of the mass.
Would *you* shoot them all ? Have they no rights ? Are
they not to be considered ? Had the planters no rights ?
Did not our Government once allow slave-trading ? Do
you know cargoes of slaves came into Bristol Harbour in
the time of our fathers ? I would have given 500*l.* to have
had the Anti-Slavery Society in Dara during the three days
of doubt whether the slave-dealers would fight or not ;—on
the one side, a bad fort, a cowed garrison, and not one who
did not tremble ; on the other, a strong, determined set of
men accustomed to war, good shots, with two field-pieces.
Then I would have liked to hear what the Anti-Slavery
Society would say. I do not say this in brag, for God
knows what my anxiety was, *not* for my life, for I died years
ago to all ties in this world and to all its comforts, honours,
or glories, but for my sheep in Darfour and elsewhere. I

confess to being somewhat tired of the length of these nego-
tiations, &c. &c. ; but it is better to be tired and worn than
that one poor black skin should have a bullet-hole in it.

Let me add to this the fact that my black secretary, whom
I most implicitly trusted and so largely paid, had accepted
bribes of upwards of 3000*l.* in three months to influence
me here and there. Needless to say, Nemesis fell on him.

SHAKA, 17 *September*, 1877.—When in 1834 His Majesty's
Government abolished slavery, they had an irresistible force,
with fleets, troops, &c., at their disposal ; also a machinery
of magistrates to carry out the emancipation. In my case,
I have nothing of the sort. The force I have may be
considered antagonistic, or, at any rate, very indifferently
disposed to such a scheme.

I read the Parliamentary papers on the Gold Coast.
They make me smile, for His Majesty gives a proclamation,
and it is over. Needless to say, that is not the case in
these lands ; the state of affairs is not parallel, and I think
that, though slave razzias may cease, the holding of slaves
will *never* cease under any government, let it be as strong
and as incorruptible as you like. Certainly, if razzias cease,
no more slaves will be made, but those now with the people
breed, and their children are slaves. Now one of the most
important chiefs of the slave-dealers is a slave; he com-
mands 400 men—the *élite;* he would laugh at my saying
he was free. In his presence, Zebehr's son said, " He
belongs to my house." With my caravans, I expect there
are 100 so-called slaves. I ask one man who those seven
women are. He says, " My wives." How can I disprove
it ? Can I risk the imputation of taking away one of his
wives ? Besides, what could I do with the poor black ? I
do not want her with me. Another says, " These three
boys are my sons." How am I to disprove it ? Am I to
go into the question whether he did beget them or not ? I
am not asking you for advice, for I know what to do, but

I

merely to show you that, if it is said I came from Shaka
with a caravan of slaves, it would be no more than what is
true.   Of course, with good authority this might justifiably
be published in the Anti-Slavery journal, and, of course, I
should not care if it was.

To-morrow (for life is a day) all actions will be weighed
and all secrets known, and we shall see why God allows
these things. I do not believe in man's free will; therefore,
if my actions are right, they are His actions; if evil, they
are the inevitable produce of the corrupt body in which I
am placed by Him.

My opinion is that the Brussels Conference is doomed to
fail. It is too mighty for God to use in His work. He
never has done any of His great works by great men.   As,
in Judges vii. 2, He would only let a few go to the war, so
His honour is engaged to work with petty men and means.
It is remarkable that no great expedition either to the Pole
or Africa has ever done as much as individuals; *vide* what
was done by Speke and Baker (in his first journey) compared with what Cameron or Baker did in their journeys
of 1869-76.

Those who hold by man's free will must consequently be
more or less elated if they do well.   Now, if you accepted
what I think is the truth, namely, that man has no free will,
you would never be elated, for you would not arrogate to
yourself your actions; neither would you be depressed by
your evil acts.   To the one you would say, "Thanks to
God for that;" and to the other, "This is nothing more
than the outcomings of my corrupt nature."   Paul says this
in his " *Wretched man that I am !*"   I feel sure no one can
be happy till he has come to this knowledge.   But it has
its drawbacks, and to some would mean loss of worldly
possessions.

I do not claim to be given this always, for I own I feared
to trust God in this slave-dealers' business; I was tossed

up and down. Perhaps physical fatigue may have been the cause. I hold to "Trust in the Lord, and lean not on thine own understanding," and He has brought me through.

I declare, however, in the *world's parlance*, that there is not a greater fool than he that trusts in the Lord and leans not on his own understanding. The world says, "It is idiotic; you must use means, your reason," &c. &c. I thank God that, though the discipline is severe, I would be quoted as a fool. You see a thing about to happen; you see how, by a little trick, you could prevent it, and *it is hard* not to use that little trick. Seven days was long for Samuel to have kept Saul waiting (1 Samuel xiii. 8-13), but he had better have waited.

Man generally works with the hope of success. I have had so many rebuffs in these countries that I work with my best will, but am rather inclined to believe that things will go on contrarily to what I expect. No country in the world is better than Africa for the "Know thyself." You and I are flies on the wheel; try and realize this, that you do not move the wheel.

As I suspected, I am convoying down a caravan of slaves. I came on them to-day—some sixty women and men chained together. What should I do? The owner of the caravan had bought them at Shaka. He had not taken them from their homes. That had been done far away by the slave-traders in the interior. Was he to blame? The *purchase* of slaves is permissible in Egypt. Would you have hanged him? If you had, you would have incurred just obloquy. Would you have taken the slaves from him?

First, it would be robbery in the present state of the law. Second, what would you have done with them? Would you have been able to feed them and care for them? If not prepared to take charge of them, you do them no kindness in taking them from the slave-merchants. In all probability

you would have done what I did, namely, order their chains
to be taken off (as scandalous) and left them with the
merchant, who, looking on them as valuable cows, will look
after them.   Don Quixote would have liberated them, and
made an attempt to send them back some forty days'
march, through hostile tribes, to their homes, which they
would never have reached.

Now, when a man is internally ill, it is no use poulticing
his toes.   So with these matters.   You must find the source
of the evil, which naturally is in the existence of the slave
razzia troops on the frontier.   But understand that, till
Shaka fell, these troops were in semi-revolt against the
Government, and I have no doubt that, till they hear of its
fall and give in, they will go on in their old ways and send
down their captives, who will be bought and passed on to
Cairo.   I dare say also that, when the stations are broken
up, their inmates, who have a lot of this merchandise on
hand, will be sending down larger allotments than ever;
so let the Anti-Slavery Society get the types ready for
" *Increase of Slave Trade,*" and for "atrocious," "disgrace-
ful," and "Colonel Gordon." *Of course,* His Highness is
delighted at some 10,000 or 15,000 of his subjects having
been in semi-revolt. *Of course* he, who gains not one
farthing, but who is menaced by this state of things, wishes
it to continue, and is only using me as a blind.   Mind and
note all these points.

I do not wish to be hard on individuals, but on the class
who are bigots, whether it be on the churchyard or temperance or any such question, who do not consider the other
side.   Men who travel much are seldom bigots (Paul was
not; he let that badly behaved Corinthian off very easily).

I consider I have been very unjust to His Highness, and
also to my corrupt predecessor (though the latter may have
deserved my criticisms for other acts), as far as slavery was
concerned.   I mean by that, slave razzias.   There is not

one Government *employé* who would not be rejoiced should these be stopped, for they directly menace their existence. The Anti-Slavery Society will rejoice far less than His Highness at the downfall of Shaka, though they may represent him tearing his hair at the *loss of revenue*, which existed only in their ideas.

I consider they all ought to sit in ashes for their past conduct; and in this I include myself (I will excuse their rending their garments, though my own fare badly enough, for the camel, heedless of its valuable charge, tears through the woods here, which are all thorns). This is a fine country, and in six months I hope to have the telegraph here (Shaka). Only one foreigner (Mason) has been here before me.

There is an odd feature in all this. The populations of Nubia, Dongola, &c., worried by the government of Lower Egypt, have migrated *en masse* to these slave negro countries. Here they have squatted, and are free from taxes, and do not know Pharaoh. It may be said, "Drive the slaves out of these lands," which is tantamount to saying, "Remove the population," for there must be twenty or thirty thousand of the inhabitants of Lower Egypt here. Every plucky boy comes up here from the Nile near Dongola. They are, in spite of their slave-stealing, a fine brave people, and far superior to the Arab of Lower Egypt.

As I was riding along, it struck me that, with respect to this emancipation of the slaves, I might ask those who press the question to tell me how it is to be done. In the efforts of the abolitionists in 1830, they did think out the *modus operandi;* and if you have read the Parliamentary papers on the Gold Coast, you will see a certain plan was proposed by the Colonial Secretary to the Government. Now, I want those who press the question to give me their plans after a study of the matter, remembering the people are not Fantees. The subject would require great research for some time, far more than I could be expected to devote to it. Frame me my rules, after taking the opinion of people of all classes, and I will then say if the plan is feasible.

We must understand that, if slavery is to be abolished, it can only be *really* so after considerable thought. An edict may be nominally published, but it will be a dead-letter unless its execution is feasible and the pill gilded in some way (20,000,000*l.* gilded the West Indian planters' pill). The question must be compromised to be effectively settled.

His Highness gave the most positive orders respecting slaves to the Mudir of Kordofan, and see, by the slave gang with me now, how those orders are obeyed. The fact is, the poor Mudir would not know what to do with the slaves any more than I do now, and so perforce he shuts his eyes. The people of England care more for their dinners than they do for anything else, and you may depend upon it, it is only an active few whom God pushes on to take an interest in this question. What misery! but He that is higher than the highest regardeth.

29 *September*, 1877.—I saw another gang of slaves asleep on the road last night. I have a regular struggle with myself—not over yet—on this subject. "The Lord is good to all; His tender mercies are over all His works" (Psalm cxlv. 9). Our whole reliance is on the truth of God, and therefore, however hard it seems, we must accept that His tender mercies are over these poor slaves. Either He deadens their feelings, or else He gives them corresponding strength. No one can dispute the truth of the above verse, and consequently one must believe that the slave does not suffer more than any other person. I am not justifying the slave-dealer in saying this. I mention it as one of the motives which prevent a somewhat arbitrary nature from acting beyond the law; justifying such acts by the suffering of the slave. Now, a king or a magistrate may be bad, yet I think that the Bible does not allow of one's taking action against either beyond the law. There are instances when

God caused revolts against kings, namely, Rehoboam and Jeroboam; but the general rule of the Bible is, that man is not allowed to take the law into his own hands, and therefore I refrain from any interference with the slaves till I see my way to act fairly according to law. The difficulty is how to draw the line between the complete emancipation of slaves and the prevention of the slave-dealers' actions. What I am cogitating (if you want wisdom ask it of God) is how, *without interfering* or *touching in any way* the question of tenure of slaves, I can frame a law to net these pedlars, and prevent these cruelties.[1]

Darfour is an intense trouble in this matter, for its population consists of Bedouin and For tribes, all Mussulmans; these tribes are possessors of slaves, which as Egyptian subjects they have a right to sell; so slaves may legally come down from Darfour to other parts. Again the For tribes are negroes, and my impression is that it is often quite forgotten that they are Mussulmans, and therefore they are sold. Altogether it is like squaring the circle to find the solution of the question. My impression is that there is no solution *short of complete emancipation,* either *by an armed force,* in which case great injustice would be done, or by *compensation,* which we have no money to make. Short of this, the best way would be to legalize the transport of slaves, in fact supervise it by the Government—which idea will shock a good many people.

I carry Homer's *Iliad* about with me, and it is odd that Achilles' wrath (of which it is a history) was on account of a slave he had captured.

19 *October,* 1877.—We are each made up of the seed of God and the seed of the devil, one blessed, the other cursed (Matthew xvi. 17, 23). Christ spoke of the latter seed, when He said, "Depart from me, ye cursed." It is thus that the world, looked on as one, is composed of good and

---

[1] *Colonel Gordon in Central Africa,* pp. 287—290.

evil inhabitants, and we are each of us types of the world—
wars, &c., against the heathen are innately in us.   It is this
double composition which makes up each individual, which
renders the Bible so difficult to understand, unless we have
the sword of the Spirit to divide the meanings and a sense
to discern.   Think over this, and with God's light it will be
quite clear to you.   The Pharisees were fleshly in their
minds, their bodily lusts ruled them, the seed of God in
them was latent.

EN ROUTE TO BERBER, 23 *October*, 1877.—The quiet of
to-day on board the steamer is delightful; a month later last
year I was coming down to you from the lakes.   What a
deal has passed since then with you and me, and in Europe.
I feel a great contentment.   A star when it reaches its
highest point is said to have "culminated."   I feel I have
culminated : *i.e.* I wish for no other and no higher post than
this one ; and I know I cannot be removed unless it is God's
will, so I rest on a rock and can be content.   Many would
wish a culminating point with less wear and tear, but it is
that very wear and tear which makes me cling to the place,
and I thank God He has made me succeed—not in any very
glorious way, but in a substantial manner.

I must confess that, little as I desire to be ever employed
elsewhere than in these lands, and much as I desire to live
my life out here, I do look forward to the time when I shall
rest from my labours.   The incessant travelling, the little
comfort to be had in any place, tends to make me wish thus.
No ; life must be some wonderful exposition of God that we
have no idea of, else why should man have such troubles?
I put my burden on the Lord, and He will sustain me.

"If they have called the master of the house Beelzebub,
how much more shall they call them of his household?"
(Matthew x. 25.)   Now, if one thinks of it, are the professing
earnest Christians of the day called anything like Beelzebub?
I say they are generally respected.   To be called "Beelze-

bub" means to be credited with every evil disposition and thought—"winebibbers," "friends of sinners"—not of reclaimed sinners, but of those who are sinners still. How little of this is credited to them ! But if they profess the true faith, then they will be condemned by the world as "Beelzebub," and as capable of everything. Then come the verses, "Fear them not therefore" (Matthew x. 26-29).

Is not the scheme of God wonderful? What opening of eyes will there be when the secret things are revealed ! What a God you and I worshipped ! How different from the true God who has now revealed Himself to us. Think of how you once regarded Him, and how you do now. They *know* Him not: they can have no communion with One they keep so far off, and to whom they allow so little power. Almighty is on their lips, but they act as if He were not Almighty. Publicans and sinners will enter into rest (Paradise) before these Pharisees. It stands to reason they must, for the latter always must think they are of some worth, while the former think of nothing but their worthlessness, everything they do tends to show them that they are nothing worth. Because ye say "We see," therefore are ye blind. Fancy the feelings of the Pharisees when addressed, " Ye generation of vipers "—men universally respected and looked up to by their countrymen.

I believe the true Christian is manifested in the bringing faith down to see that all events, small and great, occur by the ruling of God. We ought to act accordingly.

Can you imagine anything more beautiful and harmonious than the Gospel? The Gospel of the Pharisee cannot fit in with this. The Christianity of the mass is a vapid, tasteless thing, and of no use to any one. I know some of your failings: *i.e.* why God lets cripples suffer, or dogs die, &c. &c.; but I believe that, as He allows the suffering, so He gives power to support it; and as for the future existence of anything that has lived, it seems impossible to doubt it. In reality, I think, we judge God as being much less kindly disposed than we ourselves are. How much He has granted us in showing us the truth!

Look at Matthew x. 37 and Luke xiv. 26: "If any man come to Me, and hate not his father, and mother, and wife, and children, and brethren, and sisters, yea, and his own life also, he *cannot* be *My disciple*." Now these are supposed to be more dear to us than wealth or honours, and yet he who does not hate them "is not worthy of *Me*." How long halt ye between two opinions? If God is God, follow Him; if Baal, *i.e.* the men of influence, riches, good places, are gods, follow them. Now, it is said God is a jealous God and will not give His glory to another, and He will certainly make men feel that He, and not their gods, is the ruler. "Thou shalt have no other gods before me." "Thou shalt not make unto thee any graven image; thou shalt not bow down thyself to them." All this points to the absolute rule God has over all events, good or evil. "Your own reason," "your judgment," are gods to us. "Lean not on your own understanding," *i. e.* as I said before, "be a fool" in the world's language.

The comfort of even the slight emancipation I have from the ruling of my own understanding is immense. If you find great opposition to any scheme which *you* feel sure is for good, you may rely upon it that this opposition is from on high; use your best efforts to carry out your views with a due acknowledgment of His government, but be not cast down if you do not succeed.

I look upon the forcing of this slave convention on His Highness as doomed to be thwarted. Germany wanted to be made quite safe against France and took two provinces, and now is obliged to be on the continual *qui vive*.

What a contradiction this letter is! Here have I been preaching on faith in God, and yet am quite at a loss on

Walad el Michael's business; at times I get quite tired of these continual excitements, and wish I was where life would roll smooth. Walad el Michael has put his troops between Senheit and Kasala, and Senheit and Massowah, in order to wait for me, whether for good or evil I do not know.

28 *October,* 1877.—I left Berber for Dongola yesterday, and am now half-way across the bend and hope to-morrow night to reach the river where it is navigable, and then to drop down by boat to Dongola. This desert air is delight-ful; it is calm and peaceful. A poor Arab clerk whom I took from Kartoum, after several furious rushes with his camel, which he could not ride, fell on his mother earth and was sent back, only too happy to go.

A fearful accident has occurred. I got out and read through a heap of papers I had not had time to study before, and made *notes* on their contents, packed them up with reports, &c., most carefully, and gave them to a servant to give to the head servant to put in his box as mine was closed. To-day I asked for them. They had been all burnt! Fortunately I had not put my *notes* in with the letters, so I have them. It is a great loss; however, I bore it well, for in these matters I can feel God ordained it. In matters like my head camel man giving me a stumbling camel, or placing the saddle badly, &c. &c., I am not so angelic (am sorry afterwards). You may fancy the utter idiocy of these servants. Here was a nicely wrapped-up parcel quietly committed to the flames; the burning was seen by all, and indeed wondered at. However, these things are ruled by God, and certainly it is for the best. Humanly speaking, it is fiendish that one can rely on no one to do the least thing. I have to look to everything myself, even to awakening the people in the morning. I bought thirty camels, costing 210*l.*, at Berber, yet the wretch of a driver made out *after* we had started that he could not buy at

Berber (the head-quarters of camels) the proper saddles, so they had to go unloaded.

11 *November*, 1877.—I wonder if I look ambitious in your eyes. Do you think I sought this place? You should know better than most people, for you have all my thoughts in my letters. Judging myself, I fear it was so when I took the work in hand; not that I cared for the money or the honours to come from it. I think, however, my main idea was the Quixotic one—to help the Khedive, mixed with the feeling that I could, with God's direction, accomplish this work.

Such expressions as Jansen made use of, viz. "that he would be sorry in every way if I gave up," comfort me in some degree, and I should think my staying here was in some measure beneficial to the people; but it will never be of much avail, *I think*, for the work is too great and the country too vast for me to do more than very slightly scratch the ground.

I dare say these remarks come from that worse-than-Colorado-beetle disease which you know as the "doles." What a dread disease it was! One could never say what was the matter: one wanted nothing, but there was the disease. Do you ever have them now?

The lights and shadows of this land are wonderful, the clearness of the air is so great.

I wonder whether you have my letters from Shaka; perhaps they are destroyed as containing secrets not for you to see. However, you will know all things some day, and, *entre nous*, I do not think you care so much for the Soudan or what I do as for the lessons learnt, and if you care little I declare I care less *when the things are over*.

I can no longer chew the cud of self-approbation over anything that has passed; it gives me no pleasure. I only think of the work before me, and know God will help me. I think the world could not go on if God revealed all His secrets; for then nearly all motive for action would be neutralized.

Think over it and tell me: would you not feel a little, just a little put out, if I gave up this work? I feel sure you would.

14 *November*, 1877.—Such cold nights! His Highness sent up a steamer for me to Wadi Halfa, and I paid for her cost some 80*l.* I do this to indirectly point out to those new English *employés* at Cairo what I think of their salaries, &c. &c. They get many of them 3000*l.* a year, and some even 5000*l.* I declare we have bloodsucked Egypt; our people are most rapacious.

I do not know how it is, but for some days I have been very grumpy. I expect it is the effect of these cold winds on my liver.

Load the camels heavily or lightly, it seems the same thing—they do not go a bit quicker for being lightly loaded. They are queer things, and I no longer believe in the immense journeys that they are said to perform. They are very enduring, and will go on for a long time, far beyond all other animals; but they feel the fatigue, I am certain, and I also believe it is an effort to them to go without water for two and three days. They do go without it, but they would work better with it every day. They also eat dry indigestible grass and shrubs, in which you would suppose there was no nourishment. The proof that they do feel fatigue is that after a journey of five or six days, if they belonged to an Arab, they would have at least two months' perfect rest.

Have you ever thought of the expression people make use of when learning of the death of any one, " He was quite prepared," not meaning that he was ready to die, being tired of the world, that he had made his will, or other such preparations, but meaning that he had prepared himself to face God by his own acts? It is diametrically opposed to the doctrine of salvation by grace, or gift, which is so clearly stated in the Scripture.

If one could calmly argue with the Pharisaical party—which one never can, for they hate to have their rags of self-righteousness touched—how could they maintain their views? Is it not remarkable that we should have been so long blinded by the Pharisaical doctrines which are the traditions of the elders? How angry these sects get with one who does not adopt *their* views; you could not offend them more grievously; they are not angry because it is God's cause, but because you ignore them; they ought to be sad, not angry. Paul remained in the Jewish Church, although he knew the symbolic ceremonies had passed away.

At times I feel much regret at being so separated from you all, and thinking that if I devote myself to this country, as *I* intend to do (*Dieu dispose*), we shall never be able to discuss the old days again. They were most amusing to look back upon. You know in old times the "*wrestling,*" as they called it, when they had what they were wrestling for all the time, prayer-meetings every night; what bondsmen we were! What have you done with your religious library? It must have cost a mint; why, ten years ago it would have turned your hair gray to have thought of parting with it. What a terrible thing our education was! how we suffered from it!

In answer to those who would have us use our own judgment and not consider all things as ordained, let us suppose we have engaged to help us by solemn promises a person of unlimited wealth, wisdom, and power, who knows exactly the thoughts of ourselves and of the whole of those amongst whom we are thrown. It is evident that, if two persons, A. and B., are watched over by this mighty friend, and A. goes in the belief that this friend will help him out of all difficulties, he will be much more comfortable than

B., who, though watched over with equal care, thinks that
his extrication from difficulties depends on himself. B. in
reality doubts the fidelity of his mighty friend; so it is with
us and God.

It is a mistake, I think, for us to consider that the difficulties into which great people are thrown are different in
their effect on such persons from the very petty trials of a
washerwoman on her.

I dare say in Southampton are many to whose trials mine
(which are indeed petty, owing to the power given me to
support them) are not to be compared, owing to the sufferer
not having had the power given him to bear the trial to the
same measure as has been given to me. I am more and
more convinced that the actions we see done are but trifles
in comparison to the thoughts which fill us. "Things
which are seen are temporal, but the things which are not
seen are eternal," and many other parallel passages would
imply this (1 Sam. xvi. 7 ; Matt. xxiii. 28).

Another thought strikes me, that everything which has or
has had life emanates from God, who, being good, can
produce nothing evil. It must also be eternal, for, as the
life must emanate from Him, it must be of His attributes ;
while the actions of the body and all that is seen of this
life are mere garments, and perishable ; it is only the
experience gained by them which is imperishable.

I believe we may fill other places in other worlds with
higher capabilities for knowing God. One of the most
remarkable passages is in Ephesians iii. 10, and i. 22, 23,
where it says that the object of God is now made manifest,
viz. to show to powers in heavenly places the wisdom of
God by *the Church*, which is His body, of which we are
members. It is by *the Church* that the infinite wisdom of
God will be shown forth. The apparent apathy of our
Lord to the various events of the world is most notice-
able. His nation was under foreign rule, yet He never

alluded to it, except in connection with the tribute due to Cæsar.

If God puts ten pounds on a man, He will give him strength to bear twenty pounds. And if He puts twenty tons on a man, He will (if He wills) give him power to carry sixty tons. This He has done for me; and I, in saying this, do not seek the praise of any man or society or king or power. I would have your prayers—they will be heard; but no praise; for He is the GOVERNOR-GENERAL, and I am only His useless agent, by whom He deigns to work His will. Therefore bear in mind that the censure or praise I may acquire from any of my actions are as water on a duck's back, and will not make me swerve from what I think He directs me to do.

KASALA, 3 *December*, 1877.—I feel I am only a straw, yet God gave the men in Darfour courage under me. I cannot look back or forward to ever having done or to ever doing anything worthy of commendation. And yet that same feeling makes me quite happy, for I have nothing to give God, and He wants nothing from me. I find not one single spot on which I can rest and say, " There I was right," nor do I want to find one.

I do not and cannot chew the cud of self-complacency. I assure you, the angry repulsion you would feel if one of your friends said to you, " How lovely your hair is; how taper your fingers are; how finely pencilled your eyebrows are; and how beautiful your eyes are," &c., is the same repulsion I feel when praised, for I *know* (and I ought to know best) the praise is false.

I no more believe in the foresight of Napoleon or the Duke. People made out the talent and foresight after the thing was done. God gives the thought, man carries it out, for the thought is given so strongly as to force him to act thus.

I feel confident all will come right with me. Things do

not go as I would think best, but they all come right, and what have I to do with them? Nothing at all. Indispensable? Oh, dear no. A fly would be as useful as I am. Is this my general feeling? Yes, but sometimes, when in what *I think* is a fix, I am leaning on my own understanding as much as any one else; but this passes off, and I am quiet again.

You feel yourself a sinner—well, if you were ten times as great a sinner you would be happier, for you would give up that very *hopeless task* of making yourself better. What education we have had on religion! It takes a lifetime to root out our errors. I was quite surprised one day, in reading Mackintosh's book on Numbers, to see he notices the hopeless work it is to try and remedy our evil nature; it seemed to me to be so diametrically opposed to all one's previous teachings. We want to carry our decayed old body into heaven, and it cannot be.

Read Nicodemus's answer to "Ye must be born again," "Can a man," &c. The answer was inferred: You must die before you can be born again, for a birth cannot come again, except a death occurs in the interim. To me the salvation and peace resulting from the same are brought about in such a very wonderful way that *that* alone seems proof of its divine nature. It is as if you had broken a cup and had bothered yourself to mend it, and as if by your simply leaving it alone it had mended itself.

When you have ceased to struggle in the utterly hopeless task of trying to better yourself, and can say, " I give it up," then peace comes. There is one little danger when peace comes, namely, that you may be inclined to call all, who do not see it, blind, so manifest will it appear to you. One could reason on it for hours, namely, that God is incarnated in each of our bodies, which bodies are merely clothes to the real *us*.

I wish I had the time and words to express what I feel on

K

these points. Although the feeling scarcely is expressed fairly by "Don't care," yet it comes near to that when one is given the belief that *God rules all* events, good and evil, and that "His tender mercies are over *all* His works"; that whatever happens is best; that God directs *all* things in infinite wisdom, and that we must give up disputing that He does so.

We do not give God the credit of being as kind hearted as we are. Think of our trials as being for our good. No mother would oppose sending her children to school, however much she may love them and great as the trial is.

Why are you not hopeful? Is it because you are not perfect? I wish you knew yourself as a million times more imperfect, for then you would give up any expectations you may have of being so. Everything you have done, or will do, is ordained by Him, for His glory, whatever you may think of it. You would have been as bad as the chiefest of sinners, outwardly, if your way had not been hedged up. When you get well down in your own opinion of yourself, it is remarkable how well the world thinks of you, and how worthless are its thoughts *to* you.

MASSOWAH, 5 *January*, 1878.—What you ask requires me to be plain-spoken. There is not the least doubt that there is an immense virgin field for *an apostle* in these countries among the black tribes. They are virgin to my belief, and the apostle would have nothing to contend with in the fanaticism of the Arabs. But where will you find an apostle? I will explain what I mean by the term. He must be a man who has died entirely to the world; who has no ties of any sort; who longs for death when it may please God to take him; who can bear the intense dulness of these countries; who seeks for few letters; and who can bear the thought of dying deserted. Now, there are few, very, very few men who can accept this post. But no half-measures will do.

Here in this place is a Swedish mission, doing and having

done nothing for twelve years, and yet here they stay; many have died, and yet they stay on, where they can do no good among the Mussulman people. They will not go to the black tribes, though I offered them every help I could give them. They asked about letters and climate, and on my saying, "No letters and a deadly climate," they preferred staying and dying here.

A man must give up everything, understand *everything*, *everything*, to do anything for Christ here. No half nor three-quarter measures will do. And yet, what a field! The black tribes are patterns to us. You never see them quarrel among themselves (though tribes quarrel as tribes). You never hear of immoral conduct; they are pictures of nice, quiet people.

The apostle too must know himself before he could come here; and how few of mankind do know themselves! He must believe that God is the absolute Ruler of all events, good or bad. He directs the one and permits the other, but governs both for His glory. He must believe that God does even now work with His Spirit, and that He can, without words, make men realize divine truths. My dear, I do not think there are ten men in the whole world who would come up to my idea of what the man must be who comes here.

Yet, if any society wants a field in which there are virgin people of quiet disposition, who will receive the missionaries well, there is such a field in these countries, and I would do my best to help them. Whoever they are, they must expect a hard life. I claim, thanks to God, in *some* measure to have the attributes I mention as necessary to live in these lands. I naturally, in my position as a ruler, am not as spiritually-minded or as free from angry passions as a missionary ought to be. If I had not the support of a loving God ever with me, I could not stand my present position, far less that of one living among the tribes.

To tell you plainly, I think the price God asks of a man who comes out to live among the tribes is too great for man to pay. I know none, no, not one, who could pay it. You know that a mission has gone to Romanika from the Church Missionary Society. Watch if they succeed. Perhaps I may have exaggerated the price God requires; but I think not. You may rely on my doing what I could to help any who came out, but let them weigh well the question.

I cannot help thinking, looking at the difficulty of merely existing in these black lands, that God has not yet decided to open these countries to know His Son. I think that He at present blocks the way. I would mention that the life a man lives is the one which the blacks would understand better than a man's words. All men can read a man's life, and they will judge of his religion by his life. As for the countries, they are splendid. Take Albert Lake, a glorious amphitheatre of mountains with plenty of fine trees, picturesque little hamlets here and there, with grain and everything men may need, flocks and cattle, and a splendid sheet of water stretching for miles, but a stillness that is dreadful. You feel yourself at the world's end. It is this more than anything which kills men off. I have had weeks on weeks of this life, waiting, waiting, waiting for one thing or another; and often, oh, how often have I prayed to die quietly and be rid of this weariness! Now, if I feel that, what would a man feel who might have greater ties to this earth than I have? I thank God, to a great measure, *I am dead—* dead to the world's glory, its money, or its honours; and this it is that helps me. —— said that nothing would induce him to stay a year on the Lake.

The mission to Central Africa—Lake Nyassa—is called a missionary enterprise. Now, how different it is from apostolic missions will be seen. If the leader finds obstacles in his route with the natives, how will he act? Will he rely on the spiritual armour, or on his Sniders? Even ——

wanted chains for the securing of his porters. What right had he to chain men of a different nation, simply because they would not carry for him? This mission is not an expedition apostolic but one of geographical discovery and forcible suppression of the slave trade. If it is necessary for their progress (according to all precedents) they will not hesitate to chain free men. What I declaim against is the hypocrisy of terming my own or any expeditions *apostolic missions* or *missions of philanthropy*. They are not so, and under false colours will never succeed, whatever they may do in the geographical line.

I do not think the time is come for the gathering in of God's inheritance—the heathen. The first thing which has to be done is to open and facilitate communication with their countries. Next, to let the natives mix with more civilized races, so as to acquire their language, their own native tongue being so poor as not to contain more than 300 words.

Do you understand that, with a language of 300 words, any explanation, even of secular affairs, must be difficult, and how much more so must be the explanation of religious truths like the Atonement, which few of us are given to properly understand? I do not think God wills it at present. I believe sincerely that a man, spiritually dead to the world and giving himself as a sacrifice in these countries, could, by his consistent holy walk and acts, inculcate higher thoughts in the population he lived amongst. His life would be the preaching; but who would have the faith to undergo this exile?

It is remarkable that, as a rule, the apostles went to more or less civilized countries, which, though pagan, had some germ of the old truth in their religions. They all believed in sacrifices and the shedding of blood being propitiatory to their gods, and the apostles could easily draw the inferences, which the offering of sacrifices suggested, of one great

sacrifice once and for all. Now the negro does not sacrifice ;
that he believes in a higher power we see by his magic, but
to human understanding I cannot consider it possible that
they, in their present entirely virgin state, can ever be got
to understand the love of God in Christ ; but with God all
things are possible.

I look on the negro races as I would on children of three
or four years of age, incapable of understanding these truths
till more matured in knowledge. It may be possible to
teach children three or four years old divine truths, and it
is our duty to begin with them, but we are not astonished
at our teaching not being permanently successful. And so
I think with respect to the natives ; truths simple might and
may be inculcated, and by degrees, as their understanding
progresses, deeper truths may be explained ; but, as a child
must grow in age and knowledge before he attains the
fulness of the truth, so must the negro nations pass the
period of their youth before they can do the same.

Nations are as individuals in some respects. Nations
almost invariably have acquired some degree of civilization
before Christianity has taken root. In our own land the
Roman civilization prepared the way for the Gospel. I
therefore claim for my own, and other expeditions of the
same kind, that they open the way for the Gospel ; but I
declaim against their being called philanthropic expeditions
or missions. Before the ground is sown it must be torn up,
and these expeditions are the ploughs. With the exception
of the inland mission in China, our own and foreign missions
confine their efforts to the ports, where there is much more
society and comfort for their apostles than being exiled in
the interior. The Roman Catholics in China were certainly
far more self-sacrificing. I went out with some twenty
young men who definitely stated that they went out *never* to
return, and took leave of their friends as if they were going
to their execution. I never have seen or heard of any

Protestant missionary being so impelled. Was not their action more Christlike than those of our persuasion who go out to the ports with 300*l*. a year for a couple or for four years, and whose bread is sure, while these Roman Catholic students went and lived as they could among the native Chinese?

Why does the Romish Church thrive with so many errors in it? It is because of these godly men in her who live Christ's life, and who, like as Zoar was spared for Lot's sake, bring a blessing on the whole community. For self-devotion, for self-denial, the Roman Catholic Church is in advance of our present day Protestantism. What is it if you know the sound truths and do not act up to them? Actions speak loudly and are read of all; words are as the breath of man.

KARTOUM, 2 *February*, 1878.—If you read the collects, you will see everywhere proclaimed the utter inability of man to know God or to help himself. It is quite astonishing that people do not perceive it.

DEBBE, 15 *February*, 1878.—I wish, I wish the King would come again and put things right on earth; but His coming is far off, for the whole world must long for Him ere He comes, and I really believe that there are but very, very few who would wish Him to appear, for to do so is to desire death, and how few do this! Not that we really ever die: we only change our sheaths

Z—— wrote me a letter and says I have fallen into a grievous error in supposing we have two natures in us, one of God, and the other of the devil. He says it is not in the Scripture. I think it is so most clearly, but it is no use arguing the question. All I say is, that to my reading all my views are clearly shown in the Scripture; that my faith, heretical as it may appear, gives peace, which none other did; and that, though I am sorry that others have not my faith, I do not censure them as wrong, or to blame, or in

L

𝔇

error. The religion of these evangelicals gives no peace, and is a miserably poor comfort in trial.

5 *March*, 1878.—It is remarkable that, with respect to ourselves, we often forget that our evil actions are nothing more than the motions of the evil nature in us. We are apt to consider that they, our evil natures, are prompted from without, but the fact is, they come from within; *their root is in us*, and will never leave us till death. No change can be made in this root; it is evil, and will remain so, and, when we are requiring humiliation, it will be allowed to break forth into evil actions. Think over this, for it is a most important subject, and one is apt to think that, when evil actions are not prominent, we are better, so to say, than when they are. This is not so. The *root* is always in us, and, in spite of its being a stumbling-block to many, I think the Scripture shows us that God, who never changes, is not one whit further from us, or more angry with us, when our evil actions show themselves, than when they do not. As you know the Scriptures, I will not quote them to you. You will know that there are many passages which, taken isolated, would be opposed to this view; but you will, by the Spirit, discern how these passages are applied, and, if what I say is true, you will accept it. As for others, it is as they can see. It is not their fault if they are blind.

From a man's birth till his death God is the same to him; love rules all His providences to man, and it is in order to meet our infirmities that in the Scripture God is represented as angry, as pleased, and as having passions like men. He is the same, and is always set against evil and for the good, but He is against evil in the abstract, not against the sinner, who is as a diseased leper, thus afflicted to show forth to powers and principalities in heavenly places the manifold wisdom of God.

CAIRO, 21 *March*, 1878.—God never hides His face; we raise up the veil and hide ourselves, when we feel our own

vileness. . . . I have my Koh-i-noor with me, *i. e.* the
presence of God, and who can take that from me, or make
me fear?

Never was there a more cold, formal religion than that
of the Pharisees ; what comfort can you get out of a stone?
Day by day I grow more and more firm, thanks to God, in
my belief in those precious truths.

KARTOUM, 8 *August*, 1878.—I wish the great mystery of
evil was revealed to you, and the certainty of that evil dis-
appearing, as darkness vanishes at the coming in of light.
I reason thus with myself, " Do not you wish you were
perfect and sinless?" and I find myself able to sincerely
say, " I do wish to be so, and yet I find myself constantly
erring "—the spirit willing, the flesh weak. Now the flesh
profiteth nothing, it cannot inherit the kingdom, therefore
disregard it, and bear with it, and endeavour to mortify it
to the extent of power God gives.

These doctrines are not revealed, because people will not
think of them; they follow the ideas of others, without
bestowing a thought on them. Think the matter out, and
lower your pride; accept the position of the chief of sinners,
capable of anything, and that in sincerity, and thus you will
know the truth, that you are utterly vile and cannot do
anything good. It is when you are so abased that you will
see your salvation is from God's free love. You are not
low enough in your own estimation to feel the power of
these truths ; you are still clinging to some obsolete idea
that you are not utterly depraved; throw away that idea,
and then you will rest in peace. Judge yourself; think
that what is known to you is also known to God. It is at
first a terrible thought, but, when afterwards one sees that
one's evil is only the natural outcome of a sink, one feels
it could be nothing else—for what else could come from a
sink? It is the agreeing to be a sink that is hard; we
try and hide it from ourselves, and so are deprived of the

comfort of perfect peace which the knowledge of our baseness gives us.

It is not right that we should display the baseness of our hearts to fellow-men, but it is comfort to do so to God. I would say, "All-seeing God, Thou knowest my intricate machinery, my thoughts and the mystery of my body, soul and mind. Thou knowest my utter and complete hatred of myself, than whom I know no one more despicable and hateful ; and if so to myself what must I be to Thee, who art holy and pure ? Deliver me from this hateful bondage ; but, if it be Thy will to humble me still more, do not heed my cries, but do Thy will. I would be away and at peace, but Thy will be done."

Now get to pray this, and then you will have peace ; try and realize what I have often alluded to, viz. that God does positively live in your body ; this is a palpable feeling and is the key to the whole truth, typified in nearly all the types. Split off from your body and become spirit ; your body is a worn-out glove, to be thrown away ; the rest of you lives for ever, and is pure and sinless.

Did you ever realize what Mary went through before our Saviour was born ? She was looked on as an adulteress, even by her own husband. It is when we are utterly condemned by the world—*i. e.* by our sinful bodies—that Christ is born in our souls by the Spirit.

25 *September*, 1878.—And "God saw *all was good*," even the tree of knowledge of good and evil, and also the serpent. I cannot help thinking that God will make all things clear to us in such a way, with respect to evil and good, that it will be like light and darkness. I am induced to make these remarks from reading Byron's *Cain*. There is much in what he says ; he thought very deeply, and did not take heed to what the church of the world said.

It is remarkable how people writing on political economy and on science have advanced in knowledge in the last hundred years, but with respect to the knowledge of God people knew as much, and even more, of the deep truths, a hundred years ago. To read a book on the state of science written *long ago* is like reading an *elementary* work on *science of to-day,* but of the deep things the people of Luther's time knew as much and more than our generation.

6 *October,* 1878.—You cannot evade it: we are each composed of two beings—one of which we see, which is temporal, which will fulfil certain works in the world; and one unseen, eternal, and which is always in conformity with God. One is sometimes uppermost, sometimes subdued, but rules in the long run, for it is eternal, while the other is temporal. How else will you explain "This is My commandment, that ye love one another;" this is My *order?* His will or order leaves no option, and must be done; but it is given to our eternal, not our earthly nature, which will not obey and has no part or lot with Him. I wonder people will not face the great mystery of good and evil. Who made the tree of knowledge and pronounced it good? Who made the serpent and pronounced it good?

13 *October,* 1878.—I wonder, if asked this question, how one would answer it: Would you like to go through life without a pain or trouble, and return to *perfect happiness* of a small dimension, or would you like to go through a sea of trials, and return to *perfect happiness* of a larger dimension? Notice, *perfect happiness,* whatever your choice may be. What would be one's choice? I do not know; man, and *hard* as I am, I would rather not answer the question, for really this life is a terrible ordeal.

I am now, thank God, so far from the least thought of man's free will that it never enters into my calculation in these thoughts, however it may guide me as Governor-General or as fellow-man. I look on universal salvation for every human being, past, present, or future, as certain, and, as I hope for my own, no doubt comes into my mind on this subject. Is it credible that so *many* would wish it to be otherwise, and fight you about it? And among those *many* are numbers, whose lives, weighed truly as to their merits by the scale of the sanctuary, would kick the beam *against* those *they* condemn.

Once I did believe that some perished altogether at the end of the world—were annihilated, as having no souls. After this, I believed that the world was made up of incarnated children of God and incarnated children of the evil spirit; and then I came to the belief that *the two are in one.*

With reference to the doctrine of annihilation, I do not think it gives the same idea of God as is obtained from this other view. It may show force to annihilate, but we should think more highly of a monarch who would, by his wisdom, kindness, and long-suffering, turn a rebel people into faithful subjects, than of him who had the land wasted and utterly destroyed his rebellious subjects. I do not think that after the declaration, " It is *finished,*" there can be any more probation; punishment brings no one to God.

I need not point out to you the unlovable nature of these Pharisees; they are enough to sour milk, they are as full of scandal as the publicans. What do they do hanging about the purlieus of the publicans, and inquiring, "Why does your Master eat with those people," &c. &c.?

I declare the products of Great Britain have terribly fallen off. You can never get a good thing now-a-days. You were and are interested in the Eastern Question; but, my dear Augusta, I feel sure it is nearly over with us. I hope it may come after our day, but I think we are on the decline. It is money, money, money with us. We put lime in our cotton, and are full of tricks in every trade. You must see it yourself in the things you buy. It may be fancy, but, to my mind, for the last fifteen years our products have deteriorated. Now falsehood in trade shows want of morality in the nation, and when morality—*i.e.* honesty—is lacking, the end is not far off.

9 *January*, 1879.—The Creation is represented in us ; each phase was accompanied by some great convulsion of Nature, and so it is in us. People like the Law much better than the Gospel dispensation. The one is much more easy to follow : they give a lot of sacrifices, follow ceremonies and washings. The other needs circumcision of *heart* and inward purification, and is much more searching and troublesome to the flesh. That is the reason why people follow the Law. It allows them to think something of themselves, while the Gospel dispensation does not.

The *eyes* are wanting to those who do not see the truth, and no talking or writing will give eyes to the blind.

29 *January*, 1879.—I am very sorry to hear of the Queen's trouble. I would that God would give them His comfort.

10 *February*, 1879.—When "Jesus opened their understanding," it was after His disciples had gone through great troubles—after His crucifixion, and when earthly things looked most black to them. They were then able to understand, while, before they had been tried, they could not.

17 *February*, 1879.—I believe many Jews are in some way believers in Jesus. You know Peter said circumcision was not necessary, *i.e.* the rites of the Law were not necessary, but that those of the Jews who wished to observe them might, while Gentiles were not to be compelled to do so. It may be that many, though outwardly Jews, are true believers ; certainly the open profession of a faith does not make any one a member of that faith.

How unlike in acts are most of so-called Christians to their Founder ! You see in them no resemblance to Him. Hard, proud, "holier than thou," is their uniform. *They have the truth,* no one else, it is *their* monopoly. These

Jews may be truly followers of our Lord, though they may
be only night visitors to Him.

5 *March,* 1879.—I have been led to wonder why one
is so worn by anxieties, and why our Lord seemed so
patient in comparison to man. In what did He differ from
us? He was the incarnation of God, even as we are;
vide Hebrews ii. 14 and 17. Forasmuch as the children
took flesh and blood, &c. &c., it behoved Him to do the
same. He did take flesh and blood, but He was sinless
on account of His immaculate conception; He received
the Spirit of God in full measure; we, each, as members of
His body, as much as it pleases God to give to us.

Can we have more of His Spirit in us than He gives? If
you look at the similitude in 1 Corinthians xii. you will see
that some are given faith, as quite a distinct gift. Now, if
it is a gift, and by grace, not of our merits, it is evident we
cannot have it, except it please God to give it. I base on
this that it is impossible for us to have faith, *i. e.* to be holy-
minded or Christlike, unless God gives the power to be so;
and thence I deduce that we have in ourselves no power to
do good or to cease from evil.

I know one collect of the Church of England says distinctly that we have no power to do good (1st Sunday after
Trinity), and yet how many have learnt that collect and
never remarked the equivalent to it is, that it is only God
who can make us do good. Christ was man, but He was
man born miraculously. He was, as needed, the spotless
Lamb of God, without blemish, for a sacrifice.

I wonder why people do not look for themselves into
these questions. If you talked to the Pharisees and asked
their belief, they would say, " I believe in Jesus Christ as
the only Saviour. I believe God will accept me solely for
His merits." Is not that also our belief? Do they act up
to it? No, with them it is, " We are the salt of the earth."
Imagine to yourself millions of earthen vessels, some with

a little water in them, some with more, and one vessel of another manufacture *filled :* so to my mind is the world, and Christ.

To those who are what are called evil-doers we ought to be most commiserate ; they are to be pitied, not blamed. Let the Pharisees say what they like, we each and all, good and bad, are members of one family, and, when one member suffers, all suffer.

With respect to my own troubles, with respect to the politics of the world, we must judge them as the working out of God's glory.

Can you, with your strong feelings, think, when you read of the tortuous ways of some nations, that God loves them with the same love as He loves Himself or you? Can I think, when I read what Gessi writes, that God loves those Arabs with that love ? Yet He does ; and not only ought we to agree, but we ought also to love them as ourselves, for, if they suffer, we suffer ; even selfishly we ought to wish them well.

These thoughts, infinitely deeper, made our Saviour callous, in all appearance, to the sufferings of his people, the Jews.

I am glad you interest yourself in the papers and in what goes on, but you are in some way responsible, as a member of the family of God, for the acts of your fellow-members : so be lenient.

The outcome of all these troubles, both in London and elsewhere, will be His glory. His sole object in creation was to make known to the powers and principalities in heavenly places His manifold wisdom—and how? Why, through His incarnated members who existed in Him before the Creation. (Ephesians iii. 9, 10, 11, and i. 4.)

Who is it that shuts the door, *their door*, to the world ? It is the Pharisee sect. " You have not washed," say they, "you have plucked corn, &c. &c. ; *i. e.* you never go to church, never attend prayer meetings, you think every one will be saved."

When I get away from my troubles here, whilst writing such a letter as this, I feel a great wish to come back to England to spread the doctrine; but I feel God must rule my way, and I must stay on and on till I am relieved. He does help me, but in so slow a way that I forget it; it is a daily gathering of manna, and only a little every day.

7 *March,* 1879.—Did you ever read a little book which I used to like—i. e. *Watson on Contentment?* It has a soothing influence. The part I enjoyed to-day (my Sunday) most was that which urges contentment on account of the shortness of one's life and the triviality of the things one is discontented about.

Certainly discontent is a murmuring against God's will, whether we murmur, or feel anxiety about Gessi or the finances of the Soudan or the dulness of one's life; it is evident that the life we do live is the one God would have us live.

16 *July,* 1879.—No one can possibly understand the Atonement unless he understands this: many members in one body, one spirit in all; as the Head is God manifest, so the body is God manifest. This is often shown in Scripture, by the same name being applied to Christ, the Head, as is applied to the Church, His body, or all mankind. Many will take exception to *all mankind;* and if any one can in his heart of hearts say he is better than his neighbour, considering the circumstances of his birth, position, &c., in which neither had anything to do, then he may object, but I do not think any one who has lived, say thirty years, can feel that.

In Cole's *Sovereignty of God* he shows very clearly that the fleshly life of man is of small account with God in His infinite scheme; to us the numbers killed by any particular accident is appalling; but it ought not to be so, for, whether 500 die suddenly, or whether 500 die and are inscribed in the *Times*, it is all the same; 500 are dead, and it is questionable whether it is better to die from the lingering ills of old age, which sometimes continue over years, than to die from thirst as these poor slaves have done within the last few days.

The amount of suffering each human being must go through from birth to death is proportioned to the power given him to bear such suffering. I believe that, after a certain period, dying people sink into insensibility to pain. Of course sudden death to the Pharisees is terrible, for they argue *that you must be prepared*. How can man prepare himself to meet a holy God? He came from God, God incarnated him, and God liberates him. He is born, or sown, in corruption; he is raised by death into incorruption.

I feel so strongly that death is not an evil to man that, if I thought the shooting of any number of slave-dealers would be of avail in stopping the slave trade, I would shoot them without the least compunction; though, if a slave-dealer was ill and it was in my power to cure him, I would do my best to do so.

September, 1879.—What prayers we ask when we say, "Thy will be done," and, when we pray for holiness, we draw down an enormity of trouble on ourselves. Depend on it, life—*i. e.* the existence of man on this earth—is a small sacrifice. The true sacrifice is a living death, or living crucifixion. Much is said of our Lord's personal sufferings on the cross, little of His life-long crucifixion of all His feelings. All cannot be bodily crucified; all must undergo the moral crucifixion, if they will taste of resurrection joys, in this earth.

I believe entirely in the Old and New Testaments as being inspired by God. I believe that "from the beginning" Christ existed, and that, as He existed, so also His mystical

L

body, the Church, existed, made up of many members. I believe that the members of His mystical body were incarnated in the flesh in this world, and that He also was incarnated in the flesh. I believe that the members were incarnated in imperfect flesh, and that He was incarnated in perfect flesh.

I believe that the whole Church, Head and members, were in the earthly Adam, but that, when the time came, Christ was incarnated by a miracle, in order that He might expiate (by the obedience of one man) the disobedience of the first man, Adam, in whom was the whole (Church) of Christ's mystical members. The object of the incarnation of Christ and His members was that God might be known, and the means by which this manifestation was to be accomplished was by the Church, *i. e.* by Christ, its Head, and by each member of its mystical body.

I base my belief on the Scripture entirely; it is there distinctly laid down that God rules all things, that knowledge of Him is His gift, and not of man's will; it is He who stirs us up to seek Him; it is He who leads us on in all our ways, who governs all our actions.

There is only one sin, and that is unbelief, which He alone can remove. Being in temporal bodies, we seek temporal things, and will always seek them till we cease to exist. I maintain that from the Scriptures we learn that our ways are ordained in every respect, but that our bodies persist in the belief that we have free will.

Hard it is for us in the body to believe that the events of this world profit naught, except from their being God's scheme to manifest forth His wisdom to the powers in heavenly places.

To accept the doctrine of man having no free will, he must acknowledge his utter insignificance, for then no one is cleverer or better than his neighbour; this must be always abhorrent to the flesh. "Have not I done this or that?"

"Had I naught to do with it?" For my part, I can give myself no credit for anything I ever did; and further, I credit no man with talents, &c. &c., in anything he may have done. Napoleon, Luther, indeed all men I consider were directly worked on, and directed to work out God's great scheme.

Tell me any doctrine which so humbles man as this, or which is so contrary to his nature and to his natural pride.

You may remember a sermon in which it was said that "those who converted" others (as if it were possible) "would have crowns with many stars." I rebelled at this at once. I know that some of the congregation that day held their noses higher than usual. We have each our pre-existent state and position to go back to, and I expect that it will be near those of our immediate family.

To accept this doctrine at all times was more than Paul could do; he boasted that he also was an apostle, but he adds "*by the grace of God.*" The evangelicals say we are good or not as *we will;* they *slide* over it by saying it is God's grace, for they dare not say, knowing the contrary, that their goodness depends on themselves.

I have often felt rather put out in times past in thinking that others might be put over me in the future life, and I feel sure you have also thought, "Why, I have gone through so much, surely I shall have a throne above So-and-so, who has enjoyed herself." The right and left hand seats are already told off, and so are all the rest; you will have *your* place, and no other.

To expect the Pharisee folk, after the heat and work of the day, to be content with the penny, the same as those who worked only one hour! They consider they deserve more, for *they worked for it.* They argue, and Paul alludes to it: then man will sin, so that grace may abound. As I have not my Bible, I forget his answer, but, looking to my

own experience, I feel, if I sin, *I have* all the feelings and
sorrow as if I had free will, and blame myself quite as
heartily as if I believed it.   God at once prevents us
making use of this truth; it is only when I have become,
as it were, spiritually minded again, that I feel I could not
help my sin, which was the natural fruit of my evil body,
and that its production was to humble me.

You know the Bible better than I do; what stronger text
can you have than Rom. ix. 16, &c.?   You ought to be
able to point out numbers of texts that support this view,
but to expect others to be convinced we must not, for the
view depends on the standpoint from which it is seen; if
two persons regard a landscape from different points, they
will not see alike, one will see this, and the other will see
this and perhaps more.

If you *quietly* judge with charity those who do not agree
with us, you will see that they more or less care for the
world's opinion of them (whether the religious or worldly
world, makes no difference).   To the degree that we disregard the world, so we shall know truth.   David was the
man after God's own heart, because he was sincere, *i. e.* he
did not hesitate to lament his evil disposition, even in public.
Every one who pretends to be better than his fellow is a
hypocrite (Isa. ix. 17).   All the fight between our Lord and
the Jews turned on the point that He refused to acknowledge
the superior sanctity of the Pharisees.

It seems certain that we ourselves can produce nothing
good.   A good tree will bring forth good fruit, an evil tree
evil fruit.   The works of the flesh are one, and the fruit of
the Spirit another (Gal. v. 19—23).   It is over and over
again laid down in the Scriptures that we can do nothing of
ourselves, but that it is God working in us to will and to do
good.   I do not say God incites us to evil, but it is our
natural tendency, which can only be checked by Him.   As
a body will fall to the ground if not held up, so we do evil

unless prevented. The outward difference between men is that in one case a man is prevented, in the other he is not prevented; both are equally evilly inclined, and to neither is any merit due.

Now, I do not think any of our opponents would deny the above arguments, *that man can do no good of HIMSELF*, and yet they look upon the deduction that man is helpless in God's hands, *i. e.* that he has no free will, as heresy. Before the law was given, man had a law in his heart, accusing or excusing his action.

When the law was given, man was informed clearly what was his duty, and our Lord showed how deeply the law went—a breach of it in thought being equivalent to its breach in deed. Now, our opponents say, man can help doing evil; doing evil means breaking the law, yet they will own no man can keep the law entirely. They say of A. who breaks 80 per cent. of the law, of B. who breaks 50 per cent. of the law, and of C. who breaks 10 per cent. of the law, that A. is most wicked, B. more wicked, and C. wicked. A. should (and has the power to) break less of the law, B. ditto, and C. ought, in consequence, to be able to keep the law almost entirely; if it is in man's power to keep any one commandment of the law, it is in his power to keep it entirely.

You know what the Scripture says—that righteousness cannot be of the law : if man could keep the law, then Christ would have died in vain (Galatians ii. 21). If man can be better than he is, of himself, *i. e.* if he can keep nearer to the law (for being better means that), then he could work out his own salvation. How can a bad tree bring forth good fruit? A. B. and C. are equally corrupt, but A. and B. show more of their fruit than C. I had these same thoughts years ago.

With respect to the chapters on circumcision, which was the type of putting off the filth of the flesh, Paul says circumcision or uncircumcision profiteth nothing; the true circumcision is our death.

You know that, though I have alluded to a man keeping part of the law, the breach of any one tittle is equivalent to the breach of the whole law. The object of the law is to show us our imperfection, as regards what God would have us to be, and to drive us to seek other righteousness than *we* can attain.

I often thought Job was the type of a man who would lose, without murmuring, his name and position, but who fainted under the breaking out of his evil flesh. Who could bear this terrible event?

What husks the evangelical religion is! It is nothing more than the law slightly veiled; it is useless arguing with its followers, and you may notice our Lord never argued with His opponents.

He put them questions and left them to be solved in accordance with their view, if they could do so. "Show us in the Scriptures this and that," and, if you do so, they say you wrest the Scriptures, and go on arguing. If their religion suits them, let them keep it; but why need they wish us to adopt their miserable cold creed? Does it make them more kind, more tolerant, more Christ-like? I think not; and, as "it is by their works ye shall know them," let the two creeds be judged accordingly.

They preach their nostrums, but a patient has the right to question the efficacy of them if they fail to cure; and for my part I say they pre-eminently fail to comfort man, and you know it as well as I do.

To say you were worldly-minded at Woolwich is false; I believe you would have gone through any penance to have peace, but you sought it after the law, and found death, not life. Now God has shown you He wants naught from you but your trust.

Their religion is a dead one, it has no vitality in it, no

advance; with the same mouth they say salvation is of the Lord and of the law, that they can do nothing and that they can keep the law: they are for using their own judgment and for implicit faith: there is no consistency in them. A. is to blame because his flesh breaks out into leprosy, B. is blameless because his does not do so. It is right that A. should be put without the pale of society, for leprosy is contagious; but A. should be pitied. How often we see who it was who received the leper.

As surely as we break the law, so surely He strikes in return; this does not affect our eternal salvation, but, as our breach of the law is in the flesh, so is its punishment in the flesh

Light is typical of good, darkness of evil. Therefore I believe that, when our Saviour comes, evil will disappear, even as darkness does when light appears. This world has its nights, but in the New Jerusalem "there will be no night." Our Saviour's title is "Light of the world," Satan is the "Power of darkness." In many places in the Bible the dispersion of darkness by light is typical of the destruction of evil by Christ.

[1] God will rule as He thinks best in His wisdom. I feel *alone*, without any help except in God, who is all, whatever troops I may have. In China it was otherwise; I felt confident my troops would stand.

Long before you get this, I shall be out of my troubles; so do not pity me, for I have the Almighty to guide me, and death is no terror. I only wish you to know *how worn I am through having to lean on* GOD ALONE.

This seems odd, but it is diametrically opposed to our flesh to do so, and it is very trying. My flesh says, "I should like 1000 good, trustworthy soldiers, and not His

---

[1] This was not addressed to me. My brother, when inclosing letters for me to forward, often asked me to read and copy what I liked, "as then you save me the trouble of writing the same thing twice."

promise. It is utterly wrong, but a widow would prefer 15,000*l.* in the 3 per cent. consols to the promise that God will provide for her. We may talk as we like, but our flesh needs *substance*, not *promises*, and I do not believe the flesh will ever agree to accept aught else, and therefore is doomed to anxiety and suffering. After my spirit, I prefer the promise; after my flesh, I prefer the 1000 soldiers: not having them, my spirit lords it over my flesh and conquers; but the flesh suffers all the same, and I see the deep lines in my face getting deeper and deeper day by day. *Why did you go?* Well, He sent me, for I went on a toss up. He is GOVERNOR-GENERAL. I am only His agent. . . . .

With the cessation of hope of comfort in the world, there is some amount of peace. Patience is not an acquired quality. No amount of patience exerted to-day will help you to wait to-morrow.

Owing to the state of affairs in the province, I am obliged to continually lean on God and to seek His help, for I see none elsewhere. This is very painful for humanity, which likes to be strong and see its way to do this or that; when you are as dependent on God as I am, you will feel worn and tired of the servitude. I want to gather manna for four or five days, and I am obliged to do it daily. Think how seldom you are in such a fix as to really go to God to help you; for most of your days your life runs smoothly, and you have not to humiliate yourself to Him. Now, I am always in fear of this or that, and I find nothing to help me but Him, and this wears my flesh and wearies me.

After my spirit I like to lean on Him; after my flesh I dislike to do so, and long to throw off His yoke. If I ask for a certain thing to be done or to happen, my flesh says, " Ask it, *coûte que coûte*," my spirit says, " Ask it, if in accord to His will; and be content if the contrary happens." This is torture to me, yet God has much blessed me, and, if He has made me wait, He has acted bountifully towards me.

I look back on my life, and seek for a spot of self-complacency ground to rest on, and I find it not. I find naught to stand on and to say, "Here I did what I ought to have done." "Know thyself." I would say, "Much rather not, rather be ignorant of that personage."

You agree that Adam was from God, as far as his life was concerned; and that he was from the earth, as far as his body was concerned. Well, from Adam came Eve, the mother of all flesh; our Saviour was in Eve; you cannot get out of it, that is if you allow the same application to Him, as Paul points out existed in Levi paying tithes in Abraham. I do not see why this view should be disliked, viz. that we with our Saviour were in the loins of Adam, and that each of us in due time was manifested.

There are many passages[1] in Scripture which imply our pre-existence with our Saviour; for, as the children were made partakers of flesh and blood, so was He. Now the children to be made partakers of flesh and blood, must have pre-existed. As you believe in eternity one way, you must believe in it the other, and there is nothing in Scripture to contradict it; the bodily forms, which are known by certain names, are temporal, being seen, and they fill certain parts in the world's theatre. What I wish to convey is, that we were pre-existent, were incarnated in sinful flesh, and were so mysteriously incarnated in that flesh as to believe and feel we were one in body and soul, whereas we are dual, being sinful in the extreme after the flesh, and perfect in our souls.

Christ raises our dead souls by His Spirit, and then we realize the dual part in us. "For the good that I would, I do not: but the evil which I would not, that I do" (Romans vii. 19). Paul is full of the duality. If I had words I could explain my meaning, but I find them not. It is only the

[1] For instance, see Psalm ciii. 17; Jeremiah xxxi. 3; Ephesians i. 4; 2 Thessalonians ii. 13; and 2 Timothy i. 9.

perception enlightened by God's Spirit that can make clear these truths (1 Corinthians ii. 11, 13, 14).

If what I say is false, may God save you from believing it, as I am sure He will. If I speak truly, you will not be able to shake off the idea, viz. that you pre-existed in God, that you were incarnated in sinful flesh for the glory of God, that He redeemed you by His Son, that your "flesh profiteth nothing," and that you are and have been perfectly safe in His love throughout your life. As one with Christ, a member of His body mystical, He needs you as much as you need Him as your Head. I fear I have written in a hurry, and wish I had more time to tell you how comforting these truths are.

RED SEA, 6 *September*, 1879.—I am in a very angry mood. I feel sure that, doing my best, I cannot get with credit out of this business; I feel it is want of faith, but I have brought it on myself, for I have prayed to God to humble me to the dust, and to visit all the sins of Egypt and the Soudan on my head; it would be little to say, take my life for theirs, for I do earnestly desire a speedy death. I am weary of the continued conflict with my atrocious self; but, when He does smite, His arrows are almost too sharp for one to bear: I will not say *too* sharp, for He tempers His wind to the shorn lamb, but it is a wearisome life and I am tired.

Read the third chapter of Job, it expresses the bitterness of my heart at this moment; yet all this I have brought on myself, by the prayer that I may know *myself.* What a fearful desire! That His will may be done, what a wish! Better abandon prayer, ask Him to forget and pass you by, till flesh fails and you sink to the grave. The spite in my own heart and in those around me fills me with hatred of any human being. A more detestable creature than man cannot be conceived, and yet you and I are cased, or sheathed, in man

But do not fear for me, for, even if He multiplies my woes a million times, He is just and upright, and will give me the necessary strength. What *enrages* my flesh is, that I am in a *cul de sac*, a road which has no *débouché*, a hole out of which I see no exit.

Everything I do *will be misconstrued.* This shows I have not faith. I do care for what man says, though, in words, I say I do not. I have not overcome the world. Read Job vi. 4; that is the bitter feeling I have.

Job was a scoffer—*vide* chap. xii. 2, 3—and so am I in heart and tongue. Though I am cast down and angry at the injustices these people have had to endure, I feel sure that, if Johannes does push matters to extremes with Egypt, it will be to his hurt. Johannes, oddly enough, is like myself—a religious fanatic. He has a mission, and will fulfil it, and that mission is *to Christianize!!! all Mussulmans.* He has forbidden the smoking of tobacco in his country, and cuts off the right hand and left foot of any man he catches doing so! When Christ comes again, how truly He may say to us all, "I know ye not."

8 *September*, 1879.—I am better in spirits to-day, though I wish it was over with me. I have had a long talk with the Swedish Protestants, and have given them this food to meditate on: that, as we had no part in original sin, so we have not a particle of part in our redemption. Till the Atonement is understood, there is no solution of the mystery. I asked them if they could explain the Atonement; if not, let them hold their peace.

ALEXANDRIA, 8 *January*, 1880.—You will, D.V., see me as soon as this letter, so I need not write what I have to say, for I will tell you in the kitchen, where I can smoke. My God has been so faithful! and kind! all through my troubles, that I can recommend Him to you. I have received your four letters, thanks for them. Pray for me!

ROME, 21 *January*, 1880.—Fancy, I had an attack of "doles" for three hours! What a dire disease it is! However, I am all right now. At outside calculation, only seventeen years' toil before my lease is out, and that will soon pass, whilst there is always a chance of getting off sooner. I cannot make up my mind to go to the Museum. I did go and see St. Peter's, and thought it poor!!! I went to Theatre San Carlo, opera *The Jewess*, but left after one hour and a half—could not stand it. I am not going to be hunted. I go direct to you and remain hid.

LONDON, 29 *February*, 1880.—I arrived here yesterday, and dined with Sir L. Simmons. To-day I went to church, in St. James', *very nice plain service*. I wish we had one like it at Southampton. It was quite like the old service of Molyneux's. Not a bad sermon. Going to church did me good. I leave to-morrow for Brussels.

BRUSSELS, 2 *March*, 1880.—I picked up a small book here, the *Souvenirs of the Congress of Vienna* in 1814-15. It is a sad account of the festivities of that time. It shows how great people fought for invitations to the various parties, &c., and how like a bomb fell the news of Napoleon's descent from Elba. It also relates the end of some of the great men. Castlereagh cut his throat near Chislehurst, Alexander died mad, &c. &c. They are all in their 6 ft. by 2 ft. 6 in.

Really, life needs only a little patience to bear with the present. If we could only look on our lives as an affair of twenty-four hours, we could bear up in whatever position we were cast, and how little it would signify whether we were great or small. The former would feel how ephemeral their greatness is, and the latter would not care to be great. The light of some stars takes 6000 years to reach the earth. If an eye was formed to see the space which this light traverses, one would, by it, see every event of this world, from Adam till now. It would be somewhat of a *pano-*

rama, only visible at *one* moment. It would need a brain similarly enlarged to realize it.

What we need is a profound faith in God's ruling *all* things; it is not the Duke or Lord Beaconsfield, it is *He* alone who rules. Napoleon, in a book lent me by Watson, says, "the smallest trifles produce the greatest results."

LAUSANNE, 18 *March*, 1880.—It is odd that, *longing with a great desire for death*, I am now quite well, and have lost the numbed feeling I had in my arm both in Egypt and Southampton.

This world is too small, and one longs for a larger sphere in the future. "Heirs" what to? something good! something useful! something grand; a sphere where one can know one's fellow face to face, without the hypocrisy of this earth. It may be said this is not in the Bible; I think it is, for the Bible speaks of bliss and peace, of a city, and of government, not of idleness. Why, idleness would pall on one after a time !

I hope you are realizing the comfort of no anchors ; the lifting of them is painful, but the result is beneficial. Christ's own words were, that He had no mother and no brethren.

The housewife you sent me is really a splendid one, thank you much for it.

LONDON, 1 *May*, 1880.—Sir Bruce Seton came from the Marquis of Ripon to ask me to go as his private secretary to India, leaving on 14th May.

4 *May*, 1880.—I am leaving on the 13th with Lord Ripon. As a man thinks who has twenty-four hours to live, so do I with respect to this appointment. I am a good deal independent of place whilst I have His presence.

ADEN, 24 *May*, 1880.—We have got here very well; Lord Ripon very kind ; but I cannot say I like the berth, and I shall get away as soon as I can do so in a respectable manner. . . . I cannot muster up enough interest in India ever to be able to write you letters like the Soudan ones.

28 *May*, 1880.—After a hot voyage we are nearing Bombay, and there will commence a certain degree of purgatory in the way of festivities, which, as far as possible, I shall avoid. I am now quite composed, and have made up my mind to leave either in September or the beginning of October. I think it will not surprise Lord Ripon. . . .

Having the views I hold, I could never curb myself sufficiently to remain in Her Majesty's service. Not one in ten million can agree with my motives, and it is no use expecting to change their views.

BOMBAY, 6 *June*, 1880.—I resigned by letter on the night of the 2nd; my resignation was accepted the next morning, and was in the London papers on the 4th. On the night of the 4th and on the 6th I received telegrams from China, asking me to go there. In all this God has helped me wonderfully.

I should like it to be known that I resigned before I knew of the China telegram, for otherwise it would seem that I had left Lord Ripon for this affair, which is not the case; when I resigned, I knew nothing of what I should do, and thought of Zanzibar. I consider the coincidence of Hart's telegram with my resignation is wonderful.

19 *June*, 1880.—We are making good way, and if all goes well, shall be in Hong Kong on the 3rd July. It is twenty years ago since I came out to China. I am in a P. and O. cargo boat; there are no other passengers, and I enjoy it: it is a perfect rest for me, I have already forgotten the private secretaryship. I do not know what I shall do, for, after my promise, I cannot enter the Chinese military service. I do not know if I shall resign my commission and commute or not, or whether I shall stay on till October, 1882. I mean to repair the monument to the "Ever-victorious Army" on the Esplanade at Shanghai. It is odd going back again.

India is the most wretched of countries. The way

Europeans live there is absurd in its luxury; they seem so utterly effeminate and not to have an idea beyond the rupee. I nearly burst with the trammels which are put on one. I declare I think we are not far off losing it. I should say it was the worst school for young people. Every one is always grumbling, which amuses me. The united salaries of four judges were 22,000*l.* a year. A. B. had been five years in India, and had received in that time 37,000*l.*! It cannot last. How truly glad I am to have broken with the whole lot; 100,000*l.* a year would not have kept me there.

All this private secretaryship and its consequent expenses are due to my not acting on my *own* instinct. However, for the future I will be wiser. I am glad to have cast off every anchor I had to attach me to this world.

3 *July,* 1880.—We hope to arrive at Hong Kong to-day. We have had a capital passage; the captain and officers are very kind, and I have had a good quiet rest.

6 *July,* 1880.—Arrived at Canton last night. The Viceroy will see me at four this afternoon, and I go down to-morrow to catch the Shanghai steamer at Hong Kong. I do not think the Chinese will take up the reorganization of their army seriously. Of course, if they do not, your brother will not stay, for I could never have the patience again to work against all their prejudices; and if they are content with their present organization, why should I bother them?

SHANGHAI, 13 *July,* 1880.—I arrived yesterday—almost the same day as I did twenty years ago. Hart met me and put me up, and I go to Tientsin to-morrow.

Things are somewhat saddening to me; it was with difficulty I recognized this place; and when I met some of those I knew sixteen years ago, I felt that a veil existed between us. I arrived at Tientsin on the 21st July, and was well received by Li-Hung-Chang. I am lodged near him, and have got away from the inquisitive foreigners. I feel rather fagged with the worries of life.

I have met many of the people who knew me, and some of my old boys turned up, such moon-faced men, grown up out of all recollection. Nar-wang's son is a red-button mandarin, and is like an ox. Yang is dead, also Kosungling; in fact, many of the best generals are gone to their rest. Li is but little changed in appearance.

The more we see of life, the more one feels disposed to despise one's-self and human nature, and the more one feels the necessity of steering by the Pole Star, in order to keep from shipwreck; in a word, live to God alone. If He smiles on you, neither the smile nor frown of man can affect you. Thank God, I feel myself, in a great measure, dead to the world and its honours, glories, and riches. Sometimes I feel this is selfish; well, it may be so, I claim no infallibility, but it helps me on my way. Keep your eye on the ·Pole Star, guide your bark of life by that, look not to see how others are steering, enough it is for you to be in the right way. We can never steer ourselves aright; then why do we try and direct others? I long for quiet and solitude again. I am a poor insect; my heart tells me that, and I am glad of it.

HONG KONG, 21 *August*, 1880.—A good leap. The fact is, I found I was *de trop* at Tientsin, so I left. —— keeps changing his mind like any woman. *I do not*, by the way, *think women change their mind more than men;* but it is a proverb, so pray excuse it.

When I was preparing to leave Shanghai for Aden, the Consul received a telegram from the Military Secretary at the Horse Guards: "Inform Gordon—leave cancelled— resignation not accepted—return England forthwith." It did not produce a twitter in me; I died long ago, and it will not make any difference to me; I am prepared to follow the unrolling of the scroll. I wish our Lord would come; to how few God gives this wish! yet how many say it! Do not send my letters round.

NEW MILFORD, PEMBROKE, 11 *November*, 1880.—I was stationed here just before the war in the Crimea, and left this place to go out to Turkey. I well remember, when ordered to the Crimea, my sincere hope was that I should be killed there. It is odd to think what I have gone through since then, and that I still retain the wish for the other world. In *Gold Dust* is this paragraph, " May I pass through *this world unnoticed.*" Take a shilling out of my box and buy it, it has some nice things in it. The prayer to Jesus " to be delivered from the desires," &c., is very good.

I have been down to the ferry behind the fort; the old ferryman remembered my being there, for he said, "Are you the gent who used to walk across the stream right through the water?" I said " Yes."

Nearly every one I knew is dead. Odd! when I am living and have been through such dangers. This confirms one's belief that, till God has no use for you, He will keep you here; and if He does not want you here, He evidently will be pleased to use you in those other worlds I speak of. When I get alone, I think much more of God and His directing power. One's capacity is infinite, as one's being is, and one cannot be filled but by Infinity.

LONDON, 4 *December,* 1880.—I shall go down and take a lodging at Twywell, and try and disentangle myself from the world, and then see what I ought to do. It is quite impossible to be with the world and to be spiritually minded; the conflict, when one tries to do so, is enough to rend one in two. " This do in remembrance of *Me.*" I mean, with God's blessing, to try and realize the truth that is in this dying request. I hope I may be given to see the truth and comfort to be derived from the Communion. I have in some degree seen it must be a means of very great

M

grace, but of this in the future. It is a beautiful subject. Do not peck at words. Communion is better than sacrament, but communion may exist without the eating of the bread, &c. Sacrament means the performance of a certain act, which is an outward and visible sign of spiritual grace. You need not fear my leaving off this subject, it is far too engrossing to me, and is extremely interesting.

TWYWELL, 16 *December,* 1880.—I have a *True Treasure* I am sending you. I had the Communion yesterday, and felt its power very much ; and last night God gave me the wish to write again. The new paper will come soon to you.

About printing. I think the papers want enlarging, but do what you like ; now don't be weak ; the papers are not mine ; add to them what God gives you. You will see these are not discoveries; they are unveilings of the Eternal Truth. Every one of us is as it were a telescope ; it is not *my* finding out, it is God's revelation ; it is not my property, it is His, and is also the property of every member of Christ.

The Lord's Supper paper I look on as a great treasure, for I *have* derived immense comfort from Communion.

I am sending you some papers on the "Unrolling of the Scroll." Be faithful and be jealous of God's Word ; let it not be wrested by me, for then it is no comfort ; the Holy Spirit is the true Teacher.

TWYWELL, 1 *January,* 1881.—I have seen it said, " There is no mercy in consigning the largest portion of mankind to punishment." There would be great mercy in doing so, if men were not changed in their desires, for the presence of God would be, as it were, the greater hell to them. The question is not of a place of delight or of a place of torment, it is of a place where God is or of a place where He is not. Our faculties cannot judge this; God will be merciful in everything He does, for He cannot err.

" Do we wish we had never sinned ? " is a question for the body; certainly it would have been better for us not to have sinned, had such been *God's will*, for, however much we may *hereafter* realize our great gain in Christ's atonement, in the flesh we should feel the wish to be sinless. "The flesh profiteth nothing" (John vi. 63), it is merely the instrument, the disease is within, the flesh is wholly and entirely bad; there is naturally no difference, no greater or lesser sinner, all are iniquitous.

For an argument people often quote those Israelites who fell in the wilderness as not entering into the Promised Land, but they do not see that Moses was amongst them; in fact, I believe it was typical, for the law cannot take members into the Promised Land.

THAMES DITTON, 8 *January*, 1881.—I hope, D.V., to put myself in communication with some of our Scripture-reader people, and shall try and visit Christ, who is in the East end in the flesh (Matthew xxv. 34). I feel this is what I shall like; these truths were not given to make a man idle.

KENSINGTON, 11 *January*, 1881.—I believe much in instinct; I could even put it in higher words. You have been in the doles, I expect. I remark on it, because I really believe that by degrees, through God's Spirit, one grows in the quick perception of things in other members, and can read thoughts miles off. It would not signify if I was wrong in your case (which I would hope I was), if it were not good for you to be as you are.

All knowledge of mysteries, &c., is of no use, except in connection with the chapter on Charity, *i. e.* Love (1 Corinthians xiii.). Somehow I have a repulsion to talk of these mysteries to those whose life denies their power; and this resembles much the same feeling I have against the Pharisee element. You will see that I think we have free-will in the flesh, and I declare I am comforted by it, for one sees how one can contend with the evil; it is not a question of salvation that is at stake, *that* is safe, but a greater realization of Christ both now and in the future.

I saw the photographs at Pelligrini's; they are good, I think. He laughed at your brother; he says, "He is all eyes;" and *I* know it, and *you* know it. Have you one in Chinese costume on a *card?* if so, will you send it here?

I have found great comfort in the results after the Communion, and now am truly happy. I should be glad to go, but am content to stay, if it is the Lord's will.

I had a nice talk with Graham on the Sacrament. I cannot tell you how important I think it. The Communion is the peace-offering. It ought to be taken very often; if possible, at least once a month.

14 *January*, 1881.—The more we reflect on it, the more we shall believe that our Lord even now is Man, as He was when here; that He can be well pleased and grieved now as He could then; that He is in reality suffering from sickness, sorrow, &c., in the slums of the world, in the bodies of His members; and that to administer to them is to administer to Him and rejoice His heart, even as our hearts at times rejoice.

Thank you for your letter, to which I telegraphed an answer, and now send back the sermon. Somehow I think you want a sharp shake, like a tree with snow on it.

I wrote those papers in great haste; but you are the crucible, to say if they are worth printing without retouching, and if they are truly expressed. You can quietly form a better opinion of them than I can, for they are, as it were, my Benjamin. Do what you think right, it is the Spirit and not the letter that is valuable.

19 *January*, 1881.—We are having terrible weather for the poor people. He has all power over heaven and earth; He is a man to feel our infirmities, and He will do right.[1]

---

[1] This alludes to the great snowstorm of 18th January, in which traffic both in town and country was almost completely stopped.

25 *January,* 1881.—Somehow I think it is no use printing any more than what you have done, or have ordered to be done ; it is foolishness to the mass of the world. You know, when I write, I never know how the argument will come out, and sometimes I get quite bewildered at what I think is antagonistic to some of the great truths, yet they generally all come right.

Now I want to ask you, Do you cling to the Chinese flags you have?—I do not mean those that have the bullet-holes. If you do, be honest and say so; if you do not, send them to me. Mrs. W—— wants them for the Graves-end ragged school ; she does not care for them particularly, so mind and be honest.

I met —— and rebuked the carping spirit in her, telling her she was, like many others, always ready to use her tusk, and, after getting others to show their pearls, to rend them ; that she, and many others, either had no pearls to show, or would never show them. I am sure you will agree in this. The swine evidently encourage you to throw your pearls before them and *then* rend you.

Did I tell you that I much liked your remark, "that what God gave us to live upon ought to suffice"? I am sure you are right. If we want more, we want it for our lust and pride.

LONDON, 3 *March,* 1881.—I have written a paper; its title is the " Divine Germ," *i. e.* the soul. How this germ was put under ground, *i. e.* in the body, and died (was separated from God). How it sprouted and found its way through the earth (the body), and then showed forth the Christian doctrine. If God wills, it will reach home, though we may not know it now. I say in the paper, "I speak only to the germ : I may as well speak to an animal as to the body. If the germ exists, it will move ; and I believe it does both."

I wish I could hide my feelings of antipathy and its

L   D reverse more, but somehow it scarcely seems possible. What strange contradictory beings we are! I keep saying, "Is God's hand shortened?" and again, "There is no way of escape." There is nothing left for me but death to prevent my speaking evil of every one and not trusting my Lord.

I like Queen Elizabeth's lines on the Sacrament :

> " Christ is the word that spake it ;
> He took the bread and brake it ;
> And what that word doth make it,
> I do receive and take it."

It is splendid.

With respect to the acknowledgment of the views we hold, I think it is this : neither you nor I have any call to print these things, and therefore in doing so we invite the thorns. If we do not like thorns, then we ought not to publish our views ; so I would say to you, "As your faith, so your walk."

I cannot help thinking I am peculiarly formed ; that I am, and always have been, inclined to value my opinions more than any one else's ; also that I am very selfish, inasmuch as I like in a general way, and not individually.

CHELSEA, 26 *March*, 1881.—I am better, but not over well, I have been shaken to the base ; it is good for me, for it enables me to feel what power the body has over the soul when one is really suffering bodily pain. B—— said, when dying, how glad he was he had sought God in his time of strength, for when he was sinking he could not do so, and so I feel. I had looked forward to a Communion, but could not go. I must confess to putting great (but *not salvation*) strength on that Sacrament.

I am glad of this rheumatic attack ; it has taught me what a frail creature I am.

28 *March*, 1881.—I promised W—— not to write any more to any papers about *anything*, so that is over. He is pushing me to go on my own account to Central Africa, and

to continue Livingstone's inquiries; he is against my going to Syria.

17 *April*, 1881.—Easter Sunday, He is risen! He is risen! From Thursday night till Friday 3 P.M.! what a conflict, what lonely suffering! It needed a long sleep in the tomb to rest those weary members,—a sleep of some forty hours' duration. What must the reuniting of the soul and body have been, the realization of their union for ever —for ever! He that liveth, and was dead; and is alive for evermore (Revelation i. 18).

In our measure we have to bear the proportion of suffering which falls to us in virtue of our position as members of Christ's Body. The full suffering—the cup to the dregs— which He as our Head endured, must be allotted out to each member of His body, according to the position of those members in relation to the Head. The sufferings of His broken heart must have been equal to those of the heart-broken members of His Body from the beginning to the end of the world.

We are the living stones of His temple; "Know ye not that ye are the temple of God?" (1 Corinthians iii. 16.) He shapes His living stones silently, and, when they are shaped, they are put in their places, we ascend to Him—He the foundation stone, the first-begotten from the dead. Is the temple nearly completed? The heavier stones must have been placed and be already on the Foundation.

Havre, 10 *May*, 1881.—Do you know that one of my great comforts is in having cast off the cords, except the one with you, which bound me to England? I have most effectually done so now, and feel as if a weight was cast off.

Gessi! Gessi! Gessi! how I warned him to leave with me! when at Toashia how I said, "Whether you like it or not, or whether I like it or not, your life is bound up with mine!" He knew me to the depths. I almost feared this in one way. However, Gessi is at rest. It is God's will.[1]

18 *May*, 1881.—I have been turned upside down; the process dates from the time I was at Twywell and began the subject. I may say that I never could have thought so many holes and corners would have been searched out. Scarcely a quiet day elapses without something being brought out which I had thought did not exist. I used to wander, as it were, through my heart, finding nice walks and splendid palaces, in which I reposed. Then came the downfall of my Egyptian palace; it was mouldy, faded and despicable; motives were discovered to be wholly earthly, and I turned from the ruins with disgust. Then I wandered into the last-visit-to-China palace, and it was splendid. However, only two or three days ago that appeared tattered and mildewed, so I have no pleasure in that ruin. Then came the smoking, which I enjoyed. To-day I have smitten that immense serpent, and now my daily allowance of cigarettes is much reduced. There is the pledge, with trust for strength to keep it.

I suppose this cleaning out of one's heart will go on, for, as goodness is unfathomable, so is evil. It is the electric light, the thorough clearing out of all nooks and corners. Sometimes one was wont to think that really one was fairly free of the flesh, but, alas! one seems scarcely to have begun. We have, as it were, been whitewashing the exterior and leaving the drains alone.

Now the health of the inmate depends far more on the drains than on the exterior; the latter is hateful to the eyes of the inmate and of others, but the whole health of the inmate depends on the drains. So if we do not cleanse our

---

[1] This alludes to the death of Gessi Pasha, who had been with General (then Colonel) Gordon in the Soudan, and who died at Suez on the 30th April from an illness caused by his terrible privations on the Bahr-Gazelle river, where he was blocked by the *sudd*, and where four hundred of his followers died from hunger.

hearts we lose His presence, though He vacates not the
house (His temple). He will not be served in conjunction
with our idols. All, all, all, or nothing is what He will have

The cloud attending the exile to Mauritius has passed
from me, through His mercy, and I feel quite contented
about it. The things of the exterior world have but very
little to do with one, when occupied with the drains of the
heart. I like to tell you my experiences, humiliating as
they are, for it is inevitable that you also have to go through
them, now you have begun.

Here have I been complaining I have nothing to do,
wanting (though pretending not to want) to put the outsides
of the houses of other people in repair, when there was rack,
ruin, mildew and bad drains in my own house; pasteboard
châteaux, like those put up when the Empress Catherine
made a progress through Russia. It is out of the question
to be decorating other houses when my own is in such a
state. I do not think much of getting help from only one
particular set of men; I will take Divine aid from any of
those who may be dispensing it, whether High Church, Low
Church, Greek Church, or Roman Catholic Church; each
meal shall be, by God's grace, my sacrament. We have
passed the question of salvation, we now are in need of
meat, it is sanctification and glorification. Christ's religion
must be a progressing and increasing one, not a religion
which stops short on the threshold. Every agreement or
covenant between God and man is shown *outwardly* by
some symbol signifying a mystery; in old time by the sacrifices, now by the commemoration of the great Sacrifice.
Christ lives in a garret in an unventilated house; we need
Him in the best rooms, *i. e.* our hearts; but then those
drains must be remedied.

20 *May*, 1881.—To govern men of any kind, put yourself
in their position, and judge how you would feel, *i. e.* " Do
unto others as you would wish them to do to you." " This

is the law and the prophets." Put yourself into their skins. Now it is remarkable that this very maxim, which is undoubtedly the most worldly-wise mode of governing men, is true still more in respect to a spiritual life, *i. e.* endeavour to realize your identity with, and absorption in, Christ; endeavour to realize what He, as man, feels for us; endeavour to grasp His feelings, His power over all things in heaven and earth, for we are entirely one with Him in all things, and He with us. God's interest, love, and desire towards Him is the same as God's interest, love, and desire towards us. We are partners with Him for weal and woe (no partners should ever conceal anything from one another; the weakness of one is decidedly the claim on the strength of the other); indeed, it is more than partnership, it is identity of person; it is closer than the union of our souls to our bodies.

22 *May*, 1881.—My diary is getting on: of course it is very inconsistent, for I am terribly torn. After a long argument in it about staying in the army or not, the final query and sentence is: "*But it is to be considered whether it is fair on your part to go and leave after putting the Government of your country to the expense of sending you out? It certainly does not seem fair; so, my friend, stay you must, till you are relieved by your Lord.*" I thank Him for the jewel, which settles the matter.

I would like to see you over Jordan, namely, over the fear of death. I believe the pilgrimage to Mauritius will be blessed to me, for I was hanging about Jordan, *i. e.* wishing for death, and not caring to conquer the promised land or to drive out the enemies; I scarcely cared whether they were there or not; I wanted the land without the conflict. The hankering after Egypt (the mystical, not the *real* Egypt, for I do not care ever to go back there) has gone. It was an evil hankering, but the hankering after the hill country is legitimate and is sure of success.

I reason this way: to attain the closest union with Christ is certainly to follow Him, and forsake all positions, rank, and honour of this world; all these things belong to Satan's kingdom, and are drawbacks. Now I do not think a young Christian ought to enter into this line, for he scarcely knows the cost; but I think, when Christ gives a man, even to a very small degree, maturity in knowledge of Himself, then, after long and due consideration and prayer, this man may endeavour to cast off Satan's gifts. The query is and must be always, Could you find Christ sufficient if you did so? *I think so now*, but certainly could not have thought so a little time ago; there was the will, but the flesh was weak. I shall, D.V., let this thought work, and God will direct me, for I am truly anxious to act for His honour and not from self-will. Now this latter I fear greatly, for the flesh smiles a little on throwing up the things of the world.

23 *May*, 1881.—I cannot understand when one series of type ends and another begins—Israel in Egypt, Israel in the Wilderness, Israel in the Holy Land; then come Judges, Kings, &c. &c. If Israel is a type once, it is always a type. I cannot help thinking that, as the realization of our personal identity and oneness with Christ is His gift, so we are in some degree imbued with all His attributes—humility, holiness, and wisdom.

A just perception and judgment is possessed by Christ's followers, but is obscured by want of light. Ophthalmia or disease of the eye of the understanding prevents perception, even in sincere seekers; a capacity of judgment exists, but in a stifled manner; even if slight perception be given, active measures are required, which must spring from a hope of better things. Head knowledge generally precedes heart working; the result of such working is the abandonment of everything that is past, and a stretching forward towards the future.

EN ROUTE TO MAURITIUS, 29 *May*, 1881.—I think we

really never die if we realize our oneness with Christ risen. I think we have a body given us at once : we ship from one body to the other.

I dare say you have felt what I allude to; every time you eat, somehow the Sacrament comes to mind. I think our grace ought to be " May this food nourish my body to enable it to serve Thee." The whole operation of eating is a wonderful matter, the death of the animal, &c. &c., all show its mystic import.

ADEN, 11 *June*, 1881.—Paul says, If by Christ's death on the cross we got so very much, how much more ought we to get from His life in heaven. It never struck me so before. How little do we think of anything but of being saved. If Christ reconciled us and removed all obstacles between us and God by His death, how much more than reconciliation can we not expect from His life? You know the passage—Romans v. 10.

If a man bought a property for a stupendous sum, at a great personal sacrifice, is it not certain that, having acquired that property, he would expend the comparatively little required to render it enjoyable? So I think it is with Christ and man.

PORT LOUIS, MAURITIUS, 24 *June*, 1881.—I have grown since I left you, and find food in the Bible I did not get before, and am quite contented to go on quietly here. My likings and my destiny are analogous. I do not want to hang on in the army, and I *could not* be employed if I did. I have had a very great slice of this world's renown, rightly or wrongly. As long as England keeps giving rewards on the scale she does to men whose sole profession and duty it is *mourir pour la patrie*, so long shall we have theatrical displays. A soldier's *raison d'être* is simply to give his life. It can be nothing else for which his country pays him. Why then give him high rewards for doing so? . . . . No sacrament to-morrow; but it is all for the best, and every time one eats should be the feeding on our slain Lamb.

I went to the cathedral—an ex-powder magazine. The text was: "Seek ye first the kingdom of God, and His righteousness; and all these things shall be added unto you." And yet, when, and to the degree one realizes that kingdom, so the "all things" appear worthless. We are, as it were, in a fairy land, a land of magic. If we are subdued by its things, we reach not the higher land; but if we refuse them, then we enter it.

I can scarcely tell you much of this place : there is absolutely nothing to do. " *Colonel* Gordon is wanted," not *I*, for religious or social matters. I strike against garden parties, archery and lawn tennis meetings ! I cannot go through these fearful ordeals of hours' duration.

I am glad to say *Gold-dust* says much of manual labour, and I think it is the common and proper course of life for man. I have been very busy about the fortifications and defences here ; but, though I cannot write much, I believe I am growing and learning truths.

Fruit comes from union with Christ : therefore if we seek that, we have this sequence. It seems to me one ought not to strive for fruit of the Spirit apart from Him who is the source of all. One may seek for holiness for itself; but that is not the proper motive ; it must be sought for simply in Him. The great point or mark before us is to apprehend Him as He apprehends us ; that is the only acceptable motive. To seek holiness, truth, absence of malignity, or purity, for themselves, may be from unworthy motives, and will not be allowed to, indeed cannot, succeed ; for these children, as it were, are bred from the wedded life of Christ and the soul. The soul cannot bring them forth separately. The vine and its branches show this. The higher one's thoughts go, the simpler they are : we get *nearer* the Root of things, though that Root will ever be infinitely removed ; but it evidently is the complete absorption of self in Christ, by which one feeling, one body, one soul, one essence exists between us and Christ, who is God. He is our inheritance (Deuteronomy xviii. 2) ; we are His inheritance (Deuteronomy ix. 29). We become Levites ; others may not reach this; they have their portion, even as the other tribes of Israel had portions, in the Holy Land. The Levites had no portion in the land ; they had the Lord only ; and consequently, in having Him, they had all things, far beyond what the other tribes had.

How often one has striven to get rid of this or that frailty, or to acquire this or that godly affection ; but it has been denied to us, for we should have used it for itself; whereas, if we seek the Root—*i. e.* union with Christ, for His beauty and desirableness—the fruit is produced. This apprehension gets rid of so many worries : it is simple; but one thing is needful—to sit at His feet, to be in Him.

27 *August,* 1881.—It is through the word of God, by the Spirit, that the understanding, conscience, and memory are affected. The Scriptures are God's word spoken to us. He explains this Himself : Search the Scriptures ; in them is eternal life. Through them He speaks to each one of us, individually and collectively. If I want you to understand anything, I explain it either by word of mouth or by writing ; these are the means by which I do so. God explains to us by the Scriptures, which are a miracle and are alike fitted for the most experienced saint as also for the meanest reader ; this is very wonderful.

A letter written by a deeply-read scholar might be understood by a well educated, but not by an illiterate, man. Here is a letter (scripture means writing) written by God, which is decipherable to all in their degree ; its truths are equally beyond the depth of the experienced and inexperienced Christian ; yet by both they are to be understood

(Isaiah xxxv. 8). Ignorance, ignorance, is the bane; all errors are from ignorance.

Look here : if you really think it good to do this thing, whatever it may be, you do it; if you do not really think it good, you will not do it ; therefore your action depends on your knowledge, *i. e.* understanding, which God alone can enlighten, and which He does enlighten by His Scriptures. It is evident that the root of sin is ignorance, as is also unbelief. A child from ignorance resists medicine, a man from knowledge accepts the same.

SEYCHELLES, 24 *September,* 1881.—I am much interested in these isles. They are wonderfully productive ; everything grows in them—oranges, raspberries, and spices of all kinds.

I have been down for two Sundays to meet a lot of Chinese, and have spoken to them as well as I could. I have not yet touched on Jesus and His sacrifice, but spoke of God's indwelling. It was satisfactory, and they were pleased.

ORACLES.

Man has always sought to ascertain the solution of un-certain matters by applying to divine authority. In heathen temples there was a select place whence answers were given by priests or priestesses to questions asked of their god, which place was especially sacred. The answers were ambiguous, and would bear two meanings.

There is no doubt that the *Holy of Holies* (in which was the Ark of the Covenant containing the law) and the mercy seat was the oracle of God in the Jewish temple (*vide* Exodus xxv. 22). "There I will commune with thee from above the mercy seat." This was *within* the veil in front of which was the altar of incense (Exodus xl. 5). Look at 2 Samuel xvi. 23, where the counsel of Ahithophel is said to be "as if a man had inquired at the oracle of God." ("Oracle," in the margin, is changed to "word.") "Even for the oracle,

even for the most holy place " (1 Kings vi. 16). " The priests
brought the Ark of the Covenant . . . . into the oracle of
the house, to the most holy place " (1 Kings viii. 6). " Hear
. . . when I lift up my hands toward thy holy oracle"
(Psalm xxviii. 2).

From these passages I deduce that the Jews had a place
where they could refer their questions to God and obtain
answers through their high priest, who bore their names on
his breastplate. They were in communion with God, and
could be instructed, directed, and advised. Acts vii. 38
says the Jews received the "lively oracles" in the wilderness. Romans iii. 2 says, " To them were committed the
oracles of God." Is there any oracle now by which man
can question, ask advice and guidance, and be instructed
by God?

We are told that the altar, holy of holies, &c., were
patterns of heavenly things (Moses and David were to make
patterns of the heavenly things they had seen. Exodus
xxv. 9; 1 Chronicles xxviii. 11, 12). The law and Jewish
dispensation were shadows of good things to come, and not
the very image of those things. The visible temple, altar,
and oracle disappeared when in the fulness of time the Son
came. Yet the temple, &c. &c., does still exist; for the
original tabernacle and temple were only shadows or figures
of the true temple, which is in heaven itself; its holy of
holies figured the presence of God (Hebrews ix. 24). It
does exist spiritually now, and with it the oracle—*i. e.* God
—must be as ready to give answers, instruction, and guidance as before, for both in the figure or shadow, and in the
heavenly substance, it is the same God who spoke and still
speaks. In the shadow there was a perceptible, substantial
mercy seat, and a voice which could be heard by man.
Now there is a spiritual temple, a spiritual mercy seat, and a
spiritual voice, which can be heard by the spiritual man.

Out of commiseration for our dual condition, God *has*

given us an oracle which will answer any question, advise, instruct and guide us; now this oracle must be His voice, for, if not, it would not be His word. He has in His infinite wisdom incarnated His voice in the Scriptures; His voice is to be understood by the highest or lowest intellect; it gives answers, &c., through all time. To the carnal man it is an ordinary book, to the spiritual man it is alive and makes alive.

In the Jewish dispensation, the high priest went into the holy of holies with the blood and censer off the altar of incense and communed with God. Now with us we have the great High Priest who, through the torn veil, His flesh, has entered and sat down for ever, at the right hand of God, keeping the approach always open.

I do not think prayer is ever lost; but when it is answered the petitioner forgets that he ever pleaded and thus loses the comfort which the close access he has to God, through Christ, should give him, in the answer to his prayer. The Scriptures are the word of God, the sword of the Spirit, the only offensive weapon against our enemies. All the other arms of the Christian are defensive armour (Ephesians vi. 12-18).

We have the altar of incense available for our prayers through Him, and He gives us His answer, guidance, &c., through that living record of His word, the Scriptures. John (chap. iv. 23, 24) prefigured this spiritual approach to God. Why then do we not progress? It is because we do not look for the answer to our prayers—we pray and leave it; we read the Scriptures and do not follow the connection between prayer and this reading, between our request and its answer; so we are barren, lame, and dull. Now God has opened my eyes to the truth, that it is by the Scriptures that He will speak to man, and *rarely* will He speak in any other way; I would almost say *never*. Any one who asked a favour or help from a fellow-man, and who, through

N

ignorance or carelessness, did not trouble himself to listen to the answer, would be considered wanting in worldly wisdom.

MAURITIUS, 24 *November*, 1881.—I consider "Oracles" a most important paper. My belief is, that whenever we are in doubt about anything, we should place the matter before God by prayer, then take the Bible wherever we may be reading, and, having our attention fixed on the subject of our prayer, seek to get the answer and take it in just the same way as if we heard God's voice. Saul inquired of the witch of Endor, while David kept on asking God (1 Samuel xxiii. 2, 4, 9-11 ; xxx. 7, 8).

I have read the Scriptures and have got pearls from them, but as though from deduction or analogy, and not as directly from God—not as though He spoke or wrote to us.

It is difficult to explain what I mean, but what I want to say is this : I now look on the Scriptures as alive—living oracles—and not as a historical, religious book, as I have hitherto done, even when feeling its mystical character. I cannot say how important this vista is to me. I have said that, as long as the newspaper affords one more attraction than the Bible, something must be wrong.

I believe that Christ *as man*, with a sinless body derived from the Holy Ghost, and to whom the Holy Ghost was given *without* measure, obtained all knowledge, all miracle power, and all His attributes, simply because His eyes were opened by the Scripture. I have one great difficulty. It is this : If I keep on thinking "What have I done amiss to-day ? " I fall under the law ; yet there is no doubt that, if I neglect to think over the day's work, I do not advance in holiness. It is as necessary to keep count over the past, under the Gospel as under the law, but with this difference : under the law one does it for one's own righteousness, but under the Gospel in order to see what answer to prayer is given. The object is entirely different in the two cases; in one we try to justify ourselves, while in the other we notice in what way, or to what extent, our prayers are answered.

I keep on asking you to lend me 10*s.* You lend me 1*s.*, and I take no notice of it, but keep on saying, "Lend me 10*s.*" The consequence is, I may be lent 2*l.*, and yet not know it. The law says, "I have earned 2*s.*; give me credit for it;" but as we can never really earn 1*d.* we remain dead. Under the law it is a question of salvation; under the Gospel it is a question of increase of holiness.

Man is dual; he needs food for the body, so also he needs food for the soul. The body seeks its like—*i. e.* flesh (quails). The soul seeks its like—*i. e.* God (the heavenly manna); to the body this manna is tasteless. What we have to do is to gather manna *daily* from the Scriptures: "Man doth not live by bread only, but by every word that proceedeth out of the mouth of the Lord doth man live" (Deuteronomy viii. 3; Matthew iv. 4). We should force the appetite of the body to take that manna: I mean we should interest the body in the Scriptures, by reading and meditating, as being *all in all*.

The body says, "Before I give up my carnal desires, show me something better—'a bird in the hand is worth two in the bush.'" The body must have some reason before it will prefer the Bible to the newspaper, it must be so opened or represented as to be more interesting (Proverbs ii. 1-9). Now, if the body could see that the Bible contains an answer to every question, that it foretells, advises, &c., then it would prefer it to the newspaper. God has been very merciful to me in the thoughts I have had here (in Patmos) regarding the Scriptures and the motives of one's actions; and now, through His mercy, I see lakes and seas of knowledge before me.

Another point has arisen with me; I have been keeping

N 2

count, and find I have not kept my garment unspotted—
two or three very prominent breaches of God's law may
have happened, say yesterday. You will say, "Then it is
evident that, though you prayed and then sought the answer,
and, though you found it reassuring, like the verse 'Be
strong, fear not' of Joshua i. 6, 7, you have failed." Well,
that may be true in one way. God knows how prone we
are to self-righteousness, and therefore keeps the knowledge
of our increased holiness from us, for we could not bear it,
we should become proud; but He answers us by rendering
our conscience more tender, so that at night, when we
review the things of the day, we find several things turn up
which would have passed unconsidered before. Now this
is a great and growing advance, for thus conscience becomes
more tender daily, and, as it is divine and reflects God's
law, it becomes a mirror to our actions and thoughts, and
the more we strive for a perfect life, as shown by this enlightened conscience, the nearer we approach *perfect holiness.*

We can never reach this perfect life here, but it is the
prize set before us, the reward of our strife; therefore we
need not be distressed out of measure, when a review of our
actions shows how we have fallen short of our high standard,
for the more tender God makes our conscience, and the
better the reflection given from its mirror, so much more
will our failings appear in our review of our daily actions.
God in His mercy will not show too much at once, for,
should we have the *full* reflection, we should be too much
discouraged.

Another way of viewing this is: our robes are very soiled;
God would cleanse them, but He will not show us the whole
of their impurity at once, so He shows us little by little.
Heaven is not clean to Him, and angels veil their faces
before Him. Though virtually clean and perfect before
Him in Christ, actually we are not clean, and never shall
be, till He grants us light.

Our shrinking back from contact with man and society is similar to the unwillingness of the Israelites to the combats of the Holy Land. "There we saw the giants, the sons of Anak; we were in our own sight as grasshoppers" (Numbers xiii. 33). When, by the review, we see our shortcomings, and say, "I will shut myself up," we are timid and fearful, and try to avoid the enemy instead of meeting him: no conflict, no conquest. Be strong, be strong in God's Word; they are bread and prey to you. Their defence is departed. If you will not go up and possess the land, then the Amalek-ites will smite you; you will not get off fighting, but the conflict will be unsatisfactory; if you begin this warfare without the Scriptures, *i. e.* in your own strength (without the ark of the Lord), you will fail. "But they presumed to go up unto the hill-top: nevertheless the ark of the covenant of the Lord, and Moses, departed not out of the camp" (Numbers xiv. 44).

Even if I had come out to Mauritius to be given this pearl, I am repaid. Canaan was a good land unworthily occupied; its people were cast out. So it is with our body; it is unworthily occupied. The old inhabitants must be cast out, and a new people brought in.

"We know not what we should pray for as we ought; but the Spirit itself maketh intercession for us with groanings which cannot be uttered" (Romans viii. 26). The Spirit of Prayer is the Spirit of God in us making supplication; it is the Spirit of Christ, the vital part of man. To go up to the war "against spiritual wickedness in high places," a man needs defensive armour to ward off the blows of his adver-sary, such as the "helmet of salvation," "the breastplate of righteousness," and the "shield of faith" (when he has these on, though they are not exactly a part of himself, like the scales of a crocodile, they defend him in the same way as if they were). Thus equipped, he cannot be hurt, but he is still without any weapon of his own wherewith to destroy his enemies; he has nothing to strike them with. He is given the "sword of the Spirit," the Word of God. This sword is not a part of the man, he wields it or not as he likes; if he does not, then, though he may not be hurt in any vital part, so long as he has his body covered with the defensive armour, yet he may be exposed to all the blows of the enemy, and, if he does not use his sword, he will be attacked over and over again with impunity.

(1) A man with defensive armour and no sword, or one he does not use, may be safe from wounds, but he cannot destroy his enemy.

(2) A man with imperfect or no defensive armour, if he has a sword which he uses, may hurt his enemy, but may also be badly wounded himself.

(3) A man with neither defensive armour nor sword does not fight, but is a slave.

A man would prefer to attack No. 3, for he is sure to be the gainer; he would sooner attack No. 1 than No. 2, for No. 1 cannot destroy him; and, though he cannot wound him, he is always attacking him, for he runs no risk. An enemy does not *like* attacking No. 2 for fear of the sword he has; however, he does attack and wound him, from his not having defensive armour; the enemy's attacks are by subtlety.

Now apply this: the defensive armour to guard against attack is Christ; He is Salvation, Faith, and Righteousness —Helmet, Shield, and Breastplate. No other armour is proof against the enemies' weapons. It is given to man to *cover him;* and does not come from him, he has nothing to do with its manufacture; and if he tries to make it himself, it will not be proof, for, though in appearance it may look well, it would fail him in need. For the spiritual warfare man must put on Christ's gift, and must plead this whenever he is assaulted by his enemies, who taunt him with being dirty under this armour. He owns his dirtiness, but it is covered and will not affect the defensive power of the armour which is on him; it is rude of the enemy to thus taunt him; his object is to get man to manufacture defences of his own, and to put off the Divine armour.

This must be resisted; and though man may and should seek to have his body clean and free from the reproach of his enemy, yet, whether clean or not, his safety is in the *divine armour* and *not* in his cleanness; therefore the sinks we may discover in our hearts ought not to discourage, though they should humble us. Man thus enveloped in safety seeks to strike his enemy, and for this he has the sword, the Word of God; if he does not use it, it is as if he had it not, it is only by using it that he can crush his enemy. Joshua i. 6-9 shows with what weapons Israel was to go forth and conquer the enemy in high places.

Man has to contend with two sets of enemies—those from within and those from without; the flesh and the devil; unholiness, temptation; his carnal lusts and the tempter, the one proposing, the other assenting.

The sword of the Spirit keeps the tempter at a distance; when it is used, he cannot with ease communicate with the lusts, which die if they are not fed by thus communing.

A man equipped with the Divine armour and sword of the Spirit, and not using the latter, is exposed to the constant attacks of the tempter, who, approaching the lusts, entices them, and keeps the man in continual ill-ease, rendering his life a burden; though through the heavenly armour of Christ he may be safe from extinction or destruction.

Man's body is good; it is a passive instrument in itself, and can be used for either good or evil, as the affections sway it; when carnally inclined, it is unclean; and when spiritually inclined, it is clean; the members of the body are weapons either of righteousness or unrighteousness.

"Let us therefore cast off the works of darkness, and let us put on the armour of light."

"Put ye on the Lord Jesus Christ, and make not provision for the flesh, to fulfil the lusts thereof" (Romans xiii. 14, Galatians vi. 8, Ephesians ii. 3, 1 Peter ii. 11).

20 *December*, 1881.—I have gained much by this time in Mauritius, and hope now I shall grow daily in grace. Anak's sons are very strong, and they have chariots of iron; however, they will be bread to me; I hope their power is departed.

God has given me so much treasure in the Bible, that ambition (that son of Anak) is very weak and ill, and I hope he will not recover. Therefore, in a hazy way, I propose doing this: when I leave, I think I shall go to Seychelles for a month, then to Beirout and look about me. As economy will be the order of the day, I may go down to Sinai, and stop with the monks there a year, living in the mildest way and dropping my name as far as possible. If you wish it, I would come home before I went; but you know English life is a poisonous one for me in every way. It is not my fault altogether that it is so, it is not God's fault; it—English life—is, as it were, a garden of temptation, and I do not want Agag alive again. (I am talking much of self, I fear.)

I seek the substance; how can we be more holy? Not with a view to greater or higher places, but to be nearer to the delight of one's heart, one's God. I am drawn to God (He draws me) with such an affection that, even were He not Almighty, I must prefer Him. I should like any trouble with Him rather than everything away from Him. Nothing, nothing could compensate for His absence.

Remember we are not to cast our pearls before swine. If God has given us this knowledge, He can give it to others; therefore I have a strong objection to putting these papers before those whose lives deny their profession. Knowledge without an increase of holiness is a detriment.

What troubles me immensely is the way in which circumstances force me into society, for in it is the great evil of judging others, picking them to pieces behind their backs, so entirely mean and contrary to our Lord's will. All this tends to make a cloud between Him and us; and yet I declare I cannot see how I can avoid it. I try and comfort myself with the words: " Be strong, be courageous; do not be afraid of them; they shall be bread for you." In fact it is very much like war between two nearly equally matched forces: victory seems to sway from one side to the other, and it is thus we learn to fight. (" Teach my hands to war and my fingers to fight.") If we stay in our fortresses, the enemy will remain in his, and there will be no advance of anything more than unimportant skirmishes, and a correspondingly feeble life. No, we must go out and fight in the open, or we shall never dislodge the enemy; and we cannot do this without loss. In fact our enemies with their chariots of iron are ourselves.

Good-bye. I am fagged with this warfare, and you must be so also. The sons of Anak are enormous; their walls reach up to heaven. One is but a grasshopper.

2 *January*, 1882.—I think that, little by little, spiritual discernment comes to me, long before actual discernment, and it is this that pleases me and strengthens my faith. In humility I say it, and in submission to God, for I know not my own motives; I now think, wherever I go, it will not make much difference. I have found the pearl "occupation" in the Scriptures, and I believe I am growing in grace, though I would not know it, for fear of being lifted up.

It has been a great blessing to me to have come out here. For the present, the connection of the Tabernacle and man's body is closed to me; that is because I know not Christ, the Key.

Should I get away from here sooner than I expect, I will telegraph " *Stop* " from Aden; then kindly stop all letters and papers for this place, and send them to Port Said. If

I telegraph "*Easy,*" then keep them all till you hear from me.

20 *January*, 1882.—I hope our friends are comforted in their trial. I cannot say more, for it would be treason to our Lord to wish things should be different from what He rules.

Man can in a measure (which is capable of expansion to infinity) comprehend God in His love and His justice, but not in His power. I mean by this, that man can know justice and love, for he has these qualities, however they may be warped in him. What man fails to comprehend is God's power; we reason: If He is just and loving, why does He not exert His power? The reason is, that it is His great power which enables Him to bring good out of evil.

To any one to whom the union of God with himself, the indwelling, is known, the coming of Christ would not produce the least shock. It is the knowledge of the indwelling of God which makes the Christian religion differ from all others, and yet this peculiarity is rarely mentioned.

I am torn in two; the sons of Anak have shown themselves quite strong, and I sometimes find myself even in alliance with them against God, though I do it unwittingly and through forgetfulness. It is no use fighting them *directly* (*i. e.* making resolves), the only thing that can quell them and *shake them off* is union with Christ.

How I hate society; how society hates me! I never tell you the sort of life I lead, it is not worth it; for it is simply the life I led at home, being asked out, and refusing when it is possible;—when I go, getting humiliated, or being foolish. This latter is better than not being exposed— keeping one's self in cotton wool, for that brings out no knowledge of self, such as is brought out by being with others. At the same time, I think it is not right to be much in society, indeed I fight against it truly, and have only dined out about seven times since I have been here.

It is not man's praise we should seek, but our Lord's; one is fleeting, the other is for ever.

I will give you a thought. Are you eternal? When you leave the body God has put you in, do you perish, or do you live for ever?—You will say you are eternal. If you are eternal in the future, must you not have been so in the *past?* The Lamb was "slain from the foundation of the world," *i. e.* was eternal; so His members, which make up His body, must have been eternal also.

Oh! if we were content to have God's will instead of our own, we should be happy. This discontent of our people is sad; it is only for a time, and it is better to have happiness and peace than wealth and position. I was never content till I found out that this great gift came by looking on all things as being ruled by Him: those of good, His own work; those of evil, permitted and overruled for our good. There is no such thing as chance; if we are not given what we desire, does He not rule all things, and is it not better for us? When you bow to the will of God, you die to this world.

I dwell more or less (I wish it were more) under the shadow of the Almighty, and though, when I go out of that refuge, I often get wounded by shafts of ridicule, &c., I get healed again, and the shafts are not over sharp. One's inclination is to shoot back, having a quiver full of sharpest arrows. To refrain is self-denial; may I practise it more!

I know I am feared because of this, but it is not fear one would wish to meet, but love. You offer a kindness, it is repelled with a snub. If you did it in a spirit of love, not otherwise, it would be right to shoot back. Have you never experienced having a pet thing, something you have done, and which you truly dote upon and see no fault in? The mere remembrance of it makes you happy, even in the time of trouble; then all of a sudden comes a dart of thought, which shows that this pet is an abortion, is hateful, was done from evil motives : its beauty has gone, it is dead, and you never wish to hear of it again. That dart is the arrow of the Light of God disclosing the truth, and showing you that your beauty is but a scab. One comfort is that, when once it is shown up, you can no longer bear the thought of it. It is the slaying of a child of Anak.

Do you remember the day I went to the Isle of Wight, and just before I left I told you about Agag?[1]

The whole of religion consists in looking at God as the true Ruler, and above the agents He uses (no one can be at rest who regards the latter). We are as much worshippers of gold, silver, and "power" gods, as the heathen. Though we do not acknowledge it, the flesh will always look to agents. I do not mourn over past things, they are gone and nothing can recall them ; look to the end and separate yourself from the earth.

I wish God to use me as He likes. Sometimes ambition makes me think "What a waste of time to be out here!" but it soon ceases to disturb me, and I am glad I have no anchors.

With respect to spiritual matters I am content with what I have; it seems quite clear to me that we are, each of us, worlds in ourselves where all events are represented. The flesh must be broken down for true life to exist. If one looks on the future life as certain and assured, I do not think we should look on this world as dreary and sad ; " enough for the day is its evil," and nothing pleases God

---

[1] Agag—catering for notice and praise, hailing the tram of the world ! "Look what I have done ! !

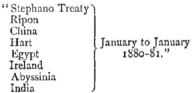

"Stephano Treaty
Ripon
China
Hart
Egypt
Ireland
Abyssinia
India

January to January
1880-81."

more than a contented spirit looking on Him as the source of all things, good and evil, as they appear to us.

I do think the incarnation was a glorious mode of showing us what God is. I wonder if there are others who realize, by God's spirit, that the soul is of God, incarnated; that it is enabled to learn good and evil, and to demonstrate to other powers the mystery of good and evil by the flesh? I feel daily more and more of this truth, and it is a life-buoy in this dull life (not that it is dull to me). The tree is known by its fruits; a selfish act is done by the selfish disposition of the doer, the disposition existed before the act which emanated from it. A loving act is done by the loving disposition, and so on. Before you judge any one, watch his or her actions, see which disposition predominates, and judge each act on its own merits.

I like these thoughts, though few ever enter into them with me. As Kingsley remarks: "Verily, however important the mere animal lives of men may be in our eyes, they have never really been so, judging from floods, earthquakes, and storms in the eyes of Him who loves and made us all." Death is nothing in God's sight, and would be nothing in ours if we recognized that our life is only a pilgrimage. It is a strange fact—better for us to ask honestly what it means, instead of shutting our eyes to it, because it interferes with our views of tenderness and of pain.

The difference between animal man and animals is that of degree. They are of the same description; but in animal man there is another Power, which, though it may be latent, ever exists, and that is the Spirit of God. In other creatures we cannot discern how far the Spirit of God in them is latent or hidden. "Man that is without understanding is like the beasts that perish." I think that the correct definition of carnal man is that his soul sleeps, while his carnal nature wakes and works; that carnal man is merely an animal, with the difference that God's Spirit dwells hidden

in him and from time to time stirs; that God speaks by His
Spirit in man and manifests Himself to the animal man, and
that then begins the strife between soul and body.   The
main point that I desire is, to test, by God's help, what I
believe, viz. that of man a part is of God, and a part is of
the world; that the part that is of God is sinless and cannot
sin ("Whosoever is born of God doth not commit sin,"
1 John iii. 9), and was such from the beginning; while that
which is of the world is sinful (" he that committeth sin is
of the devil," 1 John iii. 8), and carnal after the nature of
its root, the world, and yet by God's Spirit through Christ
can be changed in its carnal nature to turn to God.   Satan
is prince of this world and god of it.   Out of the dust of
this world God formed or shaped man.   Out of this world,
which had been delivered to Satan, of which he was god and
prince, was man shaped, and then God breathed into his
nostrils the breath of life.   All philosophers are nonplused
by the fact that in the beginning life must have been given,
even if we accepted that we came from sponges.   The
analogy between our bodies and the tabernacle is certainly
to be revealed, if God gives the Spirit to enlighten the
Scripture, which contains the solution of *all* mysteries.

I believe Christ is God, the Second Person of the Trinity,
incarnated in a sinless body, imbued with the Holy Ghost
without measure.   I believe man is *of God*, incarnated in a
sinful body, imbued with such measure of the Holy Ghost
as God gives.   In the soul's depths is implanted the revelation of God's truth; the Holy Ghost does but awaken this
consciousness.   The soul is Divine, is capable of understanding Divine things, is not to be affected by evil or to be corrupted or alloyed.   It can be dormant, retire out of view,
hindered from revealing itself, being obscured by the flesh
and sense.   God is the Creator and Almighty; the soul is
of God, Divine, unable to create, but eternal.   It is possible
for the soul to know Divine things which the body cannot

and does not know.   Children are essentially animal in every way; they are more occupied with their little stomachs than anything else, but they are spiritual as well.

3 *February*, 1882.—I have to thank God for several precious working truths—" God forbid that I should glory " is one.   It is connected with idols in one's heart.   One hugs a thought of some sort or another about politics or such like.   God shoots an arrow at it and it becomes dust.   Again, the only way to fight Anak is to keep in union with God in Christ—when one goes out or in, when one writes or receives a letter, meets or speaks to any one. This is what is meant by the jealousy of God : He will be partners with us entirely in all we do or think.

He also has been gracious enough to let me see the benefits derived from earthly snubs, they are reminders of Him, like the iron belt or hair shirt of the old monks; one is so very forgetful that one needs these thorns, though they are no longer thorns when they give this benefit, but are healthful lancet stabs.

Another truth God gave me is, that the Holy Ghost must participate in our Scripture reading ; that we must in mind keep in union with Christ.   Thank God also, I can now pray and wish that every one in the world were holier than I am—higher than I in the future world.

8 *February*, 1882.—I believe, humbly, that God will grant me this life of continual union with Him.   The great danger is in the motives for wishing it ; for if you seek this in order to speak wisdom and lord it over others, it is a wrong motive.   Wisdom must go with humility, and with a preference of others to self.   Good-bye for the moment.

16 *February*, 1882.—I send you a packet with two brooches, and also a *roll;* eat it, I hope it will do you good.   I send one paper, and I have another, a very big one, on "The Tabernacle and the Human Body," but it is not finished.   I confess to having a sort of fear of the

sacrifices and Israelitish ceremonial, they have been so twisted and written about. However, there is no doubt these details were not given for nothing ; they contain solid meat, if one can find it, or rather if God will reveal it.

I shall send you the whole paper when God gives me light, for it will serve to show you how I got involved in the subject, and how it unrolled as I went along. Look at the Tabernacle, a lot of wood and tapestry : nothing more ; yet, with God in it, it is everything. That it is the type of every man, both actually and spiritually, I think is sure ; and the solution is in the Scriptures, which are Christ. In the carnal man the Tabernacle is in ruins.

I should like to send you the paper now, for the thoughts are sketched out ; but I have got involved in the ceremonial law, and, as it needs close reading of Scripture, it requires a long time to finish it. The difficulty is to separate that part which refers to Christ, and that part which refers to man. If I knew Christ, then it would be easy to discern.

18 *February*, 1882.—What a wonderful history ! these thoughts of eatings and sacraments. Eat in *distrust of God*, and *trust in self*, and eat in *distrust of self*, and *trust in God*. It is very wonderful, as is also that the analogy should be so hidden. Eve knew no more what would happen to her by her eating, than we do by our eating.

What do you think of letting —— see the papers ? Do not do so, unless you like ; all the papers I have sent you are yours, and yours only. Do not lose patience with the Tabernacle paper ; it is full of meat, but requires some little patience. Read it quickly through first, then read it slowly again ; you will believe me when I say it will well repay you.

The creature is in bondage waiting for the redemption of the body. The present Jerusalem is in bondage and is a type of the heavenly Jerusalem, the city of the living God, His Temple. The same *is, not will be*, the mother of us all. Do you remember I used to say that you could see by the eyes of the scuttlers (boys) whether they *knew* God lived in them, or whether they did not know it?[1]

6 *March,* 1882.—I question whether the Government will let me go to Palestine. However, wherever I may go, my Lord, who is my companion, will go with me. I am wonderfully well in health.

I can assure you one does get great strength from the Sacrament. I will let you know where to send letters, &c. I feel as if I were going to embark on a strange ocean.

8 *March,* 1882.—I have come to a conclusion; may God give me strength to keep it! *Stop all the newspapers.* It is no use mincing the matter; as the disease is dire, so also must be the remedy.

These are the words which have done this: "My son, *unglue* thyself from the world and its vanities. Put on the Lord Jesus Christ, find Him thy wisdom, righteousness, redemption, thy riches, thy strength, thy glory" (*Christ Mystical*). Somehow I thought it must come to this ere long. If I ever need to know, or give my opinion on any subject, then Christ will give me the necessary wisdom. Newspapers feed a passion I have for giving my opinion; therefore, as we have no right to judge and have nothing to do with this world (of which we are not), this feeding must be cut short.

You drew a bow at a venture with your full strength, and you have done for your brother; the arrow has gone in up to its feathers. "He that speaketh of himself seeketh his own glory" (John vii. 18). Why, you have knocked down the work of years; what have I ever been talking of but self? Why do I go to Syria? Supposing I keep myself from any political work, the very looking out of that

---

[1] The boy Capsune, whom General Gordon rescued from the slave-dealers in 1879, asked the lady who had charge of him, whether she was quite sure that Gordon Pasha still kept his blue eyes, and did she think he could "see all through me now?" Another day he said he was "quite sure Gordon Pasha could see quite well in the dark, because he had the light inside him."

Arabah valley, and writing about it, is nothing more than advertising oneself. I do not know how it will end, but it must end well, for God has given me the determination to abide near Him, and He will keep me to it, I firmly trust.

On leaving this, as I expect to do in April, my route might be by the Zanzibar coast; so, if the pillar of cloud moves me, I shall go there. The giving up the papers may cause the starvation of my passion for politics, and that scab may drop off. God has shown me what the scabs are :—Evil speaking, lying, slandering, back-biting, scoffing, self-conceit, boasting, silly talking, and some few more.

I would not wish to be rid of these, *unless God so willed it*, for they keep me down, and prevent my treading on my weaker brethren, which I should be sure to do if I was rid of them. The Canaanites (Ex. xxiii. 28, 29) are good, for otherwise the beasts will increase. So that I cannot say, any more than Israel could, what I shall do or where I shall go. I believe I shall not be confounded. I asked to know Christ's life; it may be, it is being taught me, in actual experience as far as my measure. We would like to know Christ's life in our rooms, *from the Bible;* God teaches it to us actually *by the trials of this life.*

I can humbly think that my present frame of mind is a direct answer to my prayers, and can even thank God for the same. The buildings I had thought so substantial are shot through and ruined by God's arrows—one of them shot from your bow reached the mark, for which I am thankful. I wish I could—no, it is not right to do so—but I have a sort of wish that I could be rid of *Colonel Gordon.*

Mind and be not faithless, if I go to Natal and come up the Zanzibar coast. I have prayed for direction, and God will direct me; and at this moment self-conceit is out of favour. You remember Agag, he was an open enemy; self-conceit is an insidious, insinuating one.

15 *March*, 1882.—I have learnt a truth, and of necessity
was in travail ere it came forth. It is this: our Lord did not
even attempt to raise the apathy of the Jewish priests; He
only answered when they questioned Him. His words were
to His disciples, and to the multitude; He did not set up
as a redresser of wrong, at any rate; it was only when the
priests, &c. came to Him that He reproached them with
their failings.

I believe this is the "*Be still*," and if one thinks over it,
one can see that more, *in fact everything*, is done by the
Spirit, and *nothing* by the flesh. I hope this will be a
solace to you, as it is to me. It would seem that, as one
grows in grace, there is less and less to *do*, and more and
more to look after in ourselves.

Really I begin to like God's arrows, and endeavour to
seek the reason why they are shot; generally one can
ascertain. Sometimes a lurking thought exists, like a small
fibre, that the action one has taken is not quite right, yet
the bulk of one's reasoning is that it is right; all of a
sudden one sees the fibre is right and the bulk wrong.
These little fibres are often neglected in the hurry of the
moment. It is odd they should all go back to the old, old
story: "Do to others as you would wish them to do
to you."

I have been torn in ribbons; all my cherished little
conceits have been shown to be tawdry pasteboard, gilt
and rubbish. I have been robbed of all *my* jewels, *i.e.* I
found them to be shingle stones; it was painful, but I felt
the truth and rejoiced at it.

It had struck me before, in 1865, that the ordinary
Christian life of *non-assurance* was not a sufficient gain to
have come from Christ's incarnation and death; then I
learnt *assurance*, then followed the knowledge of His indwelling, then the solution in my mind of the problem of
the safety of others; and then I halted, having given up the
thought that in this life it was possible to regenerate the

body, putting down its failings as venial and connected with our human infirmities. In time it came to me that surely some growth, some improvement, ought to be made, some increased sanctification ought to be expected, one ought not to be so very barren; glimpses of selfishness, self-seeking, pride, and a certain weariness of one's *châteaux d'Espagne* came to me, and led to this—Christ dwelleth in us, and His light enlightens all dark places; the *châteaux d'Espagne* were found to be dens in which snakes had got coiled up, and when the light was turned on them out they came, making one's self-sufficiency as obnoxious as when one first knew the law, though in a milder way. Now I do think there is a great deal more to do in clearing out these places; I had before thought only death could come and deliver me, now it is different: there is still work to do, though I continue to look on death as gain.

CAPE TOWN, 4 *May*, 1882.—I left Mauritius on the 4th of April, and reached Cape Town at 4.30 P.M. on the 3rd of May. It was a long, weary passage, and I was very seedy for some days. A sailing-vessel is indeed a trial. However, God strengthened me all along, and I was given to be submissive and to consider that He ruled for the best in delaying my passage, both to teach me patience, and also that by His ordaining I was not to appear at the Cape Town stage of life until a certain day. I landed at 7 P.M., dead tired, and got unnoticed to an hotel.

Now the pillar of cloud and fire—how will it move? God will guide me. Look at the paper I send you, and you will see announcements of volunteer drill, &c.! *That* I could not do! It would end like the Ripon affair (which by the way was about two years ago). We were nearly put into quarantine, but God delivered us from that trouble. To take the volunteers of Cape Colony would be like taking the volunteers in England; and that I could not stand, I feel sure.

You will not care overmuch for my secular history, but

will say, " What did you learn on the passage ? "   Well, the
passage was truly a fearful trial ; dirt prevailed in everything ; the bilge-water literally, when pumped out from
decayed sugar, tore up the very inmost parts of the stomach,
and showed me that, if that was wrong, life was unendurable.
I am not generally sick at sea, but I was nearly dead with
it ; perhaps it was Mauritius fever coming out.   Salt water
had got into the tank and we had to drink it.   I was very,
very ill, but through it all I would not have changed one
iota of the voyage

I learnt that, to be like Christ, we must not only have
our will subordinated to His, but be *delighted* to have it so
and even seek it.   To be like Christ : what a deal it means,
and how very feebly the mass of the world realize it !   This
I learnt a little of ; then I found I had quite a scab over
my feelings, that they were not sensitive to what daily gifts
Christ gives us in the ordinary walk of life—for truly in our
natural state we have no right to anything, and, considering
the animosity the devil has against us, we might expect a
fearful series of trials, if Christ did not protect us.   Then
again I saw self-conceit more clearly, and the obstacle it is
to union with Christ.   Yet with all that, I think I shall
write on Egypt ; but, D.V., it will not be a bitter letter, for
I have asked God's direction.   He gives wisdom, and my
letter, though feeble, will be in His strength, for truly He
has given me to care little for what man says, or for the
world's honour, praise, or money.   I like very much the
hymn " Abide with me."

10 *May*, 1882.—I am a *rag*, that voyage in the *Scotia* has
killed me.   I went to Dr. Abercromby, and he told me I
was on the verge of an attack of jaundice.   I am certainly
better, but feel far from well.   Listless, worried in *body*, not
a bit in spirits, and as if I had eaten copper.   I want to get
into the position of delighting to accept and do His will,
yet I feel so very much inclined to wish His will might be
my release.

Earth's joys grow very dim, its glories have faded.   My Mauritius sojourn has quenched to a great degree my desire for anything but to be with Jesus.   Everybody is very kind here and complimentary, but all compliments are to me but sounds of the wind.   If it was Jesus' will, how delighted I should be to be called away, to be a nail in His footstool, and how willingly I would have every one to be higher than me in heaven !

I wonder whether you enter into my feelings as to those wonderful truths shown me in the Mauritius ; they are true Koh-i-noors.   I feel, since I left there, that God has said, " I have given you great wealth, and now I will hide Myself for a time, to see if you will trust Me."   I feel that, hidden as His face is, I can do so, and rejoice that I am sick and troubled.

If I go up I shall succeed, for it is nothing to Him to help with many or with few (2 Chronicles xiv. 11) ; with respect to my money affairs, " The Lord is able to give thee much more than this " (2 Chronicles xxv. 9) ; what an un-satisfactory religion it is that takes God's promises as mere talk !   Praise now humbles me, it does not elate me ; did the world praise Jesus ? and what right have we to take this praise of men, when it is due to Him ?

I do not think it would be good to send the letters round, which I write to you—what I think, and what is, as it were, between us two.   Your troubles are mine, and *vice versâ;* others do not even give me their thoughts, and I see no further reason to give them the analysis of my heart and its manifold changes.

Why am I not in the *Gazette?*   I will not move, but it seems odd.   Anyway, if they do not promote me, I shall hope for strength to bear it.   *He* is ruler, and I love Jesus irrespective of His mighty rank and power.   At Communion this morning I asked Christ to let me rest, and then He should take the post of COMMANDANT-GENERAL, and that I should be passive in the matter.   Good-bye, my dear Augusta. *fifteen years more.*

20 *May*, 1882.—I went to see Cetewayo, and felt for him, and tried to cheer him. I gave him a stick with an ivory head—a beauty—which had been given me by the Sultan of Perak, who was a prisoner at the Seychelles. When I told Cetewayo that I had always been interested in him and that he must have hope, with a deep "*Ah!*" he pointed upwards. He is a fine savage.

BEAUFORT W., 21 *May*, 1882.—I reached this at 8 A.M. and went to church here—a nice service. I am going into a regular hornets' nest. Sometimes I think, "Why did I take this burden upon me?" It seemed as if I sought it; but then things are all ruled, and I have the great comfort of my Mauritius retirement. One thing I find is, that, as we advance in union with Christ, we get more and more sensitive to our deficiencies; this is only natural, but it certainly does keep one very much alive—I expect, because one is unused to the frame of mind.

PORT ELIZABETH, 25 *May*, 1882.—Arrived here last night; had a comfortable enough journey, very nice quiet thoughts. I trust God will smite self-conceit; this demon is most powerful.

I like the Boers; they are a God-fearing people. Also I like the colonists; they are a fine set. I have hopes that the native question can be settled quietly both for the colony and the natives; and, though I say it, a grub like myself, who can put himself into other people's skins and find out their feelings, is better adapted than a bigger man for the solution of such questions. Anyway, the disarming of tribes must strike any one as a foolish, impossible thing to do, when alongside of it are broken promises.

Nothing in particular happened on the road. I was cross because —— would look after me and tired me.

I heard of my promotion yesterday, and thanked God for it. I scarcely expected it.

KING WILLIAM'S TOWN, 1 *June*, 1882.—I am very well; things do not weigh on me as in old times; Christ is the

Captain of the Hosts, and I roll the burden on Him. One
thing I cannot do just yet, viz. write papers on the Pearls;
somehow I cannot tune my harp to do so; however, I suppose now is the time of ploughing and seed time; here I
am, and if God will use me and keep me from self-conceit,
it is well. I am glad I can keep the vista before me of rest
in Jesus, and that things do not greatly move me.

I have still my Koh-i-noor—the desire to depart. I guard
that most carefully, in spite of all the worries and goings to
and fro.

5 *June*, 1882.—I send the new card. Would you kindly
write to Cox and get for your drawer the commission of
major-general, so as to complete the set? I do not go into
detail of my work here; it would not interest you. I am
using my energy as much as I can, to get things into shape
after my ideas. If you mix the contents of the white and
blue papers of a Seidlitz powder, you will understand what I
have done here : that will suffice as a description.

If I leave this place, you would not mind; for the things
of the unseen world are worth all those of the seen, and
truly a life spent in His service is of greater worth than one
spent in these temporary things, which necessarily make one
carnal to some degree; not that they ought to do so. My
constant prayer is against Agag, who, of course, is here, and
as insinuating as ever. He has some footing for his presence, as the things relate to his department. He is very
subtle. It is difficult to rule and yet be compassionate
and kind. However, if one's general line of conduct is
in that direction, perhaps in time the difficulty will
disappear.

Both clergymen here preach the great secret, the indwelling, but not as strongly as I could wish. Their churches
are full, while, where it is not preached, they are comparatively empty.

I wonder how you are getting on; I have had no letters
since I left Mauritius. If you get the general's pay at the

end of June, you will be all right as far as money is concerned to the end of the year.

F—— is a very nice fellow, and keeps me in order. Write to him; he knows all about you. He receives the truth, but has not reached the point of looking on death as life. He is more humble and better tempered than I am, and in consequence he is sometimes bullied about things; so tell him to stick up more.

I feel ashamed, but send you another gold pen *hors de combat*. However, it was not trodden upon.

7 June, 1882.—To-day F—— and I had a terrible discovery. We found, disguised in a form which we had been petting and fondling, our old familiar friend. For some time F—— would not believe it possible it was Agag, and then, when he could no longer deny it, he fell back, and said he had known it all along. I rent him sorely for not saying so. To say we have got rid of him is no use, as he will be back again and again fondled.

However, F—— has now lost some of his awe of me, so I hope he will in future be more outspoken; though, between ourselves, I believe F—— thought Agag was as fine a fellow as I did. The subject was an ultimatum to the Colonial Government of some business which we *had* THOUGHT *they ought to have shown more attention to.* This letter was rent in pieces when it was discovered. It is certainly humiliating to see the vast difference between one's words, "to leave all to God," and one's acts, so very diametrically opposite to that line of conduct. One feels inclined to withdraw from the combat altogether, and go into seclusion; but even there I expect Agag would pursue in some form.

Sometimes I think these attacks come when one has been speaking much about the mysteries of Scripture knowledge. They are arrows shot at self-conceit. Certainly self-conceit is a very powerful enemy, and scarcely to be subdued. Ask me if I have any ability or talent above others, and I will

say, "None; what I do is God's work." Yet over and over
again I find I am lording it over some poor fellow, and
taking pleasure in so doing. It is very humiliating and
good for one when one sees it.

8 *June*, 1882.—F—— this morning, in reply to an
accusation that he was Egypt to me, *i. e.* the reed that went
into my hand when I leant on it, denied it, and said he had
seen Agag all along! He was driven at for this, for the
fact that he had seen it all along proved *he was* Egypt to me.
He is rapidly losing all respect for me, and will no longer
allow it is night, because I say it is, when it is really day.

I am going to see Mr. Stewart, a clergyman near here,
who has a large industrial school.

I have said "Good-bye" to ——. I cannot make him
out. He is very gentlemanly, but he is an oyster that I
cannot open.

11 *June*, 1882.—You remember that I had asked my
Saviour to undertake the post of COMMANDANT-GENERAL;
that I then wrote my reports, and then must needs act on
my own will, and insist on an immediate answer. If you
read 1 Samuel xiii. and xv., you will see that Saul acted in
both cases in the same way. He agreed to do as Samuel
ordained, and then he lost patience and acted after his own
ideas, thus breaking the covenant with God. Hence all my
troubles. It was virtually using God for one's own ends.
"To obey is better than sacrifice, to hearken than the fat
of rams." Saul was frightened about the Philistines, and
wanted to keep the best of the spoil of Amalek. He
reasoned for himself, forgetting his compact. Faith (David)
is to reign in his place. I am comforted for Saul; Amalek
was his trouble as well as mine (Exodus xvii. 16).

What we are to do is to ask God to direct us, then to act,
and then to be patient. God lets us act, but He keeps to
Himself all the issues; but if we follow up by expediency
actions, we throw over all faith—we virtually obtain wisdom
to act from God and then throw Him over.

I have learnt from this episode; but I own that, had I been more quiet, I think God would have shown it to me sooner; but one is so mixed up with carnal things and talking, there is no time to think. It was only when in the carriage *en route* to Lovedale by myself that I was given to see my error. I have come to think that if, with a due reference to our Lord, we decide on a line of action, it matters little what that line is, provided we follow it and wait His pleasure: thus, if I decide to go to London, I should go there, unless unforeseen circumstances, over which I have no control, prevent it; but I have no right to create those unforeseen circumstances.

This is not a good illustration, but you will understand me. I wish I was out of this, but I have no right to liberate myself. I think, if the War Office refuse to give me my 500*l.* a year, I may use that opportunity; but I must not create one myself.

Somehow I do not like the carnal life I live, it wears me. Sir H. Parkes was right to say, "Be quiet." In reality I am "not moved" by the events which are around me —at any rate, "not *greatly* moved," not nearly so much as in the Soudan—the people do not interest me in the same way—yet one's natural discussion-like nature gets aroused. You would not care a bit if —— had said this or that, yet you cannot help discussing it, especially if what she had said was misrepresented by others; so with me.

No, I do not like anything which disturbs the mining operations. I had a nice Communion to-day, and renewed the covenant that Jesus was to work, and that I was not to interfere with my will with what He settled. I fear I write much of myself, but I find little else to write about, for I do not think you would care for all the routine work of this place.

Had a good sermon to-night at the Scotch church—the rich man and his barns overflowing, "This night thy soul shall be required of thee." The rich man wanted to live apart from God, God was not to have His share. It came home to me!

Good night! I fear my letters are very full of "*I*," but it is an unsatisfactory "I," so you will not mind it. All our troubles come from impatience, from not trusting God. It is like moving, when the cloud is still.

DORDRECHT (forty miles west of Queenstown), 17 *June*, 1882.—Your kind letter, dated May 17, came last night; this is the first letter I have had since I left Mauritius. Instinctively I thought you had been ill, quite apart from my not having heard from you; it is odd. Kind regards to the Beadons. I wrote to Cowell and sent him an amusing account of an assembly of Basutos, in which they say the Queen ought to bear them on her back in a skin, as they carry their own children. I am all right, and hope to be used by my Lord, if He thinks fit; but no pearls are yet to be dived for, one's life is too unsettled. I am, D.V., growing, but I cannot yet write the new truths. Good-bye, my dear Augusta, I sincerely hope you are not suffering; I dare say no more.

UMTATA, 27 *June*, 1882.—I arrived here on Sunday, and go to Kokstadt on Wednesday. I hope to be back at Capetown in about twenty days at the outside, having done most of the country, and being well up in most of the questions. I am very well, and, thank God, in covenant with Him, which is a great comfort to me. I do not write long letters for I am generally moving about, so I will say good-bye, you shall have a good letter soon.

KOKSTADT, 2 *July*, 1882.—Look at Jeremiah xiv. 21, "Do not *disgrace* the throne of Thy glory." Is not that a daring expression? "Break not Thy covenant," *i. e.* do not give us up because we give Thee up. It is the covenant of faith, or of God's indwelling, for these two words are analogous. I like this very much. Anything we do out of covenant, is worked by God, the other covenanting party, to our good; only then we have not the comfort. Agag has been pretty quiet after his late outburst.

KING WILLIAM'S TOWN, 1 *August,* 1882.—I have just come back from Port Elizabeth and have caught a bad cold, which is trying. As for the work, it does not move me now. What frets me is, that in being energetic I sometimes am not kind to others. There is one prayer in *Gold Dust* which struck me: "O God, treat me *to-morrow* as I have treated my fellow-man *to-day.*"

In the Bible version of Psalm xxxvii. 8, is "Cease from anger, and forsake wrath, fret not thyself in anywise to do evil." In the Prayer-book version it is, "Leave off from wrath, and let go displeasure, *fret not thyself, else shalt thou be moved to do evil.*" Thus it would seem that, when we worry ourselves, we risk *being moved to do evil.* Thus A. does not do what I wish; he may be wrong, and I may be right. I fret, so to say, over it, and *am moved to do evil.* Daily I am more and more convinced that the non-assertion of one's rights is great gain, though only to be acquired by a closer union with Christ.

Taking it materially and carnally, it is certain that Christ knew both this and the future world thoroughly, and He considered it much better worth while to give up His will here, knowing He would gain in the next world; for, even He needed the "hope set before Him," ere He despised the shame of the cross. One knows it is very hard to accomplish, but it is a great gain to see and to desire self-abnegation. I think if we could press on in union with Him, we should cross the hedge of separation and find self-abnegation no pain, but really a pleasure. Even with our small progress, there was a time when what we now enjoy—communion with Christ—was irksome, yet how changed that is now! for we wish for more communion and are depressed when deprived of it.

The soul must feed on the body: the feeding of the soul is death to the body, we must suffer in either one or the other; but the suffering of the body is less than that of the soul.

I have but little pleasure in the things of this world. This command eats up my thoughts and words. I discuss this and that, though I firmly and truly believe that Christ rules all things. As for what happens in Egypt, it does not move me, for I know Christ rules there, and in Him I rule also, as much as if I were actually on the spot.

12 *August*, 1882.—How odd, those leaflets being in Dutch, and my wanting them, and your sending them just as I am about to go up to the Free State, when, as in the "Auld time long ago," I shall be dropping them along the road, near the Boer towns. What hundreds I did give away; how I used to run miles, if I saw a scuttler (boy) watching crows in a field! If I or any one else went now to Gravesend and dropped them, how quickly men, now grown up, would remember that time. Send me the whole lot out unless you want them, I mean of all languages; it is the loveliest leaflet I ever saw, and it still looks fresh.[1]

[1] "Whosoever shall confess that Jesus is the Son of God, God dwelleth in him, and he in God" (1 John iv. 15).
You believe in your heart that Jesus is the Son of God? Then God dwells in your body, and if you ask Him, "O Lord! I believe that Jesus is the Son of God; show me, for His sake, that Thou livest in me," He will make you feel His presence in your heart. Many believe sincerely that Jesus is the Son of God, but are not happy, because they do not believe *that* which God tells them: that He lives in them, both in body and soul, if they confess Jesus to be His Son. You believe this statement, yet do not feel God's presence? Ask Him to show Himself to you, and He *will* surely do so.
"Know ye not that your body is the temple of the Holy Ghost which is in you, which ye have of God, and ye are not your own" (1 Corinthians vi. 19).
"Come unto me, all *ye* that labour and are heavy laden, and I will give you rest. Take my yoke upon you, and learn of me; for I am meek and lowly in heart: and ye shall find rest unto your souls" (Matthew xi. 28, 29).
"Verily, verily, I say unto you, he that believeth on me hath everlasting life" (John vi. 47).
"Trust in the Lord with all thine heart, and lean not on thine own understanding. In all thy ways acknowledge Him, and He shall direct thy paths" (Proverbs iii. 5, 6).

I am much better than I was, and hope you are also well again. We are all getting old.

I find now much more ease in prayer, can enter the Presence more freely; have less of what one may call remorse, inasmuch as I cannot pretend to anything like goodness in myself. In some degree evil-speaking of others and scoffing is still rife. It is inseparable, for the moment, from one's post of command; not that it is really inseparable, but, because I am frail. I see sparks of jewels, but, living as I do, have not time to dig them out.

I feel now that I could settle down, having no desire for posts of honour. I wonder what you really think of those jewels I sent you.

It is a year since the things in the "stone-room" were packed; I wonder if they are rotten? Do what you think best as to having them examined.

You do not know into what a whirlpool of cares I have got by this appointment; somehow they are more serious than those of the Soudan. You see, in the latter place I had supreme authority; here, though I have great influence, I have to explain everything and discuss it, but will not weary you with details of the worries. I can only say, God has often "chosen the weak things of the world to confound the things which are mighty," and it is sure that He will help me, for I *do not care* for the glory, such as it is, of success, but am willing to leave it to Him.

I have mentioned that one has vistas of great things, glimpses of jewels, by the side of which those which are behind, though invaluable, are somewhat eclipsed. I may

---

"Call upon me in the day of trouble: I will deliver thee" (Psalm l. 15).

"They shall hunger no more, neither thirst any more . . . . for the Lamb . . . . shall feed them and shall lead them unto living fountains of waters, and God shall wipe away all tears from their eyes. And there shall be no more death, neither sorrow nor crying, neither shall there be any more pain, for the former things are passed away" (Revelation vii. 16, 17; xxi. 4).

better say, however, that the glimpses are only views of the same jewels from other points of view.

14 *August*, 1882.—Fancy, since I left Mauritius, with the exception of twenty-nine days on board ship, I have been living at hotels, and, I may say, have not talked of the pearls to more than a dozen people.

A dear little lamb, aged six, son of the hotel-keeper, died this morning. I saw the dove yesterday, and it said in its suffering that it knew "Jesus." I saw his little sheath this morning, and envied the peace he was in. Now with Jesus! This time yesterday sucking an orange!

25 *August*, 1882.—I am pretty well, but still have rheumatism in my back. I am in covenant, and can realize more the personality of Christ—can think more of Him as I would of another man. He seems nearer like this, than He did before.—How glad I am not to be in Egypt now!

XALANGA, 29 *August*, 1882.—Read the enclosed papers; they will tell you of the crisis. I am pretty well, but, as you may imagine, in rather a fix, for really things look critical out here, and if a war broke out it would be one of races. Perhaps, if my conscience allowed me to take duty in it, I might be a gainer in one way, *if it was His will*, for I am tired of myself.

1 *September*, 1882.—The archers wounded me sorely for three days, so that I knew not where to turn for help; but I rose again. I have not yet been given to see why I was wounded so terribly; I may see it shortly. You will not have many letters now for a time, for I am going to Basutoland. Do not bother about the —— or ——: it is no use, and it is better to give up your own will than to be troubled. Remember what was said to me when I did not want my mother to go out in the wet; that it was because I wanted my will to rule over her.

I prefer to do what I like, and, as far as I can, I put myself into the skin of others, and think how they feel it they are thwarted. Great love is akin to great jealousy. God is "*love.*" His name is "*Jealous.*"

2 *October,* 1882.—I have my hands full, and am in doubt as to what will happen; but all will come right. I must wait till God speaks to me and shows me how to act. Much as I should like to go home and see you now you are ill, I can only pray God to put on me some of your pain, if not all; but, even in doing that, I fear I am doing you an injury, for what you suffer now will be so fully made up to you hereafter.

I have some nice thoughts, but need time to write them out. Many will agree that in man is a germ which is Divine; that the word of God calls it out from its dormant state into new life. If you consider this, you will see how very little the clergy think of this vital truth, "*Because ye are sons,* God hath sent forth the Spirit" (Galatians iv. 6); "Forasmuch then as the children are partakers of flesh and blood," it behoved Him also to partake of the same, &c. &c. (Hebrews ii. 14). It is not a question of reasoning. The clergy think a new germ is put into man by baptism, or by what they call conversion; but the germ exists dormant until God the Holy Ghost awakens it; the preacher is only a watering-pot, as it were. This is most important in preaching. Good-bye, I leave you in Jesus's hands in confidence.

4 *October,* 1882.—God is love, and He will not let us deprive ourselves of great blessings for temporary relief. I now can take things very differently. When a trouble comes and I wish it away, I think, " Perhaps in this wish I am losing something," so I am quiet. How different things look now that we see that union with God is rest, disunion is unrest! that is the whole secret; it is not what we do or leave undone, it is not this or that sin, all is summed up in *union* or *disunion.*

It is odd how little I think of Egypt or the Soudan; it is all now passed from me. If I should leave this colony, I

do not know what I should do.   Shall I go to the Congo?
For me life is ended ; I live more or less in the future life,
thanks to God.   My *Friend* is with me, and I am quieted
with the knowledge of His rule.   We are under no *punishment* now, we are only at *school;* no one likes school life
away from home.   I think, if you go *home :* who is there
that will care for my pearls of great price ?

KING WILLIAM'S TOWN, 6 *October*, 1882.—The telegrams
will show you that the Cape Colony chapter of my life is
over.   I am so glad to be free of all this turmoil.   There
will be a fearful row, but these things have not moved me
at all.   I have thought more of a scuttler who shed tears
when I spoke to him of God's living in him, than I have of
all this affair.   What a queer life mine has been, with these
fearful rows continually occurring !   They will amuse you I
hope.   I am at East London and enjoy the quiet.

"SS. KINFAUN'S CASTLE," 20 *October*, 1882.—I shall,
D.V., be in England when you get this.   I shall go by sea
to Gravesend, and on to Southampton at once.   Whether
men praise you, it does not make you better, or whether
they blame you, it does not make you worse.   God judges
by motives, men by actions (Thomas à Kempis).   When I
went to the Cape I prayed for glory to God and the welfare
of the people, so I am glad *I* got no glory out of it.

I shall be glad to see you again.   I hope I have increased
in grace ; I think God has made me grow.

The King of the Belgians may ask me to go to the Congo.
Query : Shall I go or not?   God will decide.   If I do not
go there, then I shall go to Palestine.   I am now, I hope,
getting quieter and quieter, though sometimes the old
writing mania seizes me, but it soon goes off.

3 *November*, 1882.—We passed Madeira yesterday, and
I saw some papers ; but was not much, if at all, moved by
the different news.   As for Egypt, affairs seem to move
much as I thought they would ; all things are governed to
God's glory.   I have lots of small diamonds (not Kimberley

ones) out of the Scriptures for you ; I want time to arrange and write them.[1]

LONDON, 27 *December*, 1882.—If one thinks of it, one cannot deny that the happiness of man entirely and altogether depends on God, that indeed He *is* happiness, and it cannot exist out of Him ; therefore, if any are unhappy, it is because they are hindered by some cherished thing from being in union with Him.

I truly believe that there is no limit to the intimacy I may reach with Him, if I give up all resting on creatures ; and I say it is, even humanly speaking, reasonable to seek this union. It is like this : I have a firm belief that I cannot possibly get any happiness apart from God, that I might as well seek for water from a stone as try to do so. I quite agree that *appearances* are against it, and that it does seem as though I could get happiness from other sources ; but I have my past experience and God's word against such a delusion, and I have come to the belief that it is only by such union that happiness can be obtained.

I like this thought, for it is clear and distinct ; it makes the man who accepts it free from place and circumstance ; it shows him he can do no good except in exhorting others to the same union ; I hope to push on towards it, and wish all others would do the same.

28 *December*, 1882.—I am just leaving Charing Cross. It is certain that *any leaning* on Egypt, namely, on *every person* or *thing* apart from Him, must be diametrically opposed to *indwelling*, for it is virtually saying that that is insufficient.

SS. "QUETTA," 4 *January*, 1883.—I have got this since I left you : That, as God is the source of all good and of all happiness, *He* is *Himself* sufficient to satisfy all our longings and to fill up the gap which the loss of the world leaves.

---

[1] General Gordon arrived in England on the 7th November, 1882 ; and after a short stay, most of which he spent in Southampton, he left, on the 28th December, for the Holy Land.

"Doles" are the feelings we have that we have lost the world and not gained Him. Generally when in "Doles" we try for something else to satisfy us; this may succeed for a time, but the gap re-opens; and we again try and fill it, with the same result. This goes on for a long time; it is a vicious circle, and has no advance in it: virtually it is leaving the union, quitting the directions or ruling of the Pillar. I have been given this view; and, when the "Doles" come, I seek their removal *only* from God, and set my face against any aid from other persons or things. I feel sure this is the right way, for it is God's way. The remedy for your "Doles" is the same as mine: to accept *all things* as from the hand of God, and pray for those who cross our path. If you prayed for them many times a day, I am convinced you would feel quite differently towards them, and would see that your will is to be governed by God. Remember, with regard to Saul's sin, he was in "Doles," and did not *wait* for his deliverance from God, "he forced himself," he said to Samuel (1 Sam. xiii. 12).

This is one thing God gave me: the other is, that whether we may apprehend it or not, the Scripture contains the mind of Christ, and is, when illuminated with the Spirit, as if Christ was ever talking to us. Now, we should think that if Christ was ever near to talk with us, *that* should suffice us, and consequently, *as I believe that in theory*, I try to realize it in practice. I have never known, and probably never shall know, how very requiring God is of our service. He requires *everything* from us, and, not till we give up every thought or wish for anything but Himself, will He disclose Himself to us fully. Say we have one hundred things: if we give up ninety-nine and three-quarters to Him, yet we shall not realize more than a very small portion of His Presence. One might expect that, by giving up so nearly all, one would be greatly blessed with His fulness; but no, *everything* must be given up, and I believe it is that little quarter we retain which prevents us reaping our reward.

If you look at it, you will see it is right, for the retention of the quarter means God AND some creature comfort, *not God alone.* It is asking God to serve along with idols, even if it be only a *little one.* Any particle of self must be enmity to God, and unrest.

I believe truly that this abnegation of self is to be reached; at least it is the goal set before us. Christ must *actually die,* not come *very near* death; and so must we, if we would rise. I once thought it possible to bargain with Christ; to say, I will give up half of my desire of the world, and gain, in the gap, a corresponding measure of Christ. It was no good: I lost the half, but did not get the measure filled. Then I tried to give up a little more, but with the same result; now I think God has shown me that it is not the least use trying these subtle bargains; that the giving up little by little is more wearisome and trying than *one* surrender, and *that* I trust He will give me power to make.

I have believed theoretically that I can do nothing to help my progress, and am now beginning to realize it. All I can do is to remove the hindrances to such progress; and that, I think, is in my power, thus: God gives me a desire to be in close communion with Him—I could not have that desire except from Him; also God gives me the understanding eye to see from His Scriptures that certain modes of life, speaking evil, judging others, &c., are hindrances to union.

We can do *nothing* of ourselves, *nothing;* but by the giving to us an earnest desire for closer union with Him, He works in us to remove these hindrances, and aids our efforts to do so, but, as it were, secretly. He, and He alone, can increase our growth in sanctity. A child goes along a road, a huge stone stops the way; the father gives the child a wish to remove it, and points out some nettles as hindrances for him to move; he does so, and on looking up finds the stone gone. Now, in this case the father does all, and that is the state, I think, we are in; we stop just short of peace, when one great effort would deliver us, which is more in appearance than in reality—*i. e.* it is more an effort of will than of action.

5 *January*, 1883.—I have thought over what I wrote last night, and I think it is true. Notice in your well-read Bible how, in every miracle, something has to be done by the recipient. " *Rise, take up* thy bed." " *Stretch forth* thy hand." The woman *touched* Him, and was cured. " *Go, wash* in the pool." Nearly all the miracles were accompanied by some act on the part of the receiver, except those of death, when *others led* Jesus to the dead ; also in the case of the man let down through the roof, when *others* did it ; *others* rolled back the stone of Lazarus's tomb, ere Jesus said, "Come forth." In cases where there was not faith sufficient to exercise these little efforts, no mighty acts were done—*i. e.* when man was too carnal, these miracles were not done. In the "loaves" miracles, *disciples had to distribute*.

Now here are a lot of coincidences which show the truth. If you look at the resurrection, you will see that Jesus left the tomb *before* the angel rolled back the stone. What I think is, that you read—*i. e.* eat the Scriptures, but do not digest them ; they remain crude in you ; they are not assimilated into your life as they should be, and so you have "doles." This is the case with us all.

Before anything is born again (rises from the dead) it must die (cease to exist). How can I cause "judging others" to die in me? Things die from not having food given them ; so I will try to avoid judging any one, at any rate, in words. *I will cease talking of others*, as far as I can ; then the judgments I have been so free with will die from want of food.

I know that in ceasing to "judge others," and in ceasing to " speak evil," I debar myself from much carnal pleasure, and I enter the vale of "doles." My life is flat ; but, patience ! I will stick to it, for there is an issue when God pleases, and I know that, as He is the source of comfort and happiness, He will eventually fill me with infinitely more joy in keeping His commandments than that which I lose.

Our object in life here is to *command* our own selves; to bring the body into subjection to the soul. If I reason that it is impossible for God to fill up the gap which is left by giving up these habits, I altogether deny His sufficiency. Our souls are risen, having died, and their desire is for the fulness of God's union. Our bodies are not risen, for they are not dead. The Word tells us *the mode of putting them to death*, but it will not *kill* them without an effort on our part, which effort, however futile in appearance, is all powerful.

A lady's finger launches a ship of 3000 tons. In reality it is like a feather, but it puts in motion vast powers. So it is with us. A man has a withered arm, and is told to stretch it out; he tries, and it is restored. If he reason that he cannot do so, it will remain withered; if he tries, then the difficulty is supernaturally removed by God. The effort puts in motion God's Almighty power, even as the finger launches the ship.

We see Smith coming, and are regularly upset. Events prevent our avoiding him. We meet, and find our fears are gone, have disappeared. Look at our meeting M. N. in the Avenue!

I think our spiritual nature is hungry, just as our natural nature is, and that it can only be strengthened and satisfied with certain food, which if it lacks, it becomes dull and makes the body dull also. *Neither* ought to be filled to the detriment of the other. Both have their places and nourishment; digestion is necessary for both, and the plainer the food the better. Thus the Bible is the bread of life, because through it we feed our spiritual nature (Matthew iv. 4). Often we use the Bible to fill our natural nature—viz. distort it to make it suit the condemnation of others—and then it does not satisfy us. There is a parable contained in the two natures and their feeding.

All things are types, whether we see them or not. The meat on our tables is a type of something slain for our existence, of blood shed to sustain ours. Our going to bed, and putting off our clothes, is a type of death; our rising, of resurrection; our clothes, of our earthly bodies. The world teems with types.

Thoughts like these drift through one's mind. Why do people think you must eat with them? There must be some type in the imbibing of food in common; yet, if we discussed the subject, we should be considered odd. All digestion of food is a type; part retained, part rejected; what is retained makes blood—the life. I often reason with myself that, if people say what is not true, it will have no effect in reality, as it will not really be received, even though it may please others to pretend to accept it.

In *every* man there are the two seeds, inasmuch as he is soul and body; the one of God, the other of the earth; the soul sinless, the body and affections vitiated. I consider, therefore, that the essential essence—the soul—of *every* man is perfectly safe, as it is an emanation from God; that each man is a temple of God (his soul), and at the same time a house of Satan (his body).

All mental discomfort comes from the mind of man being in divergence from the mind of God; when the two are in agreement no warfare occurs, for they work together, and the man accepts the rule of God. The less conflict, the more peace; He will have His way, and He would have us accept all events with the knowledge that He is love, whatever, and however contradictory those events may appear to *our* comprehension. It is frequently repeated in Scripture that we are virtually dead to the events of this world, and therefore can have nothing to do with them. It is extraordinary to think that He places our spiritual nature *in* the flesh with a view of separating it *from* the flesh. All events of this life tend to the willing or unwilling

death of the flesh. Life is one continual crucifixion, whether
we look on it as such or not.

PORT SAID, 11 *January*, 1883.—A man lies to another;
that other has a sore temptation to lie back. How often
we misrepresent conversations when we retail them to a
third party. What liars we are! How we colour things
to justify ourselves! All our evil actions are emanations
of death or corruption, owing to the absence of life in us.
"In deaths oft," says Paul (2 Corinthians xi. 23), "I die
daily" (1 Corinthians xv. 31). We are always either in
night or day: as naturally, so also spiritually. Our nights
are the times when we do acts of darkness, worldly acts;
for our life, in the carnal world, is as darkness ("The way
of the wicked is as darkness," Proverbs iv. 19). Our times
of spiritual life are our days. "When shall I arise and the
night be gone?" (Job vii. 4). "My soul cleaveth unto the
dust (the world), quicken thou me according to Thy Word"
(Psalm cxix. 25).

I have often thought that perhaps, while we sleep naturally,
our souls may have work elsewhere; for they are spirits,
and cannot be thought to be idle. How different the trial
of the night before appears next day. How oppressed we
are on going to bed; how strong we often feel to meet the
trial when we awake. Sometimes in nature we have the
moon at night, sometimes great storms; so is our life in the
carnal world. Sometimes we go through the world with
security, for then we have, as it were, the moon, or reflected
light from others given us; at other times we stumble
having no light. As we earnestly desire daylight when we
are stumbling along a rough road, so we should earnestly
desire inward light in our spiritual walk.

Our Saviour was crucified for imputed impiety. "He
being man" was accused of "making Himself God." He
was under the reproach of *being unclean*, of *casting out devils
by means of the devil*, of being *gluttonous* and a *wine-bibber*,

of being *mad*, of being a *friend of publicans and sinners*, of *irreligion*, of *breaking the law*, and of *sedition*.

The sin of man towards Christ personally was that, when He came as a sin-bearer into the world, we condemned Him, despised Him, ill-treated Him, and, after denying Him, slew Him, instead of sympathizing with and aiding Him to bear the burden of our sins, which were on Him. A lifetime even with our comforts seems a weary time, and *that* when we are akin to the world and without the quick sense of evil that our Lord had.

Remember me to Willie Warren;[1] he is one of Jesus' temples. I hope his "scuttle" is better.

JERUSALEM, 17 *January*, 1883.—Everything looks small and insignificant, but quite meets the idea I had of the *worldly* position of the Jews and of our Lord. In fact, the Scriptures tell the story without any pretence that either the country, people, or our Lord were of any great importance *in the world.* They are expositors of how very low the position to which He, the Lord of Lords, descended. You can realize the fact as well in England as here, by substituting a Scripture-reader of dubious birth and humble parents, exposing the fallacy of a ceremonial church-going religion, and pointing out how impossible it is to please God by such religious formalities.

We have Pharisees, clerical powers, publicans, and Sadducees now, even as they existed during Christ's stay on this earth. We have corrupt governors, thinking of expediency ; we know Judas now *in ourselves;* we get angry at some event, some expenditure on what we consider useless objects and argue that we ought to stop it. The perpetrator of such expense may snub us openly ; and we go to those who dislike him, who agree with us and tell us we are doing right. This strengthens our idea of his being wrong; so we conspire with his foes and decide we will make the man

---

[1] A Southampton crossing-sweeper.

smart for his rebuke and actions. We plausibly argue that we are doing right, and we betray him. Then, when we see this man who has offended us in the hands of his enemies, and that they will go much further than we could wish—in fact, that when agreeing with us in words they had other motives to guide them than we knew of, then we are sorry, and, as it were, *hang ourselves.* Often and often our actions are guided by the hope of a little gain. We argue : " I am doing right, and if I can gain by so doing, well, it is so much the better."

18 *January,* 1883.—I walked round the city, about two hours' quiet walking, then went in and saw the so-called Pool of Bethesda ; also the Wailing Place of the Jews. A Mohammedan (?) gave me the Psalms in Hebrew and English, open at the sixty-ninth. I read it, and it seemed wonderful how the Jews, who were kissing the stones with the greatest emotion, could not see the parallel between our Lord and the Messiah. The Jews were His church, and they are now undergoing His crucifixion. In Mark xv. 25 it says it was the third hour when they crucified Him, namely, the hour of the morning sacrifice, 9 A.M. John xix. 14 says : "About the sixth hour." Margin of your Bible says : " Some MSS. have third hour." But the new version has no marginal note, and says : "Sixth hour." Now I believe it was at the third hour, that of the morning sacrifice. All the Gospels agree that He died at the ninth hour, the time of the evening sacrifice, and when the paschal lamb was slain.

I feel, for myself, convinced that the hill near the Damascus Gate is Golgotha. From it you can see the Temple, the Mount of Olives, and the bulk of Jerusalem. His stretched-out arms would, as it were, embrace it all the day. Close to it is the slaughter-house of Jerusalem ; quite pools of blood are lying there. It is covered with tombs of Muslim ; there are many rock-hewn caves ; and gardens surround it. Now, the place of execution in our Lord's time must have been, and continued to be, an unclean place as long as the Jews held their state. The Muslim would consider such a place unclean, and it is evident the Crusaders never built on it; so, to me, this hill is left bare ever since it was first used as a place of execution, and it never can be used till the Muslim leave the country, as it has tombs on it. The little hill on the side would be just the place where the women would look on afar off, ready to run away by the road if molested. It is very nice to see it so plain and simple, instead of having a huge church built on it.

I am going to see a house three miles from Jerusalem, for there are none to let on the Mount of Olives. . . . . I have found a house at Ain Karim. It is surrounded by barren rocky hills, and will be solitary enough.

I do not care for the sites. I like the Temple, Wailing Place, *my* Golgotha, the Mount of Olives, and the Valley of Kidron; I like the *places*, not the *sites*.

Kubeibeh is the Emmaus, seven miles from here; evidently Peter had been hanging about the place of crucifixion and burial the whole day of the Resurrection, and then went off to Emmaus, as being an out-of-the-way place. He would not like to go to Bethany, where he was so well known to be connected with Jesus. All seems so natural that seeing it is a real pleasure.

It is quite unnecessary for any one to come to Palestine; just read the Scriptures in their simple words, for no one could describe it better. Put yourself in the actor's skin, and you will feel as Peter and the others did, and know their motives. The situation of Emmaus quite suits the sort of place a timid man would go to for hiding—a wild stony country with caverns all about.

I have not yet seen where Agag was hewn in pieces before the Lord, but I expect to find it (he, Agag, is still alive in all of us). —— says, he wants " quiet to realize his position."

I think it is hopeless to seek quiet in *places*, it must be quiet in *one's self*. However, he says "*he knows, feels sure*," therefore one cannot help him, except in praying for him.

19 *January*, 1883.—There are two huge heaps of cinders some twenty feet high and eighty feet long and wide, about 200 yards from the hill which I suppose to be Calvary; they are heaped up over some old cisterns. If you think of it, the red heifer was killed and burnt beyond the camp (Numbers xix.) and the ashes laid in a clean place and mixed with water, the water of separation (verse 9). This ash-heap with the cisterns in this vicinity ought to be the place, it is far enough from the hill to be clean (200 yards), while the hill, being a place of execution, was unclean. Think how many years the Jews had sacrifices, and what piles of ashes must have been collected. Another big heap of ashes and bits of burnt bone exists about 300 yards from the cistern heap, near the so-called Tomb of the Kings. All the ashes of the sacrifices for sin were taken out of the camp. The garbage of Jerusalem was burnt in the valley of Hinnom (Gehenna), so, as that is to the south and south-west of the city, and my dust-heaps are to the north, they cannot be the ashes of garbage.

I think a year here will suffice for me, and then I would go to Bow (East End). People will then have fairly forgotten me, and, D.V., I shall be well up in Palestine. . . . I have been over the Temple area, or Harem, as they call it. The rock is very curious ; it is bare, rough, and unhewn, of whitish brown stone, standing five or six feet from the floor of the mosque, and can only be touched through the bars of a railing which surrounds it; its simplicity is striking in comparison with the polished marble, mosaic, and coloured glass around : it looks just like the top of a mountain. I think it is the altar of burnt offering ; the dome covers the rock, and is 120 feet high.

I forgot to tell you that I walked over the Mount of Olives to Bethany; it is a poor little village, just as I suppose it was in the time of our Lord. From the top of the Mount of Olives you can see the Dead Sea quite plainly. To-day I went to see a model of the Tabernacle; I noted that the Cherubin over the ark had *six* wings each (see Isaiah), that in the ark of the covenant were the two tables of commandments, and on each side was a small box: the first containing the roll of the law; the second, Aaron's rod; the third, pot of manna; the fourth, mice and emerods of the Philistines. This seems to agree with the Scripture, which says in Deut. xxxi. 26, that they put the book of the law into the *side* of the ark.

Close to the dome of the rock on the *south* is a basin twenty-four feet in diameter. Now, if the rock is the altar of burnt offering, and the basin, or cup, the laver of the wilderness, or brazen sea of Solomon, it ought to be to the *east*, and the Holy of Holies to the *west;* but the man who showed me the model said that the laver was north, or south of the altar of burnt offering, so the cup now existing may be the site of Solomon's brazen sea.

I must go again and see about the Holy of Holies. You see, the real Temple was only fifty yards long and twenty-five yards wide. A, B, C, D is a raised platform; now between g and f is only thirty yards, so, if the Temple was to the west of the rock (as it must be, if the rock is the altar of burnt offering), the Holy of Holies must be now *trodden on*, as prophesied in Daniel viii. 13, by people walking between h and g. I think this is likely; the Jews will not enter the precincts, for fear of treading on the Holy of Holies. Now, I want your attention to this. E, K, L, M is the sacred square of the Muslim, and somewhere in that square was the Temple. The first thing that strikes you when you enter the square is the rock f, and the round basin R. The Temple was twice the size of the Tabernacle, being sixty cubits long and twenty cubits wide. Now, from the centre of the rock to the edge of the platform A, B, C, D is 120 cubits, and from the centre of the rock to h is 190 cubits; so the sanctuary of the Temple should lie between E, L, and *f;* but it must not touch the edge of E, L, for its end wall was that of the Holy of Holies, and between that and the edge must have been forty cubits. I think the sanctuary of the Temple must have stood one half on the platform and the other half below it.

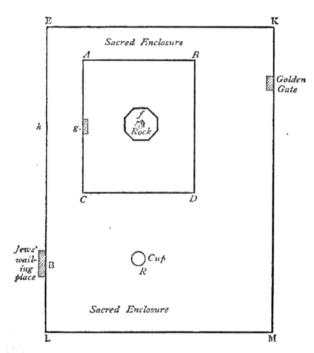

Now note the wailing place, B. When I first saw it, I said, " Evidently the Jews wail towards the *Holy of Holies;* " then it struck me that the Holy of Holies must be west of the rock, and that probably they wailed where they do (a space only a few yards—say thirty—long) because of the houses built elsewhere, all the wall really being covered, except this piece. It then struck me that they wail towards the cup, which I think is the brazen sea, or laver.

Now, entry into the Christian Church is by baptism; entry into the Jewish Temple was by the laver, thence to the altar, thence to the holy place, and thence to the Holy of Holies, *i. e.* God; for, if the Jew entered without purification, he would be destroyed (" Wash lest we die," is said of the laver and altar). This is very curious. The Jews have hammered nails between the interstices of the huge stones at the wailing place, to be witnesses to God that they have been there; there are regular rows of nails stuck in.

I hear that at my village the Greek-Russian Church give the Lord's Supper to all who present themselves, without query; they give it in both kinds—bread and wine, so I shall go there. It is odd that no queries were asked when we poisoned ourselves in Eden; but that, when we wish to take the antidote, queries are asked. It is sufficient for me that the Greek Church is Christian, and that they "show forth the Lord's death till He come."

I went to the Synagogue and saw the Jews with small knobs of leather, containing the law, on their foreheads and left arms, reading the Scriptures and swaying backwards and forwards. They do it every morning at 6.30. They evidently consider the Scripture as food.

I saw an excavation of streets fifty feet below those said to be of the time of our Lord, and those in some places are sixty feet below the present surface. Those I saw excavated are Solomon's city.

AIN KARIN, 28 *January*, 1883.—I am in my new house at Ain Karin, three miles from Jerusalem. Household cares trouble me rather, but they will settle down.

5 *February*, 1883.—To me —— is one of those "ever learning and never arriving at the truth;" most uncomfortable. I believe the real remedy is prayer and supplication He is of a querying nature, ever raising carping questions. "Whose wife shall she be?" "Is it lawful to give tribute to Cæsar or not?" &c. &c. "If so, how would the world go on?" I see in him myself, selfish and self-sufficient

We cannot get on with one who doubts the main treasures of our existence. I do not, however, mind; it is better to be thrown back on God in Christ; and Christ bore with me. I sometimes think he is an unbeliever; if silenced in his questions, he puts them in another form, which rather ruffles me. For instance, such questions as this, "With respect to *that* indwelling you speak of," &c. &c., really irritates one's flesh. Yet our Lord had these trials continually; never indeed did His disciples seem to be convinced; they were silenced, and only that; they did not understand till He had opened their eyes *after the Crucifixion*.

Take each of us as a cavern wherein things of darkness did once luxuriate. Light came in and destroyed them. It is the Holy Ghost, the Spirit of Christ, that will illuminate our caverns. We know there are interstices where darkness still exists; we would that these recesses should also receive the light, and therefore we must keep the portal open and not let things of darkness close up the entrance. If we do, though we may have a certain measure of light within us, it is only sufficient to *keep alive* the things of light, but not enough to kill the evil things. Light is knowledge—a just apprehension. They would not have "crucified the Lord of glory" had they known *Him* (1 Corinthians ii. 8). We should not speak evil, if we were quite sure that God rules all things, for we question His rule by so doing; every judgment we pass is impugning His Godhead, and is paganism.

8 *February*, 1883.—I have been looking over the books I brought out, and have come to this conclusion—they are useless for all material purposes, and it will be better to trust entirely to the Scriptures and Concordance. I dare say it may be difficult to put one's *words* clearly, but, as far as one's understanding is concerned, it is better to be without than with commentaries.

There is some coincidence between dust and water. *I believe*, but am not sure, that, if the water part of our bodies be removed, we fall to dust, and it strikes me that our natural birth was the antithesis to baptism. It is much more satisfactory to be given God's truths than to find them out with great labour from books. Take the question of our Lord and ourselves. "Forasmuch then as the children are partakers of flesh and blood, He also Himself likewise took part of the same" (Hebrews ii. 14). Now the children must be of the same nature as the parent; as He is, so we are also, but in an infinitely smaller degree, though of the *same* quality. Perhaps it will be better to keep this sort of letter to yourself.

I feel sure that nothing but a complete and entire surrender of everything to Christ will be available. *He is able to fill us*, and to render us much more happy than any worldly pleasures can do; that is an undeniable axiom. But we must, after having given up everything, be patient, and wait for the "filling up." I say this, for I am trying the experiment of giving up all hindrances to a holy life, and, though rid of those hindrances (which were pleasures to me), I am yet empty of any increase of spiritual joy. However, it is certain the increase will come, so I must patiently wait for it and avoid going down into Egypt, *i.e.* the world. The experiment is a safe one; it is like going through a severe operation for an illness, with the *certainty* of ultimate cure.

I like much your remarks and texts about giving up *everything*, for they came in with the views I was then writing to you. Certainly, if we think about it, we feel disinclined to give up anything for a doubtful something; which means, we doubt God, and is want of faith.

11 *February*, 1883.—About the invasion of Canaan: if we look at the subject, we find there a land in the possession of one set of people, who are to be dispossessed by others. This is the *literal* state of affairs. Spiritually, the land is our body, and the two races are striving in us—the one to keep possession, the other to gain it. God is the

same in this matter, whether we take it spiritually or literally; the nation that obeys God will inherit. I will not, however, say *obey*, though that is included, but that the nation in union with Him will inherit the land—*i. e.* the body. Now, it is evident that it is our self-will which represents the Canaanites (the possessors of the land), and self-denial their opponents. Now, if these two exist together, there must ever be war between them, and the body— or land—will be torn by their division or strifes. In Joshua we begin with the marching round Jericho, where self-denial had to be exercised; here however self-will gained the advantage, the wedge of gold could not be resisted, the end was trouble in Ai, and self-will was slain with Achan. Then followed peace with Gibeon, which being made somewhat on self-will lines immediately brought punishment, for Adonizedec self-righteously came to the attack, and so on. I think there is a still higher view to take of the matter, though this is the real spiritual one to us.

All this knowledge is no good, unless we draw the practical lesson from it—that success and happiness are only to be had in giving up our own will, and that we can learn as *easily!* in any country as in Palestine. I think that visiting these lands shows clearly, by their insignificant appearance, that the real matter is *in ourselves*, not in the position we occupy. In comparison to England, Palestine is an arid land; but, compared to the desert, it was paradise.

The Temple of Solomon was fine for those days, but, setting aside its Divine significance, it was only about six times as long as the room you are in, and not much wider —60 cubits = 90 feet = 30 yards long, by 20 cubits = 30 feet = 10 yards wide. You could walk round the city in less than an hour; it is not quite three miles round. Down to the Southampton docks and back would be about the distance.

We have done the Jews much harm by the admiration of the letter of their *history*. They really think they were

a wonderful people *in themselves*, and would not agree
with us in our belief that their wars are still carried out in
any "scuttler" or washerwoman. Moses frequently enacts,
or rehearses in brief historic action, what the Apostles
subsequently more fully and clearly described in words.

16 *February*, 1883.—I am just back from an excursion.
I went to Jerusalem, and then descended the Valley of Fire
(el Nar), which leads from Hinnom and Kidron to the
Dead Sea, and went to the monastery of Mar Saba, which
is built in the clefts of the rocks. Sixty monks live there,
mostly on vegetables. It was founded by Saint Saba, who
lived there in a cave, 439 A.D. A lion used to come into
the cave, and it ate the donkey that drew the Saint's water;
so Saba went to it and said, "You have eaten the donkey,
so you must bring the water yourself!" The lion agreed,
and shared the cave with the Saint. Foxes come down
below the grotto every night to be fed; I saw some six or
eight of them. I slept there, and went on the next day
through a wild, barren, queer-looking country to the Dead
Sea. I saw nothing remarkable; gulls were flying about;
the only striking thing is the knowledge that it is 1300 feet
below the Mediterranean; certainly the water is salt
enough.

We passed Gilgal, a little mound, four miles from the
ruins of Jericho, which are vast heaps. It is odd to look
on the high hills, and fancy what they saw on that day when
the walls fell down.

The most interesting and yet most dreary ride was that
from Jericho to Bethany (which is only two miles from
Jerusalem), a weary, barren track, without a house; yet it
is certain our Lord walked it. About two miles from
Bethany is a fountain, at which one must feel sure He
drank. We were tired enough, though riding! Bethany is
a wretched little village, much as it was in our Lord's time;
indeed everything tends to make one feel very mean for
grumbling, when we think that the Lord of Lords, the

Almighty God, took such a low place for our sakes. He came as a sin-bearer, and it was His death and passion that we needed to relieve us from our bondage.

As our Lord's crucifixion affected the whole creation, so also did every act of His life ; and we can imagine all the heavenly and satanic hosts watching His walk up those hills, knowing He was going to meet the power of hell in all its fury.

I went down into the so-called cave of Lazarus, but it did not seem real, for it is down a deep sort of well. A lot of Arab "scuttlers" assaulted me on my exit, wanting backsheesh, and we nearly all went down the well together.

You see Davids keeping their flocks, and you see the hills appearing to move, as it were, when the sheep go along the side. I think we are in error in supposing the Jewish kingdom was meant to be great in an earthly way. Rome, Greece, Babylon, and Egypt were all far mightier than Judea, in a worldly point of view. Solomon's kingdom was first in wisdom, but not in extent, and even allowing that the Jews will again come back as a nation, they may be first in some respects, but not in others.

To govern the world from Jerusalem would be to destroy the individuality of nations. Should there be a real millennium, our Lord will be (as He is now) Lord of Lords and King of the whole earth, yet His rule will not be as King of the *Jews*, for they, with us and other nations, are only and equally members of His body, the Church.

18 *February*, 1883.—Christ fills heaven and earth ; how is it that each individual is not filled, for we are but small cups ? I am quite happy, so to speak ; my days pass for the main part in communion with Christ, and affairs in Egypt or the Cape no longer trouble me ; but I feel it is a selfish life, and that disturbs me. By God's grace, I have gained great thoughts of our Lord's passion and His suffering on earth ; but am I to stay quiet here, where there is

little mission work I can do?   I will place this before Him, and wait His will.

23 *February*, 1883.—I have a lot to tell you.   Close to the place, which I think is Golgotha, are immense underground caverns, whence they took the stones for the Temple; you know they were to be prepared afar off, and so they were.   Some are half cut; they made a groove in the rock, put in wooden wedges, and, wetting them, split off the stone. It is right that they should have been taken from the very rock close to which the Head of the Church (His members) was crucified.   Our life now is as if we were being cut out underground in the dark (no one likes being chipped in the dark) to be placed in the Temple when ready.   More goes on inside the quarry than we know or think of.   No sound of hammer was to be heard; is it not remarkable?   Though we can do nothing to give light, I think we ought to say, "Light is there, seek for it."   Truth is a sharp razor-edge; a hair's breadth right or left is error.

28 *February*, 1883.—Wonderful are the works of God in the Soudan!   Look at His work.   He has upset the Egyptian people thoroughly, and they will get their liberty from the oppressing Pachas.   He has permitted this revolt, which will end, I believe, in the suppression of the slave trade and slave-holding, and He has humbled *me*.   I will speak about myself for one moment.

I foresaw the Egyptian and Soudan affair, and was not listened to.

I am glad I was humiliated, for the things of this world will pass away.   I expect Laurence Oliphant will go to the Soudan; there will be no end of trouble to reconquer it, and I am sorely tempted to write Lord Dufferin my ideas; but I will not, for Jesus is Lord and He knows what to do.

3 *March*, 1883.—I have great comfort in thinking that our Lord rules every petty and great event of life, both on a small and large scale.   Therefore He governs the Soudan now through A., B., and C., as much as He did when I was

there, and neither I, nor A., B., and C., have or had any-thing to do with the government, *as far* as others were concerned; with respect to the motives of our actions, it is another matter; they are the permanent residues—the things unseen. This comforts me, for I feel that their welfare, and the course of events that takes place, are being conducted by the same hand, whether I am there or not.

To me, one of my great difficulties is to try and raise others. I am sure we ought to try and ought to bear with them, but it is one of the hardest things to do.

How much did you pay for the boxes and models? You see I am sharp!

I see no one from week's end to week's end, and am very glad, for I speak no evil; query—is it good? for the evil is in me. I am working this out (but cannot yet see it), that our life is the Bible history, and that our Lord's life was the same.[1] If it is good for me it may become clear, for I feel sure it is so. It would be nice if we could see where we are, and get warned for our future guidance; say one was at Jacob, then one would be prepared for Egypt and brick-making.

The altar throughout shows the state of the spiritual life. Solomon's Temple was the improvement of the flesh up to the highest point. The *altar* we serve shows the *God* we serve. The Antichrist we serve is *self;* as long as *self* occupies the Holy of Holies, we follow and sacrifice to it. I am not troubled about the Soudan, and feel quite quiet; I had prayed for the sins of those people to fall on me, and have been spared. This is a rambling letter.

The Temple of Solomon must be utterly destroyed ere the true Temple is built. Self must utterly disappear, as it does at our death, ere we reach the Resurrection. We should anticipate death in the spiritual destruction of self.

[1] "We need never go beyond our own selves to find the Pharisee, the Sadducee, the heathen—all are within us, though, through the blindness of our hearts, we cannot discern them."

16 *March*, 1883.—I have some nice thoughts.   If Christ our Lord has united us to Himself as His bones and flesh, we can ask Him with full reason, and even with justice, to quicken our bodies.   I think still more and more of the indwelling; it begins first, " Let them make Me a sanctuary; that I may dwell among them" (Exodus xxv. 8).   David says, " I had in mine heart to build an house of rest for the ark of the covenant of the Lord, and for the footstool of our God" (1 Chronicles xxviii. 2).   David "desired to find a tabernacle for the God of Jacob, but Solomon built Him an house;" "howbeit the Most High dwelleth not in temples *made with hands.*"   " Heaven is my throne, and earth is my footstool: what house will ye build me? saith the Lord: or what is the place of my rest?" (Acts vii. 46-49).   "After this I will return, and will build again the tabernacle of *David* (*not* Solomon), which is fallen down; and I will build again the ruins thereof, and I will set it up " (Acts xv. 16).   "Thus saith the High and Lofty One that inhabiteth eternity, whose name is Holy; I dwell in the high and holy place, with him also that is of a contrite and humble spirit" (Isaiah lvii. 15).   " Ye have made it a den of thieves."   All points to the fact of the indwelling.   Self usurped the throne, but has no legal right to it, and we can claim its dethronement.

Wonderful it is how the types glide into one another. Before Abraham's death, Isaac takes his place; before Isaac's death comes Jacob.   Joshua comes before Moses dies, Saul before Samuel's death, Solomon before David's. The Temple takes the place of the Tabernacle, our Lord takes the place of the Temple.   All glide one into another till He comes, when all is concluded : dissolving views, until the substance came.

3 *April*, 1883.—I was never satisfied with Mount Ararat being the site of the Ark's resting place.   For the Ark of Noah was the Church, and nothing in Scripture seemed to denote that Armenia had anything particular to do with

Israel. I think the Ark rested on Mount Moriah, and thus was connected with Jerusalem, and the *Altar* of *Noah* was the "*Rock.*" I feel this is very interesting; to me Mount Ararat of Armenia never was the true site.

Do you remember how I went, or nearly went up it? My name is on it now, Corporal Fisher, R. E., left it there in a bottle.

5 *April*, 1883.—With respect to the rejected corner stone, I think this—It had a spiritual meaning, and was, and is, our Lord, who unites Gentiles and Jews in one Church; it means an angle-stone, uniting two walls; perhaps it may be said to be spiritually the point where the spirit and letter of Christ's religion meet, where the spiritual sacrifice is one with the actual sacrifice. Truly the Scriptures begin to sparkle with diamonds, and I can quite imagine that God may give such a thirst for them that it passes all other desire.

I am thinking of making a sort of concordance of catch-words; it seems a kind of work that is needed.

There can be no doubt that the human body was the masterpiece of all creation; that wretched, blear-eyed, wizened old man is a *chef-d'œuvre* of God, as it naturally should be, for God to dwell in. I can imagine all angels examining a raised " scuttler " with the greatest curiosity and amazement. " Let us make " implies, if it is possible, consideration by the Trinity before the body was made. Man is the gem of creation.

Look at Mr. ——'s letter; to me his sheath was *very selfish.*

Numbers xx. is instructive. The people chode with Moses. We wish we were dead. Why have you brought us into this evil place out of Egypt? It is no place of rest, or figs, and there is not even water to drink. We are driven out of the world, and think we are going to be satisfied; instead of which we find ourselves in a wilderness, and we cannot go back into bondage again. We want the figs, &c.,

of the world, but cannot like its worries ; besides, the world will not have us back, for we are a danger to it and caused the death of its Pharaoh and firstborn.

16 *April*, 1883.—I even dare now to ask God for His arrows against self and self-conceit, and can thank Him when they come ; it is a great comfort.   I am all right, and at work from morning till night.   As for Egypt and the Cape, I no more care for them ; and Lord Dufferin's despatch shows that, even had I gone out, it would have been another fiasco.

In the Scriptures one sees all specious reasonings, all fear of what the world says, all covering up of real with apparent motives, the wish for popularity, the paganism of man, the utter ignoring of God—all pointed out in a few simple touches : the key is ourselves.

23 *April*, 1883.—I get stunned by quotations from ancient authors, and fall back on the Scriptures.   It does seem very wonderful how they are hidden secrets, though, had we eyes to see them, they are indeed *open* secrets.   I find sometimes most wonderful analogies, yet they are still vague.   So to speak, it seems as though the Scriptures went out of their way to use peculiar words.

Our Lord's words are all full of deep meaning, which one sees just dimly, and then they vanish.   As Corbett says, no concordances, no books can aid in the perception of the Scriptures ; they are spiritual and not expressible.   What would be "catchwords" to one mind, would to another be unintelligible.

It strengthens our faith to find that the letter agrees with the spiritual meaning or apprehension.

It is here I think our clergy fail : there is too much secular work, mothers' meetings, &c. &c., and not enough study.   I think that the study of Scripture, the avoidance of scandal or picking to pieces, the visiting of the sick, with earnest prayer would tend towards the perfecting of a Christian ; something is wanting, if any one of these is neglected.

As God is infinite, so our growing apprehension of Him must be infinite. Your book on astronomy says that the contemplation of high subjects raises the mind, and this I think is quite true, for, the more one dwells on eternal things, the smaller appears the behaviour of Smith or Jones, or the acts of Robinson.

We are pianos, events play on us. Gladstone is no more important in the events of life than we are; the importance is, how he acts when played on. So is it with the bedridden woman; the angels and powers watch her and Gladstone alike; both are equally interesting; that broken cup is the same as the Irish troubles.

The slave trade must go on; it is the type of the spiritual bringing into subjection of the heathen in us. The death of a million is the death of a million *ones;* whether in a day or in a thousand years, it is the same to each of those million *ones.* I find very few sit down and work out a subject. *I* like my thoughts as greatcoats; others like these same thoughts as pleasant songs.

There is no doubt, I think, that very many know the fact of the indwelling of God, but how little do they meditate on what that indwelling is ! I would fain attain to the realization of Christ as sitting by me. I feel sure that the picking at our neighbours is sheer paganism; it is the great test of one's belief.

I lent some of my Cape papers to —— and he did not even take the trouble to read them; this shows how very little people think of us, or of our doings; the fact is, we are under the greatest delusion when we think people in general do care for them.

Thank you much for the payments and work you have done for me; I fear I give you a lot of trouble, my dear Augusta; I can see you bending over and doing up the papers and books; you are really very kind to me.

I have sent home my gun, and can never shoot again. Scene—morning. My servant brings up a hen partridge alive (he knew I had bought one before and let it go) ; its wings were tied, it had been captured on its nest, such beautiful bright eyes and red bill, such a beauty ! I was cross, and took it to cut the string, and whilst so doing I felt it struggle, then flutter, and it was dead. I felt it very much, and do still, though I am accustomed to death and think it no loss ; however, that day the gun was doomed.

I remember an incident when I was going to Katerif to see King John's ambassador, I was walking along the road, and with my whip flicked at a lizard, and cut off its tail ; it haunts me now.

Respecting the finding of sites, now that all vestiges are absent, there can be no way except by spiritual analogy. For my part I doubt the usual theories regarding them, because, as a rule, these matters have not been looked into from a spiritual point of view. It is wonderful how one person starts an opinion, and it is taken up without thought by the mass; we are like sheep.[1]

Saul certainly ought to have had something to say to Jerusalem and its Temple, for Saul is self-confidence and reliance on the flesh, and is a predecessor to David, who is trust only in God. The Saul in us has to die ere David comes into his kingdom (2 Samuel iii. 1). With God's blessing, I hope to fathom the Kings of Judah and Israel.

26 *April*, 1883.—I have now been to that rock where you and I were made, in Adam.

I slept at Latrun ; the hotel keeper said he expected Prince Louis of Battenberg and a lot of Russians, and that, if they came, I must go into another room. I was fast asleep when they arrived at 11 P.M., when the man knocked

---

[1] "The majority of mankind think that they think, they acquiesce and suppose that they argue, they flatter themselves that they are holding their own—when they have actually grown up to manhood with scarcely a conviction which can be called their own. An error once stereotyped goes on repeating itself by the mere *vis inertiæ*. Men go on repeating words without weighing their meaning or suspecting that, with the change of sense, they cease to convey the idea they formerly did."

at my door. I altogether forgot where I was; however, I got up, but did not realize the position at once. I mention this, because from it I feel sure that in sleep the faculty of memory and intelligence leaves the body and the animal alone remains; I have always had an idea that we are living a dual life, one in the body here, one somewhere else, yet I never saw this so plainly as I did last night.

There is a remarkable word in Scripture, "weapons"; it is sometimes used for "bodies," as though our bodies were the weapons *we* (true *we*) fight Satan with. I have not yet got it worked out by the letter of Scripture, but spiritually I think it is true.

I have been thinking over our feelings and how often it is that we are so very insincere even in prayer. I do not only mean that our thoughts wander, but that we address God as if He did not quite realize the most subtle thought within us. If we think of it, we must come to the conclusion that the life in us is of God, for by Him all things subsist and hold together. Free will does not do away with the fact that every one has the Spirit of God in his actual existence, and that the same Spirit, being God, and our life, though apparently apart, are yet one; so, any thought can be no more kept from Him than we can think a thought apart from ourselves. We are apt (though not to the same degree) to speak to God as we speak to one another; for instance, we pray for power to give up a certain habit, say evil speaking, and, at the moment of so praying, we have a thought of evil against some one, and we, as it were, whisper to that thought, "By and by I will attend to you, not now," and we go on praying against the very act we intend in our hearts to do. All this is insincere and dishonouring. Look here: if we could see one another's hearts, should we ever have the face to be insincere? I do not think so, for first, we should know it was of no use, secondly, shame would prevent us, and thirdly, our lips would refuse to utter the words of insincerity. I have seen no one for the last

fortnight, so to speak, but I know, when I go out, that I am
unchanged; I never feel dull, and always have plenty to do,
but it seems to me an idle life; yet, on the other hand, the
most active life is only useful as far as it stirs one's motives
and actions, it is never that we really guide events.

I hope you are well; tell me how your sheath is.

In the Scripture one sees the most wonderful exactitude
of God's rule, which extends over all creation, and which
tends to elevate our idea of His wonderful wisdom. He
does, or over-rules, an event in B.C., and fits that very event
into an action in A.D., which shows that He over-rules every
intervening thing. I am more and more convinced day by
day that the framework of events is fixed and determined,
but that our part in connection with them is the gain or loss
we sustain. I like this, for it equalizes *all* work, great or
humble. "Rejoice not that the spirits are subject unto
you; but rather *rejoice, because your names are written in
heaven*" (Luke x. 20).

7 *May*, 1883.—I have several very interesting subjects in
embryo, they float in one for a time and generally come out
quite different from what I expect. The Israelites mur-
mured against the law; when given light, one likes the law;
in fact, obedience to God is heaven, disobedience is hell;
thus He will make us love it. . . . Our Lord would never
have held an appointment in this world; it would not have
suffered Him to do so, though He had divine wisdom; this
thought should comfort us all in our humble positions. I
have tried my servant a good deal by telling him how Adam
excused himself, and how Eve excused herself; he now
looks quite faint when I say "*Adam.*" He used to pour
forth excuses long before any idea of accusing him was
conceived.

I had a letter from Egypt, which is not very sanguine
about the state of affairs, all because our Government will
not say they will stay; yet stay they must, whether they like
it or not. The *Weekly Times* is very good in giving the

salient points of events; now that I take no vivid interest, I like to see how things are working under His rule.

I have found a new object of interest, namely, the stars (a rest to one's eyes after Greek and small print references in the concordance), and by dint of great patience I can now tell the Zodiac and some others. It is certainly very interesting; those worlds were made without the least effort, but our salvation took a weary life of hardship and very great suffering.

I like the thought that we are so made as to be able to understand the Godhead, that we have faculties which are capable by degrees of increasing in knowledge of Him. Adam in Eden governing all animals is a type of Christ governing all powers. As there is a great gap between man and animals, so there must be a vast gap between our Lord and all powers. One thing I like to dwell on is the transcendent value of man. It would have cost no trouble for our Lord to have made another creation in our place; His taking our nature, He being God, shows that nature was such as could hold Him and be a fit habitation for His Godhead. He is God, yet He is Man, one Christ, never to be separated the one nature from the other. Now, God could never take a wholly unlike or uncostly nature to be one with Him for ever. He could only take the *chef-d'œuvre* of creation, inferior inasmuch as it (the body) is a creation, but still superior to all other created existences.

Give me a ream of foolscap and I will sign it : it may be filled with my demerits and unworthiness, which I agree to; but my so doing is a proof of how much I accept the free gift of God. Unless our Lord's sufferings were in vain, it is just that sheet of demerits that I have signed which gives me my right to Him; had I a clean sheet I should have no right to Him. It is His matter why He went through so much for me; we may not think we were worth His trouble, but He thought otherwise. If we need anything very much and it is given us, we may have a sense that we are not worthy it, but nevertheless we gladly accept it; the counting over of that great gift makes one think less of self and one's own unworthiness, and that, as a *sequence*, produces a better life—but only as a *sequence*. Fruit comes from union with the vine.

JERUSALEM, 16 *May*, 1883.—"The weapons of our warfare are not carnal, but mighty through God to the pulling down of strongholds." The members of the body are the weapons of our warfare, by which strongholds are pulled down; for we wrestle not with flesh and blood, but with powers and principalities in heavenly places: that is satisfactory. It is through our bodies that effects are produced in the spiritual world; then comes the thought that the chief of the members or weapons is the tongue: see James's account of it. The tongue has power to defile the whole body, therefore it is the chief member: a world of iniquity is set on fire of hell, restless, evil, full of deadly poison, earthly, loving the praise of men, carnal, selfish, devilish, proud, death and life are in its power (Proverbs xviii. 21). Whoso keepeth his tongue, keepeth his soul from troubles (Proverbs xxi. 23). If a man thinketh himself religious, and bridleth not his tongue, his religion is vain (James i. 26). This is a terrible indictment against our speaking evil of our neighbours, and how very guilty I have been of this. Sorry, sorry, sorry, for all this evil speaking, yet when in company I feel drawn away; it is no excuse. Who shall abide in the hill of the Lord? He that taketh not up a reproach against his neighbour (Psalm xv. 1, 3).

Now, here is where I like the Scriptures, that they give terse antidotes against defects, something practical to go on. This altogether reconciles me against seeing many people, for such-like talk is generally unavoidable; it depends on temperament a good deal. I am not wise in my words or writing; I write from my heart, and speak from my heart, which is not good. There must be a breach of union, if the tongue says differently from what our Lord would speak;

in fact, the speaking evil of our neighbours can only come from the pagan thought that He does not even exist. I consider that insight quite a jewel to me ; for why, when we try so hard, do we not realize more our living membership with our Lord? Why do we so quickly forget Him in our daily walks? It is evidently some such hindrance as this that prevents this realization.

Sins in act are not nearly so frequent as sins in word ; both are sequences of the breach of communion, of the non-realization of the indwelling of God.

Comfort yourself as to the actual fact of death ; I have a great desire for it. I think we shall leave the world with as little pain as we entered it, that is, with none ; it is natural to suppose so—a heart will beat for some time after being taken from the body.

I have become much more timid about speaking of these matters of universal salvation, yet perforce one comes to this question. If every one lives, then he must live by the fact of his possession of an emanation of the Life of Life, which must be good, and never can be evil. This emanation is the cause of his existence, his life in fact, and that I regard as the " *he.*"

29 *May,* 1883.—I will look up "sword" and "fire", I know the connection of old. The "tongue is a sharp sword"; "tongue is a fire." All those passages when A smites B with the sword are typical of verses smiting some faculty in us, if we had eyes to see (1 Samuel xv. 33; Hosea vi. 5).

If you had ever read the history of how the Bible was preserved you would wonder, for you would learn how it was pieced together and kept in a miraculous way. I can imagine how difficult, without God's Spirit, it would be to believe it, for it would seem to have been purposely left to perish, and was saved by so-called accident (we do not believe there are "accidents"). It is like God to act thus ; He in some little unobserved way interferes at, apparently, the last moment. Some of the Gospels were in fragments, scattered here and there; yet all have come together. In fact, the more one dwells on the Almighty power and wisdom of God, the less one wonders, for to guard the Scriptures, while apparently letting them follow the laws of the world, is no effort to Him who governs the universe by His will. Things which struck me before no longer surprise me in the same way.

I am glad you see the spiritual analogy between Zion and our bodies. All these things are only interesting to me as the continual showing forth of *God dwelling in us,* of which the whole Bible is full, and of which it is itself the type. "The word quickens," *i. e.* gives life.

Do you know that after one's mind is well imbued with the *letter* of the Scripture history of Samuel, Kings, and Chronicles, one will reap spiritual food. It is quite right that real labour has to be expended on it ("In all labour there is profit": Proverbs xiv. 23).

You must try to get the idea that death is a great inestimable blessing, and then you will think nothing of the slaughter of Egyptians, &c.; also that the death of one or a million ones is the same. This is a great gift, for it takes away our sorrow for the slaves, &c., of Africa.

8 *June,* 1883.—I like to figure God as a beneficent, kind God, loving His creatures, and bearing with their weakness. We can to some degree imagine how to angels man is wonderful, for it is only in Christ that they or we can see God. The heathen, indeed all men, have always a tendency to wish for a visible appearance to worship; the mind tends to long for some actual, tangible thing; hence the idols.

I was over the resting place of the ark of the covenant yesterday, it is a splendid hill; you can see the Dead Sea and the country laid out like a map, quite the place for the ark to rest upon.

I have long thought that in each of us is, in a measure, the spirit of Christ, which is our real selves, our souls; and that the weariness of our lives is from their being incarcerated in these bodies. I think the real *we* suffers in us, as Christ suffered *in* the world, *from* the world. Thus it is that all the Psalms apply to each one of us, to the corporate body, the Church of God, and to Christ.

Who is there who does not know the Aha! Aha! of scoffers in us? "You were going to do this or that, and you did just the contrary." It is only natural for us to think we can do this or that, and so we could, but for Satan's entering and our bodies giving way; for "he that is dead is freed from sin," and our real *we* never dies, so that is spoken of the body. We often, at least I used often, to think, as in the Psalms, "God will not regard." What madness! Considering our-life is a part of His, it is as much as to say, "My head does not know what my hand does." We subsist by, and only by, Him. Do not fret for power over Satan, trust in God; *without any effort on your part*, your names were written in *heaven*.

The ravines round Jerusalem are full of the dust of men, for over a million bodies must have been slain there. What a terrific sight the resurrection there will be! I suppose there is no place in the world where so many bodies are concentrated.

As God wills it, I am glad you are better. What I would wish for you is to be in His hands; and, if one thinks of it, can one wish anything better? I am trying to reach that stage. The spark of life in us is an emanation from Himself, and, as we care for ourselves, so He cares for us. To wish against God's will is to wish against one's self.

We give a shilling to a beggar because we pity him, and we chuck it to him. Here are two motives: one divine, that of pity, the other earthly, in that we are too proud to hand it. Over and over again we err in this way, spoiling kindly acts by some ill-natured word. No consistency can be expected except from the perfectly holy

R 2

or the completely carnal man, in whom only one set of motives rule. I believe very much in praying for others; it takes away all bitterness towards them.

I wonder sometimes what is written in the roll of futurity about me. I scarcely think I am to dwell thus for long, it is too quiet to last. It is remarkable, as I have said, that we know nothing of our birth, or until some time after; where were our souls before? I feel more strongly than ever the pre-existence, and believe that the next world will be no new world to us. I think, if it were possible to have our hearts broken in the next world, broken they would be when we realize His love.

I do not like to push you, but do you chew the cud? Do you study on the future and try and see it, and feel how He works all things. We are the locks, our Lord is the key.

15 *June*, 1883.—If a man makes an arrangement with his fellow-man, the greatest honour to him is to consider that arrangement as effectual and final. So it is the greatest honour to our Lord to believe His word. It is not presumption to claim the fulfilment of His promises; it is a comforting thought, indeed, it is peace, for we place our burden on Him, who is both able and willing to bear it. The prayers of the patriarchs were most simple; they took God at His word, that is all.

I like much this style of prayer, and recommend it to you: to plead with Christ to look after His own members. He knew all about those members, when He undertook the covenant. Surely, if He bore the punishment of our sins, as He did, He is not likely to neglect the fruit of His work. Why, the fact of His not doing so would be the triumph of His foes, and would be virtual failure; and we know that He could not fail. I am delighted with the prayer, I only realized it lately, indeed a few days ago; before that it was misty. I now ask Him in some way to regulate matters for my earthly members, for they also are His. I really believe we shall enter the resurrection life by such prayers, and die to the world.

There is some reason why we do not make more progress; is it unbelief—not believing or taking hold of what He says? Thus, for instance, we believe this or that, yet we will talk over the matter, and argue it, as though He did not exist. Now this is unbelief in *acts*, even though, when we are alone, we believe He rules. I feel sure that the discussing of material things, in a material way, is the source of our death-like state, and of our "being moved." We live in union with Him in the spirit, but not in the body.

In every case, it is evident by experience. that we can scheme nothing for ourselves, therefore it is waste of time. It seems to me sure that all the Levitical ceremonies, &c., are the outward signs of the Gospel dispensation, if we could see the analogy. It cannot be supposed they were meaningless.

I have really done Jerusalem completely, and got it well into my mind; it has been very interesting. Most likely I shall soon leave for Haifa; you will therefore understand, if you do not get letters for two or three mails. Kind regards to Mrs. Reid; I asked her if she had her *ticket* and was ready for the train—death!

What I dislike in ——'s letters is the sentimental part, it is to me quite painful; she is so impressive. I do hope you will try and quiet her. I am torn in two with the wish not to be unkind, and yet I wish her not to bother me. She would make me king, but I feel ill at the thought, for she will slay me when I fail, as I inevitably must do. I shall not write to her, or notice her last letter.

6 *July*, 1883.—I get dreadfully barren at times, and can see nothing; you will always know it from my letters. I feel as if I was too much alone here and too selfish.

JAFFA, 11 *July*, 1883.—I have moved down here, and have taken a pretty good house for six months. This place is well situated for going in all directions.

It is a distinguishing fact of Scripture, that it is so simple, in reality its simplicity is its depth. A writer, whose book I found in the hotel, says, "Revelation is transcendentally grand, though all the Books are grand." Revelation means revealing—unveiling—secrets; so it is what its name implies, the revealing of the mysteries of God to man. It is a book of the deepest interest.

The self-righteous preachers and religious authorities of the outward Church do all their works to be seen of men; they preach great sanctity and love, but do not practise it themselves; they like a special dress, and the place of honour at dinners. Woe unto you, hypocrites! You shut up the Kingdom of God by preaching that man cannot be saved except by good works or by belonging to this or that community.

I believe the deadness in some of the clergy is owing, firstly, to not reading the Scriptures; secondly, to not meditating over them; thirdly, to not praying sufficiently; fourthly, to being taken up with religious secular work (Acts vi. 2-4). I wonder how it is that, when a subject of the greatest import is brought up, one sees so very little interest taken in it; and how willingly it is allowed to drop with a sort of "Oh, yes, I know all about that."

I believe the smallest word one speaks by the Spirit is all that is needed; if it does not work its way, the longest sermon will not do so. The fact is, the Spirit gives life; *we* have nothing to do with the call; *that* must be made by the Spirit. Now, who would discuss a subject like this? Not one, I know; many would look on it as an insidious temptation to cease from work. In reality, the flesh likes fuss and activity and to be of importance; it thinks it is doing a great deal when it is really only hindering; still this view may be distorted and used as a temptation to do nothing.

I stick to Thomas à Kempis and think he is right and Scriptural. Our Lord never seemed pressed, but was always calm and ready to state the greatest truths. All these things are to be learnt through the Spirit; it is utterly useless to press such ideas. We are like stones of the Temple, some are nearly hewn away from the Rock they belong to, while others are not yet nearly quarried out; and we thoughtlessly imagine that all these will see the same truths from the same point of view.

Married people with families cannot possibly hold the same views as single people. I say " cannot possibly," but I mean that it is unlikely they should. What a blessing it is one was never married! Marriage spoils human beings, I think; if the wife is willing the husband is not, and *vice versâ;* how often one sees that. Somehow one feels hurt at one's jewels not being appreciated; but I will not argue; when a man says, "he knows this or that," it is hopeless. To some degree this is a cross, for it leaves but few topics of conversation and makes one appear dull; when one's mind is on a particular subject, one must either talk of it or be silent.

I know no one but you who will go on from day to day, from hour to hour, talking on these matters. I found six or seven sermons of Spurgeon in the hotel, and read them. I like him; he is very earnest; he says: "I believe that not a worm is picked up by a bird without direct intervention of God, yet I believe entirely in man's free will; but I cannot and do not pretend to reconcile the two." He says he reads the paper to see what God is doing and what are His designs. I confess I have now much the same feeling; nothing shocks me but myself.

A converted Jew preached last Sunday that God gave man a direct portion of His life; yet I believe, if you pressed that man, he would deny that each man possesses a Divine germ; he was most strong on the point, and repeated it over and over again. I suppose his spiritual man would receive it, but not his carnal man. I believe truly that the secret of work, and our defined duty, is the life in the Spirit the constant desire, even if not realized, to feel God's indwelling in us; it means, of course, the death of self, as if we lent our bodies to God to work in; I think that is the true object of a godly life, and nothing else. God in the lent body will work sufficiently and in due season, but there will be no fuss or worry. Before the fall, Adam was to till the garden, not to labour with fatigue; and through Christ we regain this position of Adam. I am sure this will be a comfort to you, as it is to me; it is the sunset of life to realize this, or rather it is the dawn of the resurrection life.

Summed up, it is "all things are ruled by God in Christ;" all working for good, all working in love, our whole work is *to be still* in His hands and to keep our temples fit for His residence. That many will agree with us is not likely, for they must be passers through of tribulation; they must have had the experience derived from the failure of any other work to satisfy; and all animal enjoyment of the world must have ceased. How few have reached or been given this! Can we wonder that we find no one who will meet us in these matters? "Be still and know that I am God," is "*Let go.*"

You know how often we are told we are saved by faith alone; most tracts, as well as the Bible, say that. Well, when we are brought to the sense of religion, what is the first thing we do? We rush off to prayer meetings, tract distributions, &c. &c.; and we torture ourselves to do all this. Yet "Be still" is the truth; all this fuss does good, *i.e.* it is turned to good, for we worry others, and we learn our own insufficiency. Yet if we did what God tells us, "*Let go,*" what toils we should save ourselves!

I quite look on this fussiness as emanating from Satan's distorting truth. It comes from the flesh; the flesh feels it is important, self-sufficient, and must be a doer of great things. Many will say, "Have we not prophesied in Thy name? and in Thy name have cast out devils? and in Thy name done many wonderful works?" to whom Christ will

say, "I never knew you" (Matthew vii. 22, 23). The will
of my Father is to be done, *i. e.* acquiesced in; that is our
sanctification.

It is remarkable that the "Be still" is so clearly put in
the Bible: Enter into rest; cease from *these* works. "It is
a people that do err in their heart, and they have not known
my ways. Unto whom I sware in my wrath that they should
not enter into my rest" (Psalm xcv. 10, 11).

If a portion of machinery were worked by any other life
or motive power than the main one, there would be a jarring
and inevitable discordance; so it is with us. "Be still, let
go." Dr. Stevenson was a wonderfully quiet old man, and
I believe he realized that truth, for he knew many mysteries
and never spoke of them.

I think that, when two on this earth get very intimate,
they rarely talk much to others, and never on some topics;
they keep others out of their intimate converse. It may be
so with God and man in union with Him. "Except the
Lord build the house, they labour in vain" (Psalm cxxvii. 1)
shows that efforts are not productive of fruit: that is the
reward of God. Look at a tree: it makes no effort, but
fruit comes from its union with the root. I consider this
view is a true gem; that by this abiding, by intercessory
prayer, and by using every opportunity God gives us for
comforting people[1] we fulfil His will. With this there is
no fuss, no hurrying.

Should events prevent our speaking, we have the conviction that, if we tell Him, we do as much, and more than
if we had not been thwarted in our words and actions.
Anna "*served* God with fastings and prayers night and

---

[1] In another letter General Gordon says: "It is one of the most
difficult things to give a person in trouble comfort; nothing but truth
will avail, and that truth must be submitted very gently, and little by
little. The comforter must get into the same position as the person to
be comforted; not in words only but in feelings. I have found this to
be the case so very often, and have felt that, when I do not sympathize
with the grief of another, whatever I may say does not give comfort."

day" (Luke ii. 37). *In* Him we reach to the end of the world; *out* of Him we are localized in Southampton or Jaffa. Reason supports this view: to be at the head-quarters of a ruler, who by telegraph can communicate orders and even supervise their execution, is certainly a higher position than to be working in one's own way in a petty place. How much more does this apply to those who seek and obtain, by the cessation of their own work, the indwelling of the Lord of heaven and earth. I think many would like these thoughts, they are calming. I want forty years more to quiet me, but, D.V., it will come at last.

One verse always comforted me: "The Lord will perfect that which concerneth me" (Psalm cxxxviii. 8); for a believer is *always* in the exact position he should be in. The rending apart of the soul and body, which is necessitated by the death of the flesh, is a most painful operation, and a lingering one; all have to undergo it at one time or another in their pilgrimage, either now or at their death. I hope these trials may break the last link that binds you to the flesh; ride at single anchor with a spring on the cable to let you go at any minute.

"*Let go.*" "Be still," even if the mountains fall into the sea. There is death in the seeking of high posts on this earth for the purpose of what the world calls doing great things; the mightiest of men are flies on a wheel; a kind word to a crossing sweeper delights Christ *in him*, as much as it would delight Christ *in* a queen. I want you to look at accidents like that at Sunderland[1] from God's point of view; we, each of us, as members of Him who is Lord of heaven and earth, are a party to His works, and acquiesce in them; for a member cannot differ from its head. Any feeling of wishing this had happened rather than that, is the raising up of the head of a rebel.

I went for a long ride along the deserted shore towards

On the 18th January, 1883, over 190 children were suffocated or trodden to death while endeavouring to leave Victoria Hall Sunderland.

Askelon, a barren sandy strip; somehow one feels nearer to you here than at Jerusalem.

14 *July*, 1883.—Continuing the subject of "Be still," we see how the fact of our being the temple of God is inseparable from quiet and rest; one cannot think that the temple should be full of noise and fuss, such as our bodies are in, when we get mixed up with much secular religious work. Those thoughts, which cause the fuss, are the money-changers and sellers of doves, whom our Lord drove out of the Temple; Mary and Martha represent this very clearly.

I had a fearful dream last night—I was back at the Academy, and had to pass an examination! I was enough awake to know that I had forgotten all I had ever learnt (I never learnt grammar or dancing), and it was truly some time ere I could collect myself and realize that I was a general, so completely had I become a cadet again. What misery those examinations were! We do not sufficiently feel for the poor young men who have to go through them.

23 *July*, 1883.—What comforts me is the thought that we are being shaped here below into stones for the heavenly temple—that to be made like Him is the object of our earthly existence. He is the shaper and carpenter of the heavenly temple. *He* must *work* us into shape, our part is to be still in His hands; every vexation is a little chip; also we must not be in a hurry to go out of the quarry, for there is a certain place for each stone, and we must wait till the building is ready for that stone; it would put out the building, if we were taken pell-mell. This also is a comfort in respect to ambition, for the things of this world are only important as tools to shape us into form. One wishes one could always feel this. I do not know whether you care for these long effusions, but they are soliloquies for me. It is truly wonderful how very accurate the Scriptures are—but then they are divine.

3 *August*, 1883.—Tell Mrs. Reid we never die, we glide

into the Lord's presence; indeed I believe we are in that presence ere we cease breathing.

I am sure of one thing, that we do lose the very sweetest times by rejecting wilfully what God gives us, *i. e.* in avoiding people and disagreeable things.   God says : I *will* preserve thee from all evil; *I* will preserve thy going out and thy coming in from this time forth; there shall no evil befall you; and yet we refuse to believe this for even a second, and go on plotting and praying, praying for more communion with Him, and then, the moment He begins to work, we flee from Him.   I want to realize this more than I do, it is evidently the reason of our deadness; there can be no confidence with distrust.   If we think we are bound to look after ourselves; if we think those strong expressions are only figurative or dependent on any particular frame of mind, they are useless to us; till we take them in their strength, we shall crawl along all our days.

What wonderful things the Spirit shows forth from the Scriptures, yet how few will study them!   Thank God, I have got to consider that salvation is a free gift.   Though clearly declared to be so in the Scripture, a due apprehension is not always given; when it is, the knowledge is a great relief.

7 *August*, 1883.—I find a certain amount of employment in my books, but have not yet managed to strike out a work to occupy me, consecutively for the term of my life.   I had hoped to do so, but the scheme fled from me; it was to draw up the catchwords which loop the Old to the New Testament, and show out the shadows in the substance. That is to be done some day, for there are many wonderful things in the catchwords.   Also, there is certainly an intimate connection between the Kings and Chronicles and our own lives, which one would like to work out in detail; one sees it instinctively, but not with power of expression.   Then, Israel is carried away by Assyria, Judah by Babylon; Judah comes back, Israel does not.

I would like to esteem the Scriptures, to *thirst intensely* for them, as those strong expressions put it; and yet, on rising from perusing them, how everything seems literally forgotten! This is remarkable, for one remembers what one has read after reading, say, Plutarch's *Lives*. I dare say you know this feeling—we agree whilst reading, and yet the sense evaporates as soon as we end our reading. I am not speaking of the vital truths over which one "chews the cud," but of the curious analogies. It may be, it would not be good for our actual present state to see all these mysteries, though the soul absorbs them all, hereafter to have them opened out.

St. Augustine says: "The man who loves God's Word reveres in it even what he does not understand, and, if anything in it seems to have an uncouth sound, he deems that he himself does not rightly understand it, and that there is some great mystery hidden there; therefore the Bible is not a stumbling-block to him, he is not *offended at it*. We now see through a glass darkly, but the time is coming when even those incidents in the lives of the patriarchs, which to some may now seem strange and trivial and perhaps offensive, will be found to be fraught with a rich store of inner spiritual meaning, and to have some mysterious relation to Christ."

God, before the flood, spoke of the *imagination* of man's heart being "only evil continually"; the word imagination is "*yetser*," which means pottery engraved with devices. God is said to have shaped or formed man of the dust, when the same word *yetser* is made use of. Here is an analogy, for the Holy Spirit goes out of His way, so to say, to use this word, and consequently there is a mystery between God's forming man, and man's imagination. Now, these are the things which would (if it was given me) delight and occupy me, if I could see the mystery. Our Lord at the transfiguration spoke of His decease which He should *accomplish* at Jerusalem, and it would seem as if the exodus

begun by Israel at the Red Sea had ended at Calvary, for
He was the true Israel.

One thing we may be sure of : that if it were good for
you and me to see these mysteries, the solution of them
would be given to us ; and though we should endeavour to
see them, we must not be down-hearted if we do not, for
God has given us the *vital* truth.   I speak of the lack of it
as depriving one of an occupation more than anything else,
for I am happy in the vital truth.   I do believe that nothing
could be more entrancing than to have this faculty, for it
would far transcend any other work in the world.   The
Holy Spirit gives us grace to believe, to be in union with
Christ by Him ; but spiritual discernment is, as it were, a
separate spiritual gift.   It is even said that, if we know all
mysteries and have not charity, it is nothing.   I expect
therefore that this desire to know all mysteries is a fleshly
desire for knowledge, which might, unaccompanied by love,
be hurtful to us.   Even now, with our slight knowledge,
one cannot avoid feeling a little vexed with our neighbours,
if they will not accept conversation on these subjects ; we
are apt to condemn them secretly.   How few will discuss
the great question, let alone these analogies.

8 *August*, 1883.—It is pretty hot, but nothing to speak
of.   I ride along the shore every evening, and walk my
horse back ; there are capital sands, and all is quiet and
peaceful.   Yes, I passed the place where Elijah killed the
prophets of Baal, it is quite identified.   He struck when
the iron was hot.   I hear two cases of cholera have broken
out at Beirout, which is some six days from here.   Truly
Egypt is giving the world trouble.

13 *August*, 1883.—Men like a God afar off ; they like
Jesus in heaven, they would not like Him on earth, for that
would be too near ; He would govern too closely, and
would be a restraint on their wills.   He would point out
that to be in union with him was salvation, not all this outside working, these prayer meetings and church-goings

Men ignore the presence of God the Holy Ghost for the same reason, for of course His indwelling would be as opposite to their wills as would be the presence of the Lord. Men like crucifixes, &c., they like a God who is dead as far as any interference with them goes.

Do you see how very important this is? This recognition of the Holy Ghost as here *in* believers, and as God Almighty? The Holy Ghost is God just as the Almighty Father and the Almighty Son is God. He wrote the Scriptures, it is by Him we believe, for faith is His indwelling. By Him we have our union with Christ and with God the Father, He is the uniting spirit. He prays in us. He teaches the meaning of the Scriptures and opens them to our understanding (His own particular work). He sanctifies, leads, guides, and directs us; His work is as essential as our Lord's redemption of us; God the Son redeems, God the Holy Ghost sanctifies.

Somehow one feels as if it were detracting from our Lord's power to ascribe so large a part in our salvation to the work of the Holy Ghost, but, if we reflect, we shall find that it is not so, for our salvation would be useless without sanctification, and we could not have sanctification or union with our Lord but by the indwelling of the Holy Ghost. Redemption alone would not give union; it makes us free from the curse of the law, but there would be no union with God in Christ: for redemption is for those who grasp it by faith. "No man can say that Jesus is the Lord, *but by the Holy Ghost*" (1 Corinthians xii. 3).

It is the peculiar work of the Holy Ghost in us to testify of Christ's sufferings, to enable us to realize them, and to glorify Christ; the Holy Ghost is the source of the love we bear to Christ.

The prevailing feature of this day is the keeping in the background the fact of the actual presence of the Holy Ghost in believers, and the result is that we are orphans having no guide. This does not hinder the working of the

Holy Ghost altogether, but it causes us to wander; hence all the sects, the low spirits of believers, the want of power in the Church of Christ, for, as the Great Guide is ignored, men seek guidance in their own inventions—ritualism, &c. We are as it were in the Church of Laodicea, in a false security, thinking we are rich when we are poor: we are lukewarm, we do a great deal in His name, but not in His way or will (Matthew vii. 22, 23).

We are believers *only* by the Holy Ghost in us: but yet we call Him "it," and we make what I cannot help calling those senseless prayers which I remember hearing at prayer meetings, "wrestling with God" for the Holy Ghost, when He is in us, if we are believers, as we profess to be.

All holiness is from the Holy Ghost working in us, in union with Christ; we are the branches, Christ is the root, the Holy Ghost is the sap. Without Him no fruit is possible. I had never realized this truth; before, it was dim to me: hence I am full of it.

14 *August*, 1883.—"Whatsoever is not of faith," *i. e.* the indwelling of God, "is sin" (Romans xiv. 23). All we do *out of communion with Him* misses the mark; this is rightly so, for we are His vicegerents, His life is in us, "for in Him we live and move and have our being." The indwelling of Christ, by the Holy Ghost, makes all texts sparkle with light. The first Epistle of John shows out this clearly, when it is thus illuminated. Do you remember the "*leaflet*"?[1]—that is the key-stone. How imperceptibly one slides into this belief. Do you remember how I used to hunt you into a corner about this?

21 *August*, 1883.—The nations and kings mentioned in Psalms cxxxv., cxxxvi., represent different rulers who strive for the mastery, causing those terrible passions in us, which we could never conquer, were it not for the indwelling of God. "The nations his enemies," Numbers xxiv. 8. "The heathen our enemies," Nehemiah v. 9. We begin our

[1] See p. 206

history in Adam in Genesis, and go all through the Bible to
the Revelation. If one considers the size of the Bible,
truly our life is one of refining in the furnace; one would
think that after the flood or exodus, or after the entry into
the Holy Land, or after Solomon, we should be quiet; but
we still have to go on to captivity in Babylon, and on our
return find that we have hardly begun. Then we come to
our Lord's day, are refined through the Epistles, and so
on to the end.

The words "Behold the man is become as one of us, to
know good and evil," are wonderful. Angels can know
good only, and devils evil only; but God and man know
both, man knows evil by this discipline. It would seem as
if our life was one continual shredding away of members,
new members sprouting, to be in their turn shred away.

It raises our thoughts of God's omnipotence and wisdom,
to think how He can work out the *same most difficult* and
intricate scheme in each man, king or peasant, during 6000
years, to us so variegated, to Him the same. How the
angels must watch the embroidery! how such teaching
would explain the Bible to them! To some of us David's
reign may occupy a week, Solomon's the same: the one
of faith, the other of quiet and decadence. What myriads
of members must be in each one of us to allow of such
slaughter!

1 *September*, 1883.—I came back from Gaza yesterday,
after a ten days' sojourn there, returning through Askelon,
where there are very fine ruins, enormous columns, marbles,
&c., lying in all directions: it is a wonderful place. Like
all the coast, it is most dreary, yet one sees that all the
country was once thickly populated. Sand from the shore
is creeping in steadily, and makes it mournful. Napoleon I.,
Alexander the Great, Sennacherib, Nebuchadnezzar, and a
host of great men passed by this route. Titus came up by
Gaza to Jerusalem. Richard Cœur de Lion was years at
Askelon. All gone, "those old familiar faces!"

I have many beautiful thoughts given to me, not yet matured; however, I will sketch one for you. You know the verse, " God breathed into Adam the breath of *lives;*" it is plural. Now, you and I believe that what God breathed into Adam was of Himself, and that it is this emanation from God in us which "does not sin." One can understand this with respect to the Believer. "What, know ye not that your body is the temple of the Holy Ghost?" Take a concordance and read the verses on " soul " and " spirit," and you will see how beautifully they come in. (The Prophets spake by the Holy Ghost.)

"Into Thy hands I commit my *spirit.*" I hear these words of our Lord are part of a prayer, still used by pious Jews, as in those days, before going to bed. (He slept in death.) They considered that God looked after their spirits (Ruach). This came from a conversation I had, that perhaps, at night, when our bodies slept (which is a type of death), we went to God. This is very wonderful and worthy of your attention.

I humbly believe the spirit of man is the Holy Ghost, and that it is only man who has " spirit, soul and body" (animals have souls and bodies). Try and get your mind free from commentators on this subject; it is not difficult, if you try and ask the Holy Spirit to teach you. What you and I have been saying of the soul being good and the body bad is thus: the "soul" we have been so long talking about is the "*spirit.*" I would not press this so much on you, if it were not so very comforting to understand; I look on this as an entrance into a higher heaven in respect to the trials of this world, so it is well worth while to study it.

I hope you will not think I am going astray. It does seem very wonderful: first, the infinite glory to which the Church is raised; secondly, the vileness of man in himself; thirdly, the incarnation of the Holy Ghost, or, what is the same thing, His indwelling in us.

Strange thoughts come to me from these very strong

words: "He hath made Him to be sin for us, who knew
no sin, that we might be made the *righteousness* of *God* in
Him" (2 Corinthians v 21) They allow of no diminu-
tion. Christ makes us *righteous* as God Himself. The
Church is *without spot or blemish* in God's sight! It is
stupendous! ——— was sometimes a trial; he was pagan,
and would talk of Smith and Jones and their acts. I tried
to get him in order by saying, "Well, we will be pagans and
discuss the matter." The fact is that none but yourself will
keep on with me in one continuous daily and hourly conversation on these matters; I despair of finding any one else.
I am more than ever convinced that there is no hope of
getting a congenial mind in any one who does not read and
study the Scriptures. Men may be spiritually-minded, and
may comprehend these questions, but they are barren of
any new light; they listen as though to pleasant songs, but
are glad to quit the subject.

5 *September*, 1883.—Jesus is Lord of heaven and earth
(He was Lord and God). It is paganism to think He
neglects to work in every little thing. Is any man likely to
have gone through what He did, and then let His sufferings
be rendered nugatory? "Sit thou on My right hand, and
look on"! Truly it is very dishonouring to doubt *His*
working. What man *in power*, wishing a certain course of
action, would be inclined to neglect the carrying of it out?

Mr. ——— is trying for funds; Mrs. ——— asked me if I
thought he would get them. I said (perhaps I did not feel),
"Yes, if God thinks it good; but you would not wish it if
He did not." She just lifted up her lip, and showed a tusk,
but I prevented her rending me. We do cordially hate
being nothing, and always have a sneaking idea that we are
doing great things. "So and So is dead; it is a great,
irreparable loss." You never see the least sign of this sort
of regret in the Scripture in the way of loss to the Church.
Men were sorry to lose Paul; they liked him, so they wept
when he said they would see his face no more.

To consider that Christ does not over-rule, watch, and order *all* things, is to degrade Him below what we would consider any man with power and will would do in His place. *He works through* means, it is true, but it is *He who works,* not the *means,* which may be straws.

I have had five live quails sent me, they are sitting like stones in the corner of my room, waiting till night to continue their journey to the south—I could not kill them. I hope animals will live again to be recompensed for our ill deeds; I think they will; at any rate, God will act justly and kindly.

6 *September,* 1883.—The quails were all killed last night by a rat! (Jehovah jireh!) I had put them in the garden, for their wings were cut, and hoped to keep them till they grew.

It is very wonderful how God's secrets are kept from so many wise and good men. Some are given to see the truth so clearly, whilst it is denied to so many millions. Many divines and writers hint at it, but never speak plainly; they know it but in part. Let those who are shown these things be humble; it is only a question of eye-opening. Whether seen or not, the truths are there, and it is He only who can open the eyes to see. I ask you whether it be possible for any man to destroy your belief in these secrets? I do not say you could dispute with them in words; but could any man alter your innate opinions? Truth is like the thin edge of a knife, there *can be no* divergence on either side.

What a deal there is in just the one verse of Genesis ii. 7, and also in Genesis iii. 6 and 19. I have nearly worn out that page of my Bible. I am very pleased with the result of these long letters; when I began, I did not know where they would lead. What a fearful thing it would have been, if they (Adam and Eve) had got at the tree of life! Truly death is a kind friend, it takes off the last shred; and, had they eaten of the tree of life, they would have lived for ever.

9 *September,* 1883.—I think that I shall move from here at the end of the year. It is now my prayer to know where

I shall go (for *He* cares what His members do, or where they go). Gaza has fallen through. You know I do not like idleness; I want to get to a place where I can find sick people to visit, feeling sure that is the necessary work for me; I think He will direct me, so I seek no advice elsewhere. I leave it to God, to decide in His time. I do not like the ways of the polished world, and my dislike has increased during the time I have been here.

10 *September*, 1883.—As the word "soul" has been so twisted and turned in our religious books, I wish you would get used to the word "*nephesh*," and understand that, when I write it, I mean the *vital essence of man, which he derived from God's breathing*. I have often used "animal soul," &c.; now for the future let us call it "*nephesh*." Truly the simple truths of the Bible have been so covered up with men's words, that one has to dig in the ruins to find them. I am sure that much obscurity arises from not using Scriptural *words*. Words like "incarnation," "classes," "fall," "animal life," and many others are not in the Scriptures, and they cause no end of trouble.

The redeemed are made "partakers of the Divine Nature." Christ was made partaker of flesh and blood. Jesus said to His disciples, "Whom say ye that I am"? Peter answered, "Thou art the Christ." Our Lord said, "Flesh and blood hath not revealed it unto thee, but my Father which is in heaven." Immediately after this Peter rebukes Him, saying, "Be it far from thee, Lord;" our Lord replies, "Get thee behind Me, Satan." Quick as their conversation was, it is evident that the Holy Ghost spoke *through Peter* in the acknowledgment that Jesus was Christ, and Satan spoke *through Peter* in the rebuke (Matthew xvi. 15—23).

No believer doubts that Christ is *one*, both God and man. On this truth hangs our salvation. Consequently we must admit the redeemed are of the Divine Nature, as much as the Divine Nature became man.

15 *September*, 1883.—If the Palestine canal is made, we

shall abandon Egypt, which will then get self-government, and will succeed under God's blessing, for He has a blessing for it. I have been writing many letters, and much about this canal, to-day, and I feel deathlike; I have for the last few weeks been in constant communion (no, not *constant*, but frequent), and worldly things make me feel tired. Somehow I think I never could work again with any comfort. Revelation is a very difficult book, and one sees very little of its meaning; but it would be beautiful if one could understand it. Dr. Mackie says, "The blessing to be looked for does not come by the comprehension, but by the reading, of the revelation God has given us in His Word" (Revelation i. 3).

I wish friends would not send me papers, &c., I pass them on to ——, who is my waste-paper basket!

A seed that is buried or sown is dead in a way, though the germ of life is in it; it is alive, though dormant (1 Corinthians xv. 36). Darkness is as the earth in which seeds of light are sown, and those seeds, enriched by that darkness, spring up into trees of light; some are long in germinating— remain long in the earth, in darkness. So I believe the germs of light—the souls of men—remain long hidden in the darkness of man's body. Somehow I do not feel drawn to write to those who criticize and yet never try to present views of their own. I do not say this from pride, but I have not time, and it is useless work to try and convince by the flesh: either men accept the truth or not; it is a gift of God to understand and see those things, and no reasoning will avail.

That was a splendid remark, "That the body is the garden of Eden;" where did you get it? It will afford me much thought: thanks for it. The serpent was good (John i. 3; Genesis i. 31), but the spirit which was in him must have been evil. The "Doles" are the "wailing place" over the ruins of the body. It is odd your writing what I have felt about our phases; but I think we have some members in each phase.

20 *September*, 1883.—My thoughts about the Wailing-place open out a vista. The Jew is the flesh seeking its own glory, justifying itself by works before men. We are all Jews *when we judge others.* "Mr. Smith does not do so-and-so; he is wrong. I do not act as he does: I am right : praise me for being better than he is." We lay all sorts of little traps to get the praise, and if we do not get it we are angry with Jones and think him stupid and not spiritually-minded. By judging others we imply that they could be better if they chose, and thus that righteousness comes by the works of the law. How very subtle the heart is! The only person we have a right to judge is ourself. Even if we could rightly judge others, we ought not to do so, for their errors are from being barren, from not being in union. Righteousness is a fruit of the Holy Ghost, which is a gift of God, and which none possess unless He gives it. *I* am very prone to this fault; in discussing these kinds of questions one is very apt to take people one knows as examples; yet the apostles used no such examples; they spoke generally. We have no right to say of any one "He is a Pharisee"; our saying so is equivalent to being a Pharisee one's self.

It is strange that the Christian visible Church drifts back into Judaism, "For if righteousness come by the law, then Christ is dead in vain" (Galatians ii. 21).

The Jew proper only thinks of the restoration of his people, good crops, universal attention and respect, *his* exaltation, and the degradation of the other nations to be his servants; so the Jew in each of us thinks only how he can be holy, never err in his judgment, have worldly prosperity, be universally respected as a good man, and feared by all those who do not live as he does. No one should wish either the Jew proper or the Jew in us to obtain his desire.

The striking feature of the literal Jew is to lend on usury. Why should this be his peculiar propensity? What does it mean? It evidently is the act of taking advantage of another when he is in difficulties; it is gain made by the

L 𝔶

troubles of others; it is profit made on the sale of help.
There must be a meaning for this peculiarity, also for their
partiality towards buying old clothes. They are a typical
people, and these things are what make them peculiar.

In the Jewish class-books they omit the fall of man and
original sin, so virtually do all who judge others—all who
think they can attain righteousness by the works of the
Law. This is the most invidious of all doctrines, and no
one is free from it while in the flesh. In fact, as long as the
flesh exists, we are under the Law; when *it* dies, *we* are free.

The world must end when Christ comes again; all who
believe in its restoration in this age are Jews, for they imply
that the world can, if it will, attain righteousness without
Christ.

The Jew is the flesh, the Christian is the spirit. The
Church is built up of many members, her children. Eve
was a mosaic, the Church is a mosaic. The omissions of
Scripture are not mistakes; silence is as suggestive as a
statement. How remarkable it is that there can be no
quiet, except with humility; courts, camps, &c., all are torn
by discordant elements owing to pride. Kings cannot
favour A. for fear of making B. jealous; C. intrigues against
D.; even such little things as wearing a bit of red riband
here or there causes strife; the one who has it not is jealous
of the one who has it. The greater the king, the greater the
discord; but God dwells in the man of a poor and contrite
heart, who trembleth at His word (Isaiah lvii. 15). Any one
who has ever been a ruler knows how miserable it is, when
disposed to be quiet himself, to have those under him who
are proud and cruel; he can have no rest. Those who
enter *that* city will be humble, for *their* righteousness will be
plainly seen to be but filthy rags; they will be tired of self
and will love God for Himself, not for His gifts.

I have been much comforted for myself and you in the
realization that in this life the position we occupy is as
nothing: each is in his right place. If Paul was not wanted

for the time he was in prison at Cæsarea, we may rest assured he was kept idle—no, not idle, but inactively employed—for some good purpose. Every one is doing work quite as important as any one else, whether on a sick bed or as Viceroy of India; it is our folly which makes us think otherwise. I am very pleased at this, for I have often thought it hard for others to be laid up, yet in reality, if we could realize it, the worry of command is no joke; up and down, early and late, troubled on all sides, eaten up with anxiety, plotting and counter-plotting—it is not, as I know, an agreeable life. We all like activity and to be employed, but I veribly believe that non-employment is the salutary trial we have to go through.

28 *September*, 1883.—The ——— were both at the wailing-place the day before yesterday, and distressed me, for I never know how to deal with them except by prayer. It is quite pagan in us when we attack the deeds of others; we deny His being the Lord of heaven and earth. The only remedy with me, dating from Gravesend, is to pray for every one who worries me; it is wonderful what such prayer does. In heaven our Lord intercedes for us, and He governs heaven and earth. Prayer for others relieves our own burdens. God turned the captivity of Job *when he prayed for his friends*, who had been as thorns in his side. I feel strongly that the grace God gave me to pray for my enemies in the Soudan led to my success, though I certainly used the sword of Cæsar on them.

Should God continue His mercy to me, as He gives it now, I shall be a bad companion, for I cannot, without a *twinge*, discuss any one; and I believe that is from intercessory prayer, for, though one may begin such a discussion, if we pray for another, that remembrance would check us.

One great altitude to be lifted up to by the Holy Ghost is the feeling that the sorrows of others are our own sorrows, inasmuch as we are members of one body. Another is, to have a humble and contrite spirit. To exemplify a truth or an error, we can find the example in ourselves. Paul rarely used the names of others: only, I think, Demas, Hymeneus, Alexander, Phygellus, and Hermogenes. John signalizes Diotrephes as "*prating;*" and those were inspired writers. This is one great reason why I never desire to enter social life, for there is very great difficulty in knowing people and not discussing others.

Having plenty of time, I get up at seven, read and pray till eleven or twelve, work till four, then go for a ride, and read and write till ten or eleven P.M.: that is my day. Very rarely do I see any one. If I were in England, I should get up earlier, and thus have some three hours to go to the sick.

Graham writes from Egypt that he is likely to go from there at the end of the year: that looks as though we should evacuate it. I like watching how God governs all things there; He acts to us as we act to others.

To speak evil is Satanic and Satan's work, and it is evident he is in every man, and, being the prince of this world, he can, with the permission of God, impel men.

My correspondence has dropped off a good deal, for I find that, when the mind is on one thing, we can only write on that subject, and it is difficult to open out any matter when one does not write continuously. Most people only nibble at these great subjects; in their letters they seem more inclined to cavil than to accept.

A natural babe refuses strong meat, it will not take it; so in like manner does a spiritual babe. When we do not know the Scriptures, we naturally do not know the tendency of certain verses; consequently, when we read any new view, we have not the knowledge of the Scriptures to fall back upon, which another, knowing them, has. There is a material, actual study of the Scriptures necessary in order to know them, which we cannot have if we do not give the time to such actual study, which few of us do. These latter are the babes, and, to write to them, we have far more fully to quote the Scriptures than to the spiritual adult.

Some of us know the Scriptures, especially the clergy ;
but, though they may understand, they do not care for the
subjects, and the beauties are only appreciated for a moment.
When we have much secular work or dealing with others,
even when we know the Scriptures, if we do not act up to
them, our minds are on the secular things, and we cannot
find time to think even of such a question as whether the
breath of God is eternal or not. When I think my reader
does not care for my subject, it damps my writing.

"And the Lord God formed man of the dust of the
ground, and breathed into his nostrils the breath of life ;
and man became a living soul" (Genesis ii. 7). I believe
that thus was made of twain one man, and that God put
this dual man under restriction as to his earthly desires, on
pain of death—*i. e.* separation from Him. The spirit of
evil tempted the carnal man to transgress against this restriction by representing to him that by so doing he would
become like God in knowledge, as he was in image. I
believe that the spiritual man was not in the transgression,
but that death, *i. e.* separation from God, fell on him by
virtue of his union or oneness with the carnal man.

I believe this to be true of all men and of each individual.
Instead of regarding the various generations of the world's
population as so many million units, they may be regarded
as one man [1] with many members, whose life would be as
the duration of the world ; the history of the world's population is the history of that long-lived man, and I believe
that history has its analogy in every individual who has ever
lived. The sins of the multitude are the sins of that long-
lived man, his sins again are the sin of Adam ; for the
single sin of Adam was the mother of this prolific brood.
I regard Adam as the pristine man, into whom God
breathed the breath of lives, and I believe that even as he
held all mankind after the flesh in his loins, so he held all

---

[1] Bishop Temple says, "The human race is one colossal man whose
life reaches from the creation to the day of judgment."

mankind after the spirit in his spiritual loins, and that the
inner man—the living soul which God exhaled into man's
carnal body—was one with Him and of a divine nature,
"heirs of God and joint-heirs with Christ," though under
bondage until the fulness of time, when God sent forth His
Son to redeem them—"the prisoners of the Lord" and
"His hidden ones." I believe that they were "set up from
everlasting, from the beginning, or ever the earth was," as
members of His Christ, "bone of His bone and flesh of
His flesh," and that their names were in the Book of Life.
I believe that the Holy Scriptures contain the history of the
carnal man and of the spiritual man, including the creation,
fall, and restoration of the former, the emission, separation,
and restoration of the latter ; that they faithfully portray, as
only God could, the strife between the two, the one acting
under the impulse of the spirit of evil, oppressing and striving to destroy, the other supported in the warfare by God.
As the history given in the Holy Scriptures is true for the
whole generation of mankind, so I believe they contain the
analogous history of each individual carnal and spiritual man,
and the strife between them until death for a time separates
them.

The Psalms are the utterances of the spiritual man under
the bondage of the carnal man, both in the outward world
and in each individual man. I believe that by this view
alone can be understood "a man's foes shall be they of his
own household" (Matthew x. 36). "Think not that I am
come to send peace on earth ; I came not to send peace,
but a sword" (Matthew x. 34). I believe that the promises
of God are to the spiritual man, and that the curses of God
are against the carnal man. The spiritual man needs the
water and bread of life for his existence, as much as the
carnal man needs earthly water and bread (Matthew iv. 4).
As far as the spiritual man is enabled by his union with the
Lord Jesus to curb and mortify the members of the carnal
man, so far will he be enabled to realize spiritual things.

I believe that, while here, the spirit of evil and its existence will remain a mystery. God in due time will reconcile all things to Himself by His Son our Lord Jesus Christ; but how, I know not. Let it suffice us to know the mystery of our reconciliation with Him. As the wheat and the chaff are one seed, so the spiritual and carnal man are one.

Remember the tenets of your faith, pre-existence, incarnation, fall into sin, atonement, and rise with the knowledge of God into your former state. I trust the Pilot to-day, though I fear the voyage among so many rocks and quicksands. Like Paul, it may be the loss of the ship, but no loss of life; no one likes the loss of his ship!

1 *October*, 1883.—It is very wonderful that not only is the reading of the Scriptures necessary, but so are even the *very* words. The greatest mistakes may grow out of not attending to the words. Take this subject: "The Lord God formed *man* of the dust of the ground, and breathed into his nostrils *the breath of life*, and man became a *living soul*" (Genesis ii. 7). "The Spirit of God hath made me, and the breath of the Almighty hath given me life" (Job xxxiii. 4).

1. Had *man* life till God breathed into him the breath of life (lives)?

2. Whence did God form *man*?

3. What gave *man* life?

4. Where did the *breath of the Almighty* come from?

5. If it came from the Almighty, was it created?

6. With whom did God make the covenant of works— "Eat and ye shall die, do not eat and ye shall live?" (Genesis ii. 16, 17.)

7. Whence did God take the rib? (Genesis ii. 22.)

8. Who ate of the tree?

9. Who was sentenced, because of eating, to go back to dust, and was told he was dust?

10. Are we not living souls?

11. Of what are we made up?

12. Who broke the covenant of works?

13. Could the breath of the Almighty sin?

14. Had the breath of the Almighty free-will?

15. Had *man* (the word of Genesis ii. 7) free-will?

16. If *man* (the word of Genesis ii. 7) had not free-will to choose or refuse, why have made the covenant?

17. What was the origin of the breath of the Almighty?

18. What was the origin of *man* (the word of Genesis ii. 7)?

19. Do not things seek their origin?

20. Are not the man of Genesis ii. 7 and the breath of the Almighty the living soul?

21. What caused man to be a living soul?

22. If the covenant of works was broken by man (Genesis ii. 7), was it not broken *imputatively* by the breath of the Almighty, which gave life to that man and made him a living soul?

23. Does not the *man* (Genesis ii. 7) die?

24. Can the breath of the Almighty die?

25. Is not death cessation of life?

26. What is the equivalent of death to the breath of the Almighty? Is it not separation from God?

27. What was the penalty of the breach of the covenant? Was it not death on what could die, and separation from God on what could not die?

28. Unless the justice of God was satisfied, would it not entail the eternal death of the *man* (Genesis ii. 7) for his breach of covenant, and the eternal separation from God of the breath of the Almighty (from its oneness as a living soul with that man) for its imputed guilt?

29. How many men were in the man (Genesis ii. 7) who broke the covenant?

30. Had the first man (Genesis ii. 7) not broken the covenant, would those in him have broken it?

31. Did not the first man (Genesis ii. 7) sin one sin, which was the mother to all sins?

32. Thence was there not one man (Genesis ii. 7) and one sin?

33. If an innocent man came and bore the penalty of that sin and took the place of that first man (Genesis ii. 7), would not the law be satisfied?

34. Did not Christ make an offering of His own body (Hebrews x. 10)?

If you will only take the trouble to write in pencil your answers to the above queries, you will gain; at any rate I have done so in writing them. Remember *man* is formed of the dust of the ground. God breathes into *man* thus formed the *breath of life* or *lives*, and *man* becomes a *living soul*. You must keep these terms clear before you; that is not much to ask.

I will make a recapitulation. (Genesis ii. 7) "And the Lord God formed man of the dust of the ground,"—the first distinct step,—"and breathed into his nostrils the breath of life or lives,"—the second distinct step,—"and man" (*vide* first step) "became" (owing to the second step) "a living soul."

Mark that the covenant, "eat and die," "do not eat and live," was with the *man*, and its breach was by the *man;* the sentence was on the *man* who covenanted, and the *man* was driven out.

The woman was taken out of *man* (Genesis ii. 23), so she was in the *man*.

The mass of the Bible is on the *man* and *man's* doings.

In Exodus xxiv. 3, 7, Israel said, "All that the Lord hath said will we do"; the covenant of Sinai was only the renewal of the covenant of Eden, accompanied by shadows of the new covenant of grace. If we live much in the flesh, we must be under the law of works and at the wailing-place. Sensitive minds are more prone to this than more callous ones; they worry themselves because they do this or that. If we agree that we can do no good thing, we ought not to blame others for not doing good things. And I am sure, for myself, one of the great hindrances I have is the habit of judging others; by so doing I imply that I am under the law of works, for I say, they should do this or that which I think right, whereas I know *I* cannot do this or that without the quickening Spirit. There is no mystery in this evil speaking or judging others; it is Satanic and hurtful, and diametrically opposed to our Lord's words: I have grievously offended in this particular.

I believe the sin of the world and its offspring sins are entirely obliterated by our Lord's atonement; we may not all know this, for we are tied to a garment which is so intimately connected with us that we think it is ourselves. When shredded off by death, or torn off piecemeal by our dying to the world before death, then we may feel this truth, though we may still work in accordance with the will of this garment, be mixed up with its concerns, with its treatment by others; and, to the degree we are so, we shall feel we are one with the garment, and suffer accordingly. The garment's idea is that God is a Being whom it must propitiate; it loves Him not, it knows its doom, and would make you feel that you and it are one, and doomed equally to destruction. It is not so; *it* certainly is doomed to destruction, but it is false when it tries to persuade you that you are doomed with it.

It is a necessary covering to you and me while we sojourn in this world: what God has joined together let no man put asunder; but it must be a slave and not the master: it has much power, for, though we are not really *of* it, it is so intimately connected with us, that we feel its wants and are happier when it is well and comfortable. I like my garment and I hate it; I would leave it and yet I would keep it; it very often rebels and does not as I would it should do, while it does what I would it should not do (Romans vii.). We live in warfare; sometimes, nay, often, *it* rules, while sometimes *I* rule; it is a perishable garment, every day tells me that.

And now, my dear Augusta, I am going to put you in the corner and cross-examine you. Do you believe these words? Tell me, as far as human language goes, are they intelligible as to my reasoning? God only can make spiritual truth known. If what I have written is truth and fact, it is only a statement of what exists, and He may make it plain. Here is an old illustration : a ship approaching land; one of the crew may see the mountains, another may see mountains and trees, another may see mountains, trees, and houses; so with regard to the truth, we each may see it in whole or in part only; but, as the mountains, trees, and houses exist, whether seen or not by the crew, so with these truths : whether apprehended or not, they exist. There is no credit to the man who sees the mountains, trees, and houses, more than to the man who sees the mountains only; the first may say, " Look *lower*, and you will see the trees and houses," and, under his directions, the mountain-seer may distinguish objects which he had before overlooked. And so it is with spiritual truths : God may reveal them to some, and they, by directing the attention of others to them, may cause things revealed to be received. I come to you again now : Are you not too reserved and shut up in yourself? I want you to flow out ; you must not be barren, for, as sure as you are, you will be a sufferer from the " Doles." I say to you, Die, throw away your pride, *your " medal*," and be free.

In birth, man is put into bondage; in death, he is liberated from bondage. As the body decreases in power over the soul, so a man dies : this is brought about by the decay of the body in old age. Happy are those to whom this death is given before the natural decay.

Man must die to the things of the world before he can produce any fruit : *this is certain*. What is death to the things of the world? It is to be counted an idiot, an idealist, an impossible sort of person, a theorist, an indiscreet person, an (apparent) condoner of evil, an enthusiast,

T

a mean-spirited person, &c. &c. It is *not* prayer-meetings, or church-going, or parish-visiting.

I speak of myself. In my spiritual nature, I despise the world, its praise or blame. I know of nothing to be admired in my body or its actions from my birth to this day. The world's praises are satires on me; its blame is just, though not from right motives. In my bodily nature, I scheme and work as if everything depended on my sending this or that telegram, or my ordering this or that; but, thank God, my spiritual nature rules, and I can, when exposed to rebuffs, fall back on that spiritual nature and be comforted.

2 *October*, 1883.—God drove out the *man* formed from the dust, and sent him forth to till the ground out of which he was taken; that is clear, is it not? Before the Fall, Adam called his rib, woman; afterwards he named her Eve.

After the Fall they knew they were naked, and extemporized coverings of fig-leaves; they had lost some natural covering connected with obedience to God and union with Him; the Lord God *made* them coats of skin, and clothed them. What they lost may be termed the livery of God. One can scarcely think that coats, in our acceptation of the word, were made by God and put on them by Him; I expect that more is meant. "Though after my skin worms destroy this body, yet in my flesh shall I see God" (Job xix. 26). What were those coats of skin, made and put on by God? What means the serpent's remark, "your eyes shall be opened," "and the eyes of them both were opened and they knew that they were naked"? This refers to the *man* formed from the dust.

Disunion was the result of the Fall, and selfish thoughts sprang up which neither Adam nor Eve cared for the other to see; so they extemporized coverings. I think that is the correct interpretation : naked means bare, open to view, *i. e.* revealed.

3 *October,* 1883.— —— came this morning. "Could I

do him a great, very great favour?" I said, "Yes, and that
I knew what it was," and said "godfather?" Of course it
was right; I knew it long, long ago, when it was coming.
He said, in reply to my remark, that the last child, three
years old, was jealous that the other was born; she had
been sulky all day, saying she was the baby: and I expect
it was her first true grief.

One of my horses died this morning of pleurisy; it had
been ill four days; I am glad it is out of its suffering. ——
gave up his appointment on *conscientious* grounds; of these
we can often find plenty and very plausible ones, when we
give up things we do not like for work which pleases us
better.

· Read the Targums; I have extracted all that is curious
about the Creation and Fall. It makes one laugh; when
speaking of the embrace of Esau and Jacob, it says that
Esau wept at the embrace because of the pain in his teeth,
and that Jacob wept because of the pain in his neck; they
apparently embraced with force.

5 *October*, 1883.—As for translations, the Scripture is
God's Word, the Teacher is the Holy Ghost, therefore there
can be no mistake; even a literal mistake is used for good
by the Teacher. Get that idea of the Holy Ghost, and no
change of translation, which is overruled by Him, can or
ought to shake our belief. All idea of human effort must
be abandoned. The Bible is *in us ;* He shows us what is
in us by the Word. The Bible is a revealing or pulling
back of a veil away from *things which exist*, therefore no
new translation can touch that; if a mistranslation exists,
and the thing it reveals does not, then we cannot see that
thing which is mistranslated. The "in" you mention—
"He dwelleth in me"—is corroborated by the Holy Ghost
in me. While He gives me grace, no human proof of any
sort could do away with the "in"; and so, if the whole
Bible were, humanly speaking, disproved, its truths are in
us, and it would not signify what people said. Think of

this, for it is the truth. To me faith is identical with God's living in us; see Paul's great verse, "The just shall live by faith," *i. e.* by the indwelling of the Holy Ghost, by whom we are in union with Christ and God the Father.

How often we feel vexed at our faults, and, if we investigate them, we find it is because our fault brings vexation on us from outside; we are not vexed because of our fault, but with its consequences, which bring thorns on us. We think we have sinned against A or B, we do not think of our sins against God. We say an unkind word; that does not vex us so much as the thought that the person to whom we said it will be disagreeable or repeat it.

6 *October*, 1883.—I am getting out of letter paper and envelopes; could you send me some in small detachments by book-post? I like large double paper.

I was at the Wailing-place to-day because of the "New York Herald" letter, but, thank God, I have now left it.

9 *October*, 1883.—Truly the Scriptures are wonderful! their minute accuracies raise one's belief very much, and show that one mind, namely, the Holy Ghost, wrote them all. It is odd how often I am barren for days, then a subject comes. During the barren times I read a good deal. "When the enemy shall come in like a flood, the Spirit of the Lord shall lift up a standard against him" (Isaiah lix. 19).

14 *October*, 1883.—There is nothing that may not be perverted; the Sacrament, reading the Bible, intercessory prayer, all may be made gods of—of this there is no doubt. We tend to make gods of everything we do. If we can, as it were, get a pull over our neighbours, then we think we are better than they. We should look on everything as a means of realizing *His indwelling;* the Scriptures only do *that*, the Sacrament only does *that*, intercessory prayer only does *that*.

In all things we should be very humble, for we really know nothing of ourselves; I own day by day I know less, and am glad to give up any ideas I have.

15 *October*, 1883.[1]—I do not mind at all how the answer about the Congo is given; at least, God helping me, I am undisturbed, if I have His grace.

If things are good to my view, I am grateful; if not, I remember that He despised the world; if He keeps me alive, it is for some purpose; when the fruit is ripe, He puts in the sickle : the fruit is all one should care for. Any thoughts, except those on divine things, are *vain* and use-less. I am quite comforted about the Soudan; He is working out an intricate scheme to our eyes, but I know it will be good. I know that the people liked me, and, humanly speaking, my reign caused the rebellion, for I and the people agreed in our feelings against the Turkish pashas.

I will end this, for it may be that the steamer will go early.

25 *October*, 1883.—I have received a telegram saying that my going to the Congo is allowed; so I shall go to Brussels, unless Mackinnon says to the contrary. It has not moved me in the least; the true temple is shadowed on earth, so all things on earth are shadowed from some real things in heaven; the heavenly are the only things which last.

27 *October*, 1883.—I hope you will be better for your trip to Brighton. I look forward to some fifteen years at the very outside, and on looking back it seems a day. I am like a man who, with others, has to catch a train at sunset. I have hurried on and got to the station two hours before time, while others who have not hurried will catch the same train. I mean, I have lived my life too quickly; however, God has ruled, and does rule it. I expect now to have a barren time.

I find the minor Prophets most interesting, but they are difficult. In my old Bible[2] you will see some dates; these

---

[1] On the 15th of October, General Gordon received a telegram asking him to go to the Congo, and was waiting to know whether the Government would authorize his accepting.

[2] Mentioned in the Preface.

were made long ago, when I worked at the subject of the Bible events being carried out in us.

5 *November*, 1883.—Should my going to the Congo be settled, I hope you will not mind; you know what little rows I get into when in England, and I am far better away. If I could have got into work in the East End, it would have been all right; but I fear I should have always been dug out, and could not have lived a quiet life. I shall not be sorry to go, if I *do* go, as I feel it will be much better for me and my surroundings. Man cannot help man, except in a very small way, and more often hinders than aids him.

12 *November*, 1883.—I sincerely hope you will keep the papers, *if you like them*, for you are the principal reason for my writing them, and all others are quite secondary considerations. I feel quite conscience-smitten at your being at so much trouble. Pray do not let the sending of the letters hurry you; they are written more for you than others, and are only on loan to Mr. B——.

I am sorry to hear of Mr. Wilberforce's illness. We are weak, frail creatures at our best, and the nearer we seek God, the more imperfect we seem to be. I have felt this very much of late; I long for my rest from the wear and tear of this life: wherever we are, we must have worries, whether in Southampton or Palestine.

How very easily I am deceived, with all my experience! Every time we fall, we get scattered like little bits, and then we gather together again; life is one succession of falls, scatterings, and gatherings: in fact, winnowing or sifting—first is a threshing out, next a winnowing, and then a gathering, and all is the work of God. I am daily more and more convinced that help can only come from God. In no country in the world does one see such money-seeking propensities as in this, yet I believe that, though they show out as most offensive in these lands, they are just as prevalent in our own country, only they do not present themselves in such a gross form as to attract our attention. We are only varnished, our civilization is superficial. Here, in the Holy Land, as is right, they are in their nakedness; in Christian lands, they are more or less clothed.

The feature of the people out here is self-exculpation on every subject; a lie ready on the tip of the tongue, sometimes for no reason, especially is they think to please. These characteristics are universal, but we do not notice them elsewhere; here you cannot help doing so, where, I think, it is allowed in order to keep it a typical country.

I am of a much more material mind than you are, I think much more of the risen flesh as material. I think I am right, for else, why is so much said of the inheritance of the earth (by earth, I think universe)? This is why I have even a carnal desire for departure from this world. I am in a hut, I want to go to a palace; now, a palace is only a superior style of hut, but it is of the same nature—namely, a dwelling-place. I cannot, with my mind, desire a state of existence altogether different from this: I mean *different* in the way of our being shadowy spirits. Everything seems to me to point to a material spiritual body; we are miracles in our formation, and it can scarcely be that we were so created only for this earth.

17 *November*, 1883.—It is very curious, the telegram about my going to the Congo having come thus altered: "The Secretary of State has *decided* to sanction your going to the Congo," the message intended being, "*declined* to sanction." I think you have the original of the one I received; I cut off the tag ends and sent it to you. I was not moved at the information which told me the true version. You can continue to write, for, if nothing is changed for the present, I shall stay here for some time. Sorry I have no gum, so have to send the sheets loose, and give you trouble.[1]

---

[1] Alluding to the custom General Gordon had of writing on half sheets, and gumming together the left-hand corners, as the letters consisted generally of many pages.

Your two long letters have just come, many thanks for them; they please me more than any other letters I get. You are quite right, to my mind; we must continually err in order to be humble, our frailty and sins are the tools God uses. I have felt this much lately. We may be sure God does right, and in love far surpassing our love, for we pick holes in one another.

20 *November,* 1883.—I hope you will not mind my going to the Congo, if God so wills it; my only care is how you would take it. I would it were given to all, as God has given it to me, to look on death as a thing to be desired.

25 *November,* 1883.—As time draws on for me to leave this land, I feel the more attached to it, and after the flesh am loth to leave it. I do not think I have forced events, but certainly I am too comfortable and selfish here, so am not surprised at being turned out of it.

As for the Soudan, I am much interested, but should feel repugnance to going back there; and that is a great gain, for I *had* a sneaking desire to return there, when I first came out here. As for the Congo, I have not much choice left me.

I shall be glad to see you again. I hope you are well, as I am, and also happy.

[The facts of General Gordon's intended expedition to the Congo, and the change of plan caused by his being asked to go to the Soudan, and all that happened after, are too well known for me to add any note here.]

Brussels, 1 *January,* 1884.—I arrived here this morning at 8 A.M., having come on from Milan, through the St. Gothard Tunnel, passing the end of one year and the beginning of another in the train. We had a bad voyage from Acre; however, it is all over now, and I am all right, in peace and tranquillity. I telegraphed to you: "*Arrived,*" from Milan, as I expect you did not know where I was.

I am glad to have escaped Christmas and New Year's Day; I will not express my wishes, except that you may daily be nearer our Lord. I would be the dust of His feet, and have a desire that all should be higher than myself. I am sorry for Mrs. Hicks. I feared what would happen, but our Lord, who is the Rock, rules all things. I have sent the King a model of the Rock; he, as Duke of Brabant, was the first to visit that spot.

2 *January,* 1884.—I have seen the King, he wishes me to go to the Congo: I said I would, and hope you will not mind; thus, my dear Augusta, I shall be with you in a few days, D.V., so keep all letters of import. I shall come direct to Southampton.

3 *January,* 1884.—Is Carter dead? is Colonel Jenkins dead? I have had no notice of either of their departures. The King is very kind. I am content about the Congo now, for I feel our Lord has so ruled it. The King has spent 400,000*l.* on the Congo; it is stupendous, is it not? He liked the "Rock" model and recognized it at once.

I went to see Malet and he was very kind; we only discussed the surface questions of Egypt, and avoided all resurrection ones of things gone by. I showed Colonel Strauch all the treasures; he was delighted, and will show them to the King and Queen.

4 *January,* 1884.—Will you order twelve small copies of Thomas à Kempis for me? I will not stay here a day longer than I can help. Thanks for your letter received this evening, I am truly glad you are not upset by the trial, I am now quite content and happy about it. The King wants to pay my hotel bill, and also my outfit; the last cannot be *allowed.*

5 *January,* 1884—D.V., I shall leave on Monday morning and reach Charing Cross at 5.30 P.M., and will come down by the next train from Waterloo. I have ordered you three copies of the Sheath.[1] It is odd that *tears* are salt like the *sea,* Satan's element.

[1] His photograph.

L

LONDON, 18 *January*, 1884.—I go to the Soudan to-night to finish a work, then to the Congo. I am not moved, and hope you will not be so.

BOLOGNA, 20 *January*, 1884.—I think of our last quiet Sunday. I hope you, as myself, are not moved, for all works for good. I am hopeful of success in the Soudan.

AT SEA, 21 *January*, 1884.—If people ask after me, tell them they can greatly help me with their prayers, not for my earthly success, but that my mission may be for God's glory, the welfare of the poor and wretched, and, for me, what He wills, above all for a humble heart.

CAIRO, 25 *January*, 1884.—I go up the Nile, D.V., to-morrow night; you will not hear much from me now, but may trust that He will hide me in His hand. I was met by three of my poor old adherents, they were truly rejoiced to see me. I am glad there is no smell of smoke in the house. Good night, my dear Augusta, *I am not* (thanks to God) *moved* even a little.

26 *January*, 1884.—I leave for the Soudan to-night. I feel quite happy, for I say, If God is with me, who can or will be hurtful to me? May He be glorified, the world and people of the Soudan be blessed, and may I be the dust under His feet.

ON THE NILE ON THE WAY TO ASSOUAN, 28 *January*, 1884.—I am on the Nile, on my way to Kartoum, and am quite well; the confidence of so many praying for me is a great comfort, and I like to lean on our Lord. I am as safe as at Southampton; mind, and keep that in view. Every one was kind at Cairo, and I have met many old friends. I have got back one of my old servants and hope to get the other. Graham and his A.D.C. go up with me as far as Korosko; I am glad to have him; Stewart also (my companion) is a capital fellow. To-day is my natal day fifty-one years ago. I have but little inclination to write you details, for nothing that I could tell you would be very cheering, and I have much to do.

My poor black secretary[1] knew he was going to his death; he said so, before he left Kartoum with General Hicks. Altogether things are very bad; but I am comforted in the affair, for I do trust Him to give peace, and am confident all will be well. I am sorry this is such a poor letter; but you can imagine I have had much to do and think over.

30 *January*, 1884.—The rising is by all accounts that of the Soudan people, and not of the slave-dealers, though of course those men are with them.

KOROSKO, 31 *January*, 1884.—Arrived at Korosko. God willing, I hope for a satisfactory solution of the affairs. The Mahdi is a nephew of my old guide. This guide knew Capsune, who is with Miss Felkin.[2]

1 *February*, 1884.—I start through the desert to-morrow, D.V., and am all right. Graham has come up, and has been a comfort to me. I am quite happy, and know that many are praying for me.

I want the king of the Belgians to let me take the Equator and Bahr Gazelle provinces for him: this would save me returning to Cairo and starting afresh for the Congo—this would also stop the slave-trade, and, D.V., we should soon join those provinces to the Congo at a place called Karurn: you will see it on your map.

I have not had time to write you a proper letter since I left; however, I shall now be quiet again, I hope. Watson and Mrs. Watson were exceeding nice and kind, and did a lot for me. I was only at Cairo from Thursday till Saturday. Huge dinner parties; ere I left, Nubar embraced

---

[1] Bazati Bey. Under a photograph of him, given me by my brother, is written: "For three years my brave and faithful friend, known by European scoffers as the 'black imp.'"

[2] See note, p. 193.

me ! I was glad to get away from the *fêtes* and troubles. I managed to get up early every day.

ABOU HAMED, 8 *February*, 1884.—I got here last night, and did not suffer in the desert. All the people were glad to see me again ; the Soudan is much quieter than I expected, and I hope all will be settled in six months, D.V. One of my guides had on a sword and belt belonging to one of Hicks's army. . . I got on a fresh camel as I entered the place, and it ran away with me ; I feared a fall, for it would have been a bad omen with these superstitious people ; however, I was saved. I deduce from this that God will bless my efforts, but that it will not be to my glory, for I fear the insidious snake—" pride."

BERBER, 13 *February*, 1884.—I arrived here on the 11th, and am quite well, but overwhelmed with work. I have great hopes that God will bless the mission. It has been a great pleasure to see my old friends, and to be so well received. I have no apprehension as to the future ; and, though I am worked very hard, am quite well. I will write to you when I am settled, D.V. Now I have not a minute to spare.

KARTOUM, 22 *February*, 1884.—I arrived on the 18th February, and was well received by the people. I have had much to do, and hope things look better.

To-day is the Mussulman Sunday, and I made those who came to see me a long sermonizing speech as to trust in God, which was well received. I mean to order the troops to have regular morning and evening prayers, as the Turkish troops do. They worship the one God *Jehovah*.

I am all right, and am supported in all this turmoil.

I expect you get all the news from the *Times*, whose correspondent is here—a nice young fellow named Power. I saw Bazati Bey's little black lamb. I miss him very much and feel quite left-handed without him. I have all my old servants back, and it is like old times again. I have not minced matters with the Pashas; it was useless to do so. We have thousands of petitions daily. I have ordered an Arabic text, "God rules the hearts of all men," to be put up over my *throne*, to which I can refer when people come to me in fear. Of course, I have not heard from you since I came up. I liked the delight of the small black boys, who were yelling about the remission of taxes when the little chaps had never paid a sou; the women were yelling out their joy, and were delighted to see me.

Raouf Pasha commenced a mosque here, and called it after his name, which I have cancelled, and given it the name of El Soudan. Raouf it was who did all the harm here; I had turned him out of the Equator and out of Harar, and had protested against his being sent up here. However, through him and the Mahdi the Soudan has got its independence. I have let a lot of Arabi's companions out of prison, and they will go down to Cairo; this is a good thing. There is, of course, a very mixed sort of feeling here about the evacuation of the Soudan; the civil *employés* do not desire it, for the half taxes will cause their pay to be diminished by half, and the *personnel* reduced.

26 *February*, 1884.—Thanks for your kind letter of 19th January received yesterday. I am glad you are "not moved" with my rapid departure. I hope you are well. I am truly glad to hear I am prayed for; it is the only thing I can lean upon.

I am torn in two with the thought of my impotency and God's omnipotency. If He is Almighty, He will work His will; and He *is* Almighty, so why should I trouble? Yet trouble I do, and am worn in the fight. I got the small seal all right, but I now use a larger one.

I thank Mr. Maund for the little book.[1]

You will know how I am situated, and excuse details.

---

[1] It was *The Dream of Gerontius*, by Cardinal Newman. My brother gave it to Mr. Power, who sent it to his home.

There is a great deal of misery here, and much fear; sometimes I get quite faint-hearted, but our Lord will support me.

There seems no chance of the Mahdi coming out of Obeid to this place, but of course I cannot be sure. In all these things one has to trust, and to think enough for the day is its evil. I got the gloves; they are splendid ones.

27 February, 1884.—I have sent Stewart off to scour the river White Nile, and another expedition to push back the rebels on the Blue Nile. With Stewart has also gone Power, the British Consul and *Times'* correspondent, so I am left alone in the vast palace of which you have a photograph, but not alone, for I feel great confidence in my Saviour's presence.

The peculiar pain, which comes from the excessive anxiety one cannot help being in for these people, comes back to me at times. I think that our Lord, sitting over Jerusalem, is ruling all things to the glory of His kingdom, and cannot wish things were different than they are, for, if I did so, then I wish *my will*, not *His*, to be done. The Soudan is a ruin, and, humanly speaking, there is no hope. Either I must believe He does all things in mercy and love, or else I disbelieve His existence; there is no half-way in the matter. What holes do I not put myself into! And for what? So mixed are my ideas. I believe ambition put me here in this ruin; however, I trust, and stay myself on the fact that not one sparrow falls to the ground without our Lord's permission; also that enough for the day is the evil. "God provideth by the way, strength sufficient for the day."

1 March, 1884.—We are all right at present, and I have hope, but certainly things are not in a good way; humanly speaking, Baker's defeat at Suakim has been a great disaster, and now it has its effects up here. "It is nothing to our God to help with many or with few," and I now take my worries more quietly than before, for all things are ruled by Him for His glory, and it is rebellion to murmur against His will. Excuse a long letter.[1]

3 *March*, 1884.—Very many thanks for your letter 30th January, received to-day. I never see newspapers now. . . . . Mr. A. B. now sees all the glories in his home; I am always interested when any one I pray for dies.

You see everything in the *Times* that is of interest; Power, the correspondent, lives here; he, Stewart and I get on all right. . . . I rely upon the prayers of my friends, and I feel that God will through great tribulation bring me out of my troubles.

5 *March*, 1884.—We are getting on all right, thank God, and I sincerely hope we may have no more bloodshed. I owe all to God, and nothing to myself, for, humanly speaking, I have done very foolish things. However, if I am humbled, the better for me.

I expect the French Consul up here to-day. Several prisoners have come in from Kordofan, and I believe the Mahdi is in a greater fix than I am, for he fears his *own* people, which I do not. It will be very wonderful if the outcome is the rising of the slaves against their masters, which is not an improbable event.

I hear very little from Cairo. Baring only telegraphs officially. I hope much from Zebehr's coming up.

7 *March*, 1884.—Only a short note, for I have no time. Things are still in the balance up here, but I hope that God may turn the hearts of the people to desire peace.

11 *March*, 1884.—This may be the last letter I send you, for the tribes have risen between this and Berber, and will try and cut our *route*. We have lots of food for five or six months. They will not fight us directly, but will starve us

---

[1] This letter of 27 February and 1 March has been presented to the Trustees of the British Museum, and is now exhibited in the Department of MSS.

out. Thank you for sending the *Thomas à Kempis,* but I doubt if they will get through now.

I am tired of myself, and I feel for Sir Bartle Frere. I like to take my mind off myself and the things up here. I am indeed glad of the prayers offered for me.

Our Lord's promise is not for the fulfilment of earthly wishes; therefore, if things come to ruin here, He is still faithful, and is carrying out His great work of divine wisdom. What I have to do is to submit my will to His, *even* however bitter may be the events which happen to me.

15 *March,* 1884.—We are all right. The enemy has established himself some six thousand strong nine miles from here, and we hear his drums from the Palace. We are well off for food, and the people are in good spirits; oddly enough, the supplies come in better than they did before, and we shall, D.V., go on for months. The steamers are a great advantage to us.

I have a great deal to do, so you will not expect long letters; in fact, we can scarcely expect that the rebels will let many posts go down. . . . . Your prayers help me, I feel.

12 *October,* 1884.—I send down my journal up to date, with this letter; it may be the last you will get for some time. The Mahdi has come down to pay us a visit, and is about four hours distant on our west front on the left bank of the Nile. He has all the Roman Catholic mission with him, except two, a priest and a nun who refused to change their faith—these two he left at Obeid; he has also Slatin Bey and all Greek merchants with him—a strange medley —and he has brought all his guns; he means to starve us out, not to attack directly. We are all right, thank God, and the town people are not put out by his coming.

20 *October,* 1884.—The Arabs are pretty quiet. I am sending down two more steamers towards Berber, to aid any advance which may be made. You will eventually get

all the news from the journal which I keep daily and have sent to Stewart. I think God will let us scramble through this ordeal.

5 *November*, 1884.—Your kind letter 7th August came yesterday. We have the Mahdi close to us, but the Arabs are very quiet.

Terrible news! I hear the steamer I sent down with Stewart, Power (British Consul), and Herbin (French Consul), has been captured, and all are killed. I cannot understand it—whether she was taken by treachery, or struck a rock, is unaccountable, for she was well armed and had a gun. With her, if she is lost, is the journal of events from January 3rd, 1884, to September 10th, 1884—a huge volume, illustrated and full of interest.

I have put my steamers at Metemma to wait for the troops. I decline to agree that the expedition comes for my relief; it comes for the relief of the garrisons, which I failed to accomplish.

I expect Her Majesty's Government are in a precious rage with me for holding out and forcing their hand.

King John wrote to me, but the Mahdi caught the letter. I sent you by Stewart a small packet with the bullet which came through my window,[1] and I sent Brocklehurst also a lot of swords, &c., but all I expect are captured. All is for the best, and is overruled for good. I am very well, but very gray with the continual strain on my nerves. I have been putting the Sheikh el Islam and Cadi in prison ; they were suspected of writing to the Mahdi; I let them out yesterday.

I am very grieved for the relatives of Stewart, Power, and Herbin.

14 *December*, 1884.—This may be the last letter you will

---

[1] The lid of the small box was found in a hut where Colonel Stewart was murdered, and was sent to me, having been so directed by my brother.

U

receive from me, for we are on our last legs, owing to the delay of the expedition. However, God rules all, and, as He will rule to His glory and our welfare, His will be done. I fear, owing to circumstances, that my affairs pecuniarily are not over-bright. . . . .

Your affectionate brother,

C. E. Gordon.

P.S. I am quite happy, thank God, & like Lawrence, I have "tried to do my duty"

" Sown in weakness, . . . raised in power;
Sown a natural body, . . . raised a spiritual body."

APPENDIX.

EXTRACTS FROM LETTERS OF GENERAL GORDON.

[1] Boldly and humbly study the Scriptures—God's dwelling in us is the key to them; they are a sealed book as long as you do not realize this truth, which is sure and certain, whether you feel it or not. Look on all trials as inevitable; you cannot make one hair white or black. No circumstances or annoyances are preventible or accidental.

It is hard for the flesh to thank God for trials, but it is our duty to do so. The blending of our will with His is the perfection of worship; no prayers, almsgiving, or church-going are so acceptable to Him. Die now, and ye will never die ("Ye are dead, and your life is hid with Christ in God").

I am at present two men: the one violent, brutal, hard, and in every way despicable; the other would hurt no one. Torn by these conflicting factions, my only rest at times is in thinking over my union with God; there and there alone can I find peace.

I have had many enjoyable things after the world's estimation, but there is nothing in any way to be compared to the study of God's word. How wonderfully it fits in with the various events of life! Examine all things through the microscope of His Scriptures, how He turns this and that event; how some are blinded for a time, and the very things they decry are done by them; it is an analysis which nothing escapes, and which shows each man to be the same weak creature as his brother; ostriches we are, all of us, to ourselves, and generally to others. Poor, poor indeed were the religion of Christ, if it did not contain more than is generally accepted. Where is its comfort? Where its support?

[1] The dates of these extracts have been lost; they are therefore placed here in the Appendix.

It is a delightful thing to be a fatalist, not as that word is generally employed, but to accept that, *when things happen and not before*, God has for some wise reason so ordained them : *all* things, not only the great things, but all the circumstances of life—that is what to me is meant by the words "ye are dead." We have nothing further to do, when the scroll of events is unrolled, than to accept them as being for the best ; but, *before it is unrolled*, it is another matter, for you would not say "I sat still and let things happen." With this belief all I can say is, that amidst troubles and worries no one can have peace till he thus stays upon his God—*that* gives a superhuman strength.

You are aware I look on death as being life. The end of our term on earth is much to be desired, for at the best it is a groaning life. I do earnestly desire that I were *ripe ;* but I suppose I am not, for here I stay and am well, while others are gathered. I believe we have no more pain in leaving the world, than we had in entering it, yet, to the eye the body seems in pain ; how odd also it is that for years we know nothing, though we live and give plenty of trouble. I do not believe we die : we sleep ; and the opening of our eyes in the next world will not be in a world which is a new scene to us, for I believe in our pre-existence, and that we are only put into the flesh to teach us how bitter a thing it is to be separate from God, and to know Him more than we otherwise could have done. God's indwelling is all in all, the great secret. We all have to go through the same path, and nothing we can say will cause any change ; the experience must be made for each by each. I for my part feel caged on this earth, for the Bible has such very comforting promises, which all fit in so beautifully, that one longs to realize the future.

The inspired Paul says, "Know ye not that your body is the temple of the Holy Ghost?" God dwells in you. He speaks of the body being the temple in which the Holy Ghost was, and is, incarnated. What a wonderful thing we cannot be joined to Christ but by the Holy Ghost! if He who is the bond of union is absent, there can be no union. "No man can say Jesus is Lord, but by the Holy Ghost" If the Holy Ghost is incarnated in us now, He must be incarnated in us for ever, for His absence would break our union with the Lord; so that in heaven God the Son is incarnated, and God the Holy Ghost is incarnated, yet there are not two, but one, for the Head, Christ, is one with the body, the Church. I speak of a great mystery—Christ and His Church (Ephesians v. 32). About the pre-existence, I take the verse "Forasmuch then as the children are partakers of flesh and blood, He also Himself likewise took part of the same" (Hebrews ii. 14). The making of the children flesh and blood did not make the children, it only incarnated them in *flesh and blood;* this is the strongest verse on the subject I can think of for the moment, but there are many others. The master key of the Scriptures is *our union with Christ, by God the Holy Ghost in us.* That is the life by faith, for if you examine, you will find that faith is distinctly the Holy Ghost's living presence in us.

Any one, to whom God gives to be much with Him, cannot even suffer a pang at death. For what is death to a believer? It is a closer approach to Him, whom, even through the veil, he is ever with.

The mind must have food, and, if it does not feed on spiritual matters, it will on carnal things. You know how fearfully dull we all are, how we mope—to me studies like these prevent it, and that is great gain; things do not move me as before; such thoughts lift one up and are most interesting, far more than worldly things ever were. I would wish to avoid laying down the law: you may look at a plate and see it is round; I look at it, and see it is square; if you are happy in your view, keep it, and I keep mine; one day we shall both see the truth. I say this, because we often are inclined to find fault with those who do not think as we do, "who do not follow *us.*" Why trouble others and disturb their minds on matters which we see only dimly ourselves? At the same time I own to repugnance to the general conversation of the world, and of some religious people; there is a sort of "I am holier than thou" in their words which I do not like, therefore I prefer those subjects where such discussions do not enter.

To Mr. Laurence Oliphant.[1]

JAFFA, *September*, 1883.—I can assure you I am not at all scared by your views. Why should I be? Truth exists undivided and eternal; neither you nor I create it by our own apprehension of it. We are all in different vessels reconnoitring an isle; one thinks the isle is one shape, and one thinks it another, but our thoughts change it not: it is one shape, and was ever so.

However, I will grant the apprehensions of men differ; and when they differ it is difficult to discuss very deeply the same truth. I think an object is blue; you think it is yellow: no argument will suffice to change our inward sight any more than any argument would change our natural sight. From different lines of thought we lead up to the same main point—*i. e.* a great desire to be *sincere* and *pure*, and on this we agree entirely. . . .

KARTOUM, *March*, 1884.—Thanks for your very kind letter, dated February 6th, received to-day. You are quite right in what you say, and in the conversation we had. I hope I may cure that "stinging" way I have too often given way to. It is unkind, evil, satanic, and utterly un-Godlike to be so bitter, and I have no excuse, for so many are kind to me. . . .

What you say is quite true: we would wish to be His instruments, and yet to act as if we were the first cause,

---

[1] In giving me permission to print the above, Mr. Oliphant writes:—
"What you have copied can only reflect the highest credit on the honesty and genuine humility of your brother's character, and can only do good. What was so extraordinarily attractive to me in him was his underlying meekness and contempt for himself, except as an instrument for Divine ends.

"The absence of all cant, combined with this intense desire for service, however humble, made me feel him to be the most Christ-like man I ever knew."

like a saw which wishes to be used, but wants to cut in the way it likes. I must try and be passive, while doing what He thinks best.

To Colonel ffolliott.

KARTOUM, 5 *March*, 1884.—I came up here very weak in human means, but have been much blessed by our Lord, and things will turn out for the best. It is odd to be here in this vast ruin of an empire, but my long lonely rides now bear fruit by His blessing. What a defeat Hicks's was! It is terrible to think of over 12,000 men killed; the Arabs just prodded them to death, where they lay dying of thirst, four days without water! It is appalling. What a hecatomb to death! I dare say you know all the details, from the papers, of his defeat. My resource is in constant prayer, to accept His will in all things without murmuring, that He may be glorified, these people blessed, and I humbled to the dust, for then I realize more of His indwelling; He will not dwell in a proud heart, which I have in excess; so you will know, if I get humbled and the people blessed, that my prayers are answered, and you will not mind the humbling for me. "Lord, it is nothing with thee to help, whether with many, or with them that have no power . . . thou art our God; let not man prevail against thee" (2 Chronicles xiv. 11). "We have no might . . . neither know we what to do: but our eyes are upon thee" (2 Chronicles xx. 12). What comforting words, and how I need them! If God so wills, I hope to be out of the Soudan in five months; I shall not (if I can help it) go again to England, but to Brussels, and thence to the Congo.

Respecting one of his young Nephews.

I never pretended to *him* that I was consistent, for it would have been no good; also, I wanted him to see that it is nothing to acknowledge one's human failings; it is useless to try to keep up appearances, for you would be sure to fail. We all take kindness as due to us; *he*, like all

of us, does the same, and that is why I wish him to write to
the people I have named. I want him to understand that,
even in a worldly point of view, it is worth while being civil
to outsiders. I have been far more helped by little people
than by great. I take more pains *to answer letters from*,
and *to help* (if it is in my power), the small, than I would
the great. I would refuse a great man's dinner, to give
pleasure in having tea with my old housekeeper. Tell *him*,
when in trouble, to read his Scripture promises: they meet
all the diseases of the soul.

I am sure that it will interest my readers to see some of
the kind and feeling letters which were written to me, expressing sympathy in our loss. It has been most gratifying
to receive such touching words of appreciation concerning
my brother as those contained in the letters from His Highness the Khedive, whom General Gordon so loyally served,
and for whom he did all in his power to save his "lost
Egypt," and I think all must feel the *true* tone of regret
that runs through His Highness's letters. This feeling of
sorrow at the loss of a "friend" is also clearly shown in the
letters of those who served under my brother. The four
officers, from whose letters extracts are given, were in the
steamers which were sent by General Gordon to Metamma
to meet the force advancing to the relief of Kartoum, and
which also conveyed the six volumes of journals, *my
brother's last legacy to me*, the final resting-place of which
will be the British Museum.

The chief command of these steamers was held by
Nushi Pasha, an Egyptian, to whom all General Gordon's
orders and instructions were given. Khashm-el-Moos Pasha
is one of the Shagiyeh tribe, and still bears the title of "El
Melik," the King, from his influence and family connections.
Khashm was the highest of the four commanders. Mahmond
Talaât Pasha and his brother, Ali Riza Pasha, are Circassians
in the Egyptian service. Colonel Watson, in forwarding these
letters, says: "You would be glad to hear how the officers

who were with your brother at Kartoum speak of him. Ali
Riza, who was an undemonstrative man, quite broke down
in speaking of him, and says he never seemed to sleep, but
was always working and looking after the people. Mahmond
Talaât has also asked me to send you one of the gold Kartoum stars, which he thought you would like. It is *not* his
own star; *that*, he says, nothing could induce him to part
with. You will see in their photographs, as in that of Nushi
Pasha, that they are wearing the Kartoum star. The three
officers came down with Sir Charles Wilson; and the ranks
your brother gave them were at once confirmed by the
Khedive. They so much like talking of your brother, and
of all he did at Kartoum. It is quite wonderful the influence
he had with all who were there."

LETTERS FROM HIS HIGHNESS THE KHEDIVE.[1]

ABDIN PALACE, CAIRO,
February, 1885.

MADAM,—Although I do not wish to intrude upon the
great sorrow which has befallen you in the death of your
distinguished brother, the late General Gordon Pasha, yet,
as Egypt and myself have so much reason to deplore his
loss, I desire to convey to you my heartfelt sympathy in
the terrible bereavement it has been God's will you should
suffer.

I cannot find words to express to you the respect and
admiration with which your brother's simple faith and heroic
courage have inspired me. The whole world resounds with
the name of the Englishman whose chivalrous nature afforded
it, for many years, its brightest and most powerful example
—an example which, I believe, will influence thousands of
persons for good through all time.

To a man of General Gordon's character the disappointment of hopes he deemed so near fruition and the manner
of his death were of little importance. In his own words,
he left "weariness for perfect peace." Our mourning for

[1] These letters are printed with His Highness's sanction.

him is very true and real, as is our loss ; but we have a sure
hope that a life and faith, such as Gordon's, are not ex-
tinguishable by what we call death. I beg to renew to
you, Madam, the assurance of my sincere sympathy and
respectful condolence.

(Signed)   MEHEMET TEWFIC.

December, 1886.

MADAM,—I thank you for the kind thought of sending
me the portrait of your brother, General Gordon. It is a
real pleasure to me to accept from you the likeness of the
man whose character all the world admires, as it deplores
his sad loss. I have hung the portrait in my room, and
shall always value it as a remembrance of the hero who died
for me and my lost Egypt, and as a proof of delicate attention
from yourself.

I beg you to accept in return my own portrait, which
I send to you as a slight token of the dear esteem and
sympathy of,

Madam,

Your sincere friend,

MEHEMET TEWFIC.

LETTERS FROM GENERAL GORDON'S OFFICERS.[1]

CAIRO, *December* 12, 1885.

MADAM,—I consider it a great happiness for me that the
echo of the sincere attachment I was animated with towards
your regretted brother, the Right Honourable late General
Gordon Pasha, has had the favour of being noticed by you.

I have been utmostly honoured with the portrait of the
late General, which you have kindly sent me, and I really
do not find sufficient words for expressing my gratitude for
your remembering me with such a precious object, representing that single man in the world, who sacrificed his
fortune and life for his country and for humanity.

---

[1] I have preferred, in giving the letters of these four officers, to let
the translations which accompanied the Arabic originals stand just as
they sent them. The simple style, even though ungrammatical, pleases
me.

It was only through my bad luck that I could not get the same fate as the gallant General, in partaking his glorious death. Will you, Madam, be good enough to oblige me by accepting my humble photograph, which I respectfully address to you herewith as a proof of my everlasting fidelity to the memory of the Hero?

(Signed and Sealed)   Mohamed Nushi,
Pasha.

CAIRO, *February* 16, 1886.

Madam,—I gratefully acknowledge the receipt of the letter of which the gracious lines were kindly traced in my name by the respectable sister of that single man who sacrificed his matchless life to the altar of civilization.

I thank you most warmly for the goodness you have shown in accepting my humble photograph, and chiefly for your intending to put it with the late General Gordon's relics. By this generous action you will have fulfilled, beyond my real hope, the ambitious feelings I ever was animated with and which I durst not profess openly.

The Lord will overwhelm you with blessings for the care you are taking of approaching my photograph to our precious martyr's precious relics, for such a circumstance has indeed the power of attenuating somewhat the pain and regret I always felt since I was unfortunately deprived of partaking the character of the fate which covers his name with an everlasting glory.

I beg of you to accept of my distinguished respects, and allow me to be,

Madam,

Your sincerest and most obedient servant for ever,

(Sealed)   Mohamed Nushi.

Khashm el Moos, Pasha, to Miss Gordon.

ASSOUAN, 24 *August*, 1885.

After presenting my compliments—I am highly pleased and honoured to receive the photographs of one, than whom

I never had a better friend and adviser, and whom I will
ever remember with great admiration and respect. These
likenesses will ever remain amongst my most valuable treasures. I am, moreover, extremely proud to make the
acquaintance of the sister of that illustrious hero, hoping
it may be my fortune at some future time to have the honour
of meeting Miss Gordon personally, so as to be able to
better express my sense of unexceptional love and esteem
to her dear brother.

I strongly urge resignation and acceptance of God's will,
and am positive of Gordon Pasha's resting-place—Paradise.
As to the sad event, Miss Gordon may rely with confidence
on my statements ; and, as to the last stage of the drama,
I can truly say that Gordon Pasha only died after he had
done his duty like a man, or after he could resist no longer ;
to say nothing of the sufferings of famine he so bravely
stood.

General Gordon Pasha leaves a name indelibly chronicled
on the heart of even every Soudanese.

MY LADY,—This is a consolatory ode on the Governor-
General of the Soudan, Gordon Pasha. I beg your acceptance of the same. I wish you well. (Dated A.H. 1302.)

The Soudan was darkened after his loss,
After the setting of that Sun of Righteousness, Gordon Pasha,
The gallant hero, abounding in virtues,
The enricher of the destitute, the uplifter of the down-fallen.
He fell upon the enemy with a sharp-edged sword ;
Weak-heartedness never led him astray—God forbid !
The hearts of his men drooped when they missed him,
Lamenting him, but without avail ;
And the Pasha Khashm el Moos with tearful eyes
Will weep for him while his life shall last.

CAIRO, *8th February*, 1886.

DEAR MRS.,—I am very anxious to see you, but much
grieved for the death of your brother. Ah ! Alas ! Aye—I
am very sorry. How that grieved me ! I am much pained
at it. I was very anxious to see him before his death ; but

how unhappy I am, for all seems to go contrary to my wishes.

After such misfortunes it only remains for me to die for the kind man whom nobody can equal.

His death grieved all the inhabitants of the globe. So the trees, with the animals, felt the greatest sorrow at his death. What a misfortune for such a brave ! Ah ! there will be no more happiness for me in this world after his death, for we were one heart.

The death of all my family did not grieve me like his ; but what can we do now ? That was our Creator's order.

Be patient, and remember where are Adam and Eve, and also the high class of men. Are they not under the ground ? Are we not going to die ? I think we will all be the same. But myself prefers death than to suffer his departure.

You send to me to send you my photograph with my name written upon it. Here it kisses your feet before your hands. If I had time I would offer it you myself, in order to express to you my displeasure and grief for his departure.

I have the honour to be your truly friend,

KHASHM EL MOOS,
Pasha.

Dear ;
Be sure of my gratitude.

CAIRO, 10 *July*, 1886.

DEAR MADAM,—I earnestly hope that you may, in your moments of leisure, be pleased to write once in a while to one who was fortunate enough to be favoured by the friendship of your regretted brother. Hardly ever out of your thoughts, he is constantly present to all those who knew him, for his is an image that never fades. . . . I do not believe his desperate straits ever caused him a moment's dread, for he was a man utterly devoid of fear, actually not knowing what such a feeling was ; and the prospect of death had no terrors for him. When shall we ever see his like again ! . . . The photograph you have sent me has caused me both pleasure and pains, because it has renewed the sorrows lying inside my heart. His Excellency, while at Kartoum, had issued decorations to all the Government employés, of which I received three; one I have given to H. E. the Acting Sırdar, in order to send it to you, and one I shall keep as a mark of distinction. . . .

The design of the decoration was drawn by General Gordon himself in Kartoum. He then caused several goldsmiths to cast a model from the drawing, and then chose the best one. He had the whole number of decorations struck under his supervision.[1]

I remain, dear Madam, yours sincerely,
MAHMOUD TALAÂT.

I HAVE the honour to express to you my best thanks for the photograph of your late brother, which has caused me both pleasure and pains, because it reminded me of his good inclination and devotion to all.

I have the pleasure of inclosing in return my own photograph bearing the decoration which was granted to me by your late brother, hoping that you would accept it for the sake of the decoration.

(Sealed)   ALI RIZA, *Lt. Col.*

The following letter, which I have lately received from Mr. E. A. Maund, contains particulars regarding *The Dream of Gerontius*, the book referred to above (p. 285), and other details which will be read with interest :—

LONDON, 30 *January*, 1888.

DEAR MISS GORDON,—On my return from Africa, I heard you were writing reminiscences of your brother, General Gordon, and at the same time I recollected that there had been some controversy about that little book, *The Dream*

---

[1] General Gordon used the Medjidie as a model, with an inscription in Arabic round the medal : " The siege of Kartoum," and date.

of Gerontius, which he gave to Mr. Power at Kartoum, and which the latter mentions in his letters home and afterwards sent to his sister. It may be of interest to some to know how it was that General Gordon had this little Roman Catholic poem with him in Kartoum.

The day he left, your brother related to me how his spiritual life was changed by what he experienced at his father's death-bed, as, gazing on the lifeless form, he thought: "Is this what we all have to come to?" This led to a long discussion on death, when I remarked that some of his ideas reminded me of Dr. Newman's little book, *The Dream of Gerontius*. Whereupon he said he should like to read it; and I promised to send it after him to Egypt. Your brother in a post-card, dated from Kartoum, 7 March, 1884, acknowledging the book, says:

"MY DEAR MR. MAUND,—Your letter 25 January arrived to-day. I am glad my old friend is at rest, and I hope your kind family are comforted. What a sad trial you have all gone through for a year, far worse than the burden on me. Thanks for the little book. My prayers shall now be for my old friend's family. I assure you that I intercede more for my friends, now I am up here, than when I was in Palestine. When Job prayed for his friends, then God turned his captivity (Job xlii. 10). Your prayers are my host. With kindest regards to all,
"Yours sincerely,
"C. G. GORDON."

This card not only shows General Gordon's strong belief in intercessory prayer, but seems to convey an idea of his forlorn and almost hopeless state at Kartoum, even at that early date. That he had presentiments of failure, I knew; for, on parting, when I wished him God speed and success, he said: "Every one has to fail, or we should have too high a belief in our own powers. As yet I have been successful: I have still to fail. I wish for humility, for God's guidance, and for resignation to God's will."

Believe me yours very sincerely,

E. A. MAUND.

I close this volume with a Greek epitaph on my brother, written by Professor Jebb, of the University of Glasgow, together with a translation which has been kindly furnished by a friend :—

ΕΙΙΙ ΚΑΡΟΛΩΙ ΓΕΩΡΓΙΩΙ ΓΟΡΔΩΝ.

μνάμαν ἀίναον λελοιπὼς
οἴχεαι, τοῖος θανὼν οἷός περ ἔζης,
πτωχοῖσι μὲν ὄλβος, ἀθύμοις δ' ἐλπίς, ἔρεισμα δ' ἀμαυροῖς.
παντοπόρον δ' ἀπόροισιν ἀνταίρων
λῆμα καὶ τρομεροῖς ἐνέσταζες βίαν.
εὐεργεσιῶν δὲ χάριν σύνοιδέ σοι τυραννίδος
ὠγυγίας ἐν ἕδραις ἔτ' ἀσφαλὴς Σινῶν ἄναξ·
Νεῖλος δ' οὐ συνάγει δίπορον σθένος ῥείθρων
εἶδε καρτερέοντα πόλις,

φρουρᾶς δωδεκάμηνον ἀλκὰν
πὰρ σέθεν πλειστόμβροτος λαβοῦσα μούνου,
εὖτ' ἀμφιχανόντα φονώσαις Αἰθιόπων στρατὸν αἰχμαῖς
παννύχιος κατά τ' ἦμαρ ἠμύνου.
οὐκ Ἄρης σ' ἕλεν, ἀλλ' ἁμαρτίαι φίλων.
πάτρας τε βροτῶν τ' ὄφελος σὺ κοινὸν ἦσθα σὺν θεῷ·
χαῖρ', ἀμίαντε μαχητά, χαῖρε, τρὶς νικαφόρε·
ζώεις· τοὺς δ' ἐπιγιγνομένους σέβειν διδάξεις
μῆτιν ἀθανάτοιο πατρός.

R. C. J.

IN MEMORIAM C. G. G.

Leaving a perpetual remembrance, thou art gone ; in thy death thou wert even such as in thy life : wealth to the poor, hope to the desponding, support to the weak. Thou couldst meet desperate troubles with a spirit that knew not despair, and breathe might into the trembling.

The Lord of China owes thee thanks for thy benefits ; the throne of his ancient kingdom hath not been cast down.

And where the Nile unites the divided strength of his streams, a city saw thee long-suffering. A multitude dwelt therein, but thine alone was the valour that guarded it through all that year, when by day and by night thou didst keep watch against the host of the Arabians, who went around it to devour it, with spears thirsting for blood.

Thy death was not wrought by the God of War, but by the frailties of thy friends. For thy country and for all men God blessed the work of thy hand. Hail, stainless warrior ! hail, thrice victorious hero ! Thou livest, and shalt teach aftertimes to reverence the counsel of the Everlasting Father.

Richard Clay and Sons, Limited, London and Bungay.

Ingram Content Group UK Ltd.
Milton Keynes UK
UKHW022238210723
425591UK00005B/163